Reach Sport

# KING ERIC

## Portrait of the Artist
## Who Changed English Football

### BY WAYNE BARTON

# Reach Sport

www.reachsport.com

Published in Great Britain and Ireland in 2020 by
Reach Sport, a Reach PLC business,
5 St Paul's Square, Liverpool, L3 9SJ.

www.reachsport.com
@Reach_Sport

Reach Sport is a part of Reach PLC.
One Canada Square, Canary Wharf, London, E15 5AP.

Hardback ISBN: 978-1-911613-51-0
eBook ISBN: 978-1-911613-52-7

Photographic acknowledgements:
Reach PLC, PA Images.

Design and typesetting by Reach Sport.
Book editing: Simon Monk. Jacket design: Chris Collins

Printed and bound in Great Britain by Bell and Bain Ltd, Glasgow

# CONTENTS

"A player like Cantona only comes along once or twice in a lifetime."
(*Sir Bobby Charlton*)

"If he is here today, tremendous, but if he is gone tomorrow we just say, 'Good luck, Eric, thanks for playing for us, you were brilliant'."
(*Sir Alex Ferguson*)

"The more I find it easy, the easier it becomes. I try to convince myself it's easy. And when you're confident you find freedom, from freedom of expression comes genius, euphoria and fire…"
(*Eric Cantona*)

Author Wayne Barton has numerous books about Manchester United to his name and has been described as "the leading writer" on the club by *The Independent*.

His biography of Jimmy Murphy, *The Man Who Kept The Red Flag Flying*, also published by Reach Sport, was critically acclaimed while his book about United's 1974 relegation, *Too Good To Go Down*, was made into a BT Sport film, which Wayne co-wrote and produced.

# MARTIN EDWARDS

M

# 'A man of integrity'

E ric was not only one of the most influential players in the history of Manchester United, but of British football too. He was the catalyst for so much change, so much of the personality and so much of the success achieved by the club while he was there. Meanwhile, his influence on the club after he departed was arguably just as significant.

The story of how Eric signed is part of Old Trafford folklore. He had been on my mind because Irving Scholar, the former chairman of Tottenham Hotspur who lived in Monaco, watched a lot of French football and would rave about this player called Cantona. He told me Eric was made for Manchester United. When the chance came to sign him we were delighted.

He came with a reputation but he was always very pleasant with me. I always got the impression he spoke much better English than people thought, and he had a good sense of humour when using that to his advantage. I always appreciated his honesty. We negotiated a contract with him during his most difficult time at the club and when I explained we were in a predicament, Eric understood, and, as I explain later, his response was surely something that will delight United fans.

Even after what happened at Selhurst Park, Eric did not want to leave the club until it seemed the FA might make it impossible for him to stay when they insisted he could not play in friendly games. Alex convinced him to stay, but we were never tempted to sell. Eric was pivotal in helping us get that first championship and was so crucial in the years that followed. I am certain we would have won three doubles in consecutive years if he was not suspended in 1995. Most players would not have been capable of the skill and composure required to score the goal that won us the Double in 1996.

He was a man of integrity, brave enough to stand up for his team-mates when he was captain. One year I altered the bonus scheme. Eric looked me in the eyes and said: "The bonuses are an opportunity for the directors to show respect to the players." Then he paused and added: "I do not think these bonuses are showing enough respect."

He was a man who did right by his team-mates, as the story about him splitting a bonus between Paul Scholes and Nicky Butt when they were just young lads shows.

His attitude as a player and a professional helped our young players – on and off the pitch – and I'm not sure that without his contribution, those young players would have had the confidence, arrogance or work ethic that helped them win more Premier League titles and the Treble in 1999. Eric was a truly magnificent player for Manchester United and will go down as one of the greatest, most important and most influential.

This is also an opportune moment to give credit to the author of this book. Wayne is probably, currently, the pre-eminent writer on Manchester United. Historically accurate and written with clarity, his books have such a forensic attention to detail that it allows the reader to trust what they are reading and that it also comes from an authentic place.

**Martin Edwards, October 2019**

I owe plenty of thanks to plenty of individuals who have offered practical and moral support during the writing of this book.

Thank you to Martin Edwards, Paul Parker, Ben Thornley, David May, John O'Kane, Harry Gregg, Jon Newsome, John Moncur, Richard Shaw, Kevin Pilkington, Ian Herbert, Gabriele Marcotti, Rob Smyth and Danny Taylor. I am indebted to Paddy Barclay; thank you so much for your support. Thank you to Dave Murphy, your friendship and extra pair of eyes throughout writing this book have been appreciated in equal measure.

A big thanks to Dan and Kim Burdett, to Hayley and Elfyn Roberts (and Gruff), and to Gemma and Steve. Oyvind Enger, Matt Galea, Nipun Chopra, Luke Smalley, Tyler Dunne and Eifion Evans. Mike Pieri, for going an extra mile, and Stel Stylianou, for all his support. Also to Mikiel and Phil Gatt, and Stan Chow. To Paul Dove, Simon Monk, Chris Collins, Claire Brown, Rick Cooke and all at Reach Sport for their work and enthusiasm on this book.

To all of my family, especially my beautiful wife, my biggest supporter. For Freddy and Noah.

**Wayne Barton, January 2020**

# PROLOGUE

# The Enigma

On Thursday 29th August 2019, Eric Cantona received the UEFA President's Award on stage in Monaco before the draw for the Champions League group stages. Fully bearded, wearing dark jeans, an untucked red shirt with the top three buttons undone and wearing a flat cap, Cantona accepted the award and quoted from King Lear.

"As flies to wanton boys are we to the gods, they kill us for their sport," he said. "Only accidents, crimes, wars, will still kill us but unfortunately, crimes, wars, will multiply. I love football. Thank you."

The speech had gone 'viral' even before cameras panned to the audience, including the bemused Cristiano Ronaldo and Lionel Messi. The pair had battled it out for years to be recognised as the best player in the world; both are often now included in discussions about the greatest player in history.

Eric Cantona rarely is. The reasons for that will be discussed within these pages but it was certainly not due to a lack of talent. Perhaps it is a resistance to his refusal to conform to expectations before, during and after his spell at Manchester United from November 1992 to May 1997. Because people could not understand him, it made it harder for them to empathise; thus, Cantona attained cult status in his home country and quickly gained a new audience wherever he went afterwards. He remained faithful to his ideals and his eccentric way of articulating them even when his career was threatened in 1991 and 1995, just as he did when the pressure was off in August 2019. It is a spectacle, a performance, but the character of Eric Cantona is true.

As someone who has embraced the idea of an outsider, Cantona has achieved a rare place in history; that of a man who transcended his profession as a footballer, assuming the role of hero, villain, artist, vigilante, activist, and, infamously, executor of social justice.

He insisted football could be classified as an art and this concept was greeted as derisively by some as the news that he enjoyed poetry and philosophy. When he arrived in England, football was undergoing a reinvention, with the governing bodies trying to steer it away from its working class roots. Cantona, a man with a working class background and attitude, also had the cultural expression of the middle class.

And, as a divisive outsider who firstly moved to a team in Leeds United whose own reputation was controversial, the Frenchman therefore existed in a limbo of his own; misunderstood by the man on the street who was more into page three than poetry, and derided by the middle class, who felt he had more in common with the terrace hooligan of the 1980s than a family-friendly figurehead for a cleaner game.

Even when he enjoyed remarkable success at Old Trafford,

there was still a childish giggle whenever Cantona expressed himself in his own inimitable turn of phrase. Some would maintain the Frenchman was foolish, or insist they misunderstood what he was saying, even if the meaning was obvious.

Still, he convinced hundreds of thousands that football could be art; an idea given weight by the way he played the game, and his innate sense of timing, often on the biggest stage, to deliver the performance which would last longest in the memory. More than any other footballer to have played in England before him, Cantona inspired the idea of storytelling; creating this notion that sport was theatre.

Since his retirement, there has been a more universal appreciation for Eric's personality. There is a period of time where English sport was inextricably linked with Cantona, a period when football changed and Manchester United changed. His influence on that change was significant.

There was football before 25th January 1995, and there has been football afterwards. Picking up this book, I will assume some familiarity with the significance of that date on your part. Whilst many people use the 1992 introduction of the Premier League as an arbitrary resetting point, the truth is slightly different. Football has always been the 'working man's game' and has long been the UK's most popular sport. The 1990 World Cup did much to grab the public's attention. It helped that England got to the semi-finals. It helped that such a journey was dramatic, and that in Paul Gascoigne, England boasted one of the tournament's most talented and enigmatic protagonists. The nation fell in love with Gazza and his tears, giving him the flaw that always helps to cement a British hero in the public's affections.

When Lazio made overtures to sign Gascoigne in 1991, there was an even greater exotic feel about the sport, enticing more casual fans. Gazza suffered a serious knee injury in the 1991 FA Cup final which delayed the move, but didn't stop the speculation; talk of the transfer dominated the sports pages. A star British player moving to Italy was nothing new but Gazza was 'the star'. His eventual transfer coincided with Channel 4 launching their *Golazzo* show about all things Serie A.

Back on British soil, the 1990s were ushering in revolutionary times. The creation of the Premier League had been announced when most clubs were moving to all-seater stadiums following Hillsborough. English clubs were also allowed to compete in Europe again after a five-year ban and Manchester United had just won the European Cup Winners' Cup, defeating a great Barcelona side in the final. It gave weight to the hope that English teams were as good as their European counterparts.

United's players believed that success over Barcelona (and a win over Red Star Belgrade in the European Super Cup) had established them as the UK's top team as they aimed to end a quarter of a century without a title. Liverpool's dominance was over but Arsenal were not quite ready to take their place, despite winning the league in 1991. United were well-placed but there were a number of contenders jostling for position.

United challenged for the 1992 Division One title – the last before the Premier League – against Leeds United. In January 1992 Alex Ferguson's team eliminated Howard Wilkinson's from both domestic cup competitions. This, eventually, would contribute hugely to Manchester United's failure to win the league. There were of course other factors. In January 1992 it was still a rarity for British teams to sign foreign players. It was a matter of great interest when Eric Cantona – a controversial French forward – announced he was on his way to the UK following a 'retirement' in his homeland. Cantona signed for Leeds and was instrumental as they won the First Division title. Later that same year, he signed for Manchester United, and the rest is history.

Three players have statues on the Old Trafford forecourt. They are three of the four players who have won the European Footballer of the Year award while playing for Manchester United. At the time of writing, 110 players have played more times for United, and 24 players have scored more goals. So how can one justify the idea that Eric Cantona is the most important player to have represented the world's most famous football club? Pure statistics won't cut it. They won't even come close. How do you accurately convey the idea that this one player stands above every other in the pantheon of outrageously talented stars? Perhaps it requires a certain investment from the reader. It requires a belief in the beautiful intangibles of the sport; a willingness to accept that some things in football transcend events on the pitch.

Cantona filled the void left by Gascoigne. His exploits on the pitch transformed Manchester United. And on the evening of 25th January 1995, Cantona completed his transformative impact on British football. Before, the sport had been, mostly, the exclusive property of the back page. Sure, there were players who had flirtations with the front pages. George Best had walked that line with Manchester United before. But Cantona's indiscretion marked a permanent shift, one where footballers would become front page news, and people of public interest, as opposed to simply sportspeople.

Football's fluid ability to present heroes as villains depending on your allegiance was always a potential goldmine for the tabloids but Cantona's prior indiscretions had been consigned to the pitch, tantalisingly out of reach. At Selhurst he had quite literally crossed the line and changed the game as we know it.

Some could reason that Cantona and Selhurst were the perfect storm that British newspapers had been waiting for since Hillsborough. The scandal which emanated from the disaster in April 1989, with repercussions that continue to this day, had revealed the general interest that was still alive in football. That Hillsborough had followed a period where hooliganism was rife made it easy to demonise the average supporter, and a working-class tragedy that was of significant public interest.

Gascoigne and Italy increased that interest, the Premier League's introduction and more live football on television kicked it up a gear, and Manchester United's ascent into a truly great team with Cantona as the key influence had helped to make the game more popular than ever.

His misdemeanour at Crystal Palace made him a safe target for the newspapers – a pantomime villain in the context of football, to steal a reference from Eamon Dunphy. It was a groundbreaking moment in the history of the game, and the length of Cantona's punishment gave the interest space to grow and run wild. By the time he was back on a football pitch, it was a different game altogether.

# KING ERIC 1

# Shy and Retiring

F ar from the impression of Eric Cantona as a journeyman who ended up in British football, the Frenchman was a highly-rated young player in his homeland. However, his career had been blighted by numerous controversial episodes, starting when he was just 21.

In February 1987 Cantona head-butted Auxerre team-mate Bruno Martini after a training ground row. Martini was left with a black eye but manager Guy Roux refused to punish Cantona, as he felt it had been a misunderstanding, and Eric was a player he was trying to nurture. This approach had also helped indulge Cantona on a previous occasion that perhaps serves as a foreshadowing; in a pre-season game in Poland, the locals had not taken kindly to the forward's showmanship in a game where he scored a spectacular overhead kick.

As the teams walked off, one fan threw an egg at Cantona – Eric responded by charging into the stand to find the culprit. He was unsuccessful, but even this early on, it was clear

Cantona was an individual who favoured a more personal kind of justice.

Roux was fond of Cantona and his approach was mostly rewarded with impressive form. On 2nd April 1988, Cantona scored in a 2-0 win over Marseille, and three days later took his place in his team's attack in a cup game against Nantes. Defender Michel Der Zakarian paid Cantona close attention – too close. As Der Zakarian ran with the ball, Eric launched a waist-high drop-kick. Anticipating the fury of his victim's colleagues, and the punishment of the referee, Cantona simply raised both hands. He was duly sent off.

Cantona was met in the Auxerre dressing room by Roux and club directors, who were furious. So were the French football federation. With punishment on the cards, Roux threatened that if Cantona was given a harsh suspension, he would make the player unavailable for international selection too.

The French under-21 side was due to play England in their European Championship semi-final, potentially with their star player unavailable. To make light of the incident, Cantona claimed in an appeal that he and Der Zakarian were friends from the same neighbourhood and his 'tackle' had been a joke. The suspension was reduced to two games.

Auxerre exited the French Cup and Cantona, sensing that was as close as he would come to glory, submitted a transfer request, knowing that the top clubs in the country would be interested. Two days later, Eric put on a show against England, scoring twice in a 2-2 draw at Highbury to secure a 6-4 aggregate win and a final place against Greece.

His performances had attracted the attention of his hometown club Marseille, who paid a national record fee of FF22m (approximately £2m) to acquire his services. Cantona had grown up a Marseille fan but his return was far from the dream he had hoped.

In August, Cantona was dropped from the national squad for a friendly against Czechoslovakia. On Friday 16th August, Cantona scored for his club against Matra Racing in a 2-0 win, and was asked about his omission. He railed against coach Henri Michel in an impassioned diatribe which concluded with him referring to the coach as "a bag of shit", adding he would not play for the side while he remained in charge.

Cantona apologised, but the damage was done. He was banned from international football for a year. More was to come. In January 1989 Marseille played a benefit game against Torpedo Moscow in Sedan; Cantona was frustrated with the poor pitch and Marseille coach Gerard Gili withdrew his player after an altercation with the referee. Cantona's frustrations turned to his manager as he tore off his jersey and threw it away. His club suspended him for a month.

Marseille president Bernard Tapie responded by saying the club would put Cantona in a psychiatric hospital if they had to. Cantona fled to Barcelona, followed by the French press. The forward's hero was Johan Cruyff, the then-Barca coach, and Tapie, ever the opportunist, intimated he wouldn't be averse to a swift sale of his record signing. Bordeaux took the chance on loan, with Cantona scoring six goals in 11 games there, starring in a squad that included Belgian legend Enzo Scifo and former Manchester United winger Jesper Olsen.

The success of the short spell did not convince Tapie to take Cantona back but only made the forward, in his eyes, a more appealing asset to sell. Bordeaux couldn't pay and PSG's advances were rebuffed when it was revealed they planned to hire Henri Michel as their coach. Instead, another loan move was agreed, with Cantona surprisingly going to Montpellier. His form was mixed as the club endured a dismal start to the campaign. In October 1989, following their eighth defeat of the season, Eric overheard team-mate Jean-Claude Lemoult complaining about Montpellier's problems in front of goal. Offended, Cantona hit Lemoult with his boot, sparking a meleé. The club chairman responded by vowing to 'fire' Cantona (in effect, terminating his loan), but Tapie refused to take the player back, and instead he was banned for ten days.

However, there was to be a reprieve, with Cantona turning things around and enhancing his reputation. By the end of 1989/90, Montpellier had won the Coupe de France against RC Paris. Tapie ordered Cantona back to Marseille, where he would work under German legend Franz Beckenbaeur. Eric's international career had also been given a reprieve; Henri Michel had been replaced by Michel Platini, a big fan of Cantona, who restored him to the squad. Everything was going swimmingly, until Cantona picked up an injury, and Raymond Goethals replaced Beckenbauer as coach. Goethals changed tactics, playing Jean-Pierre Papin as his sole striker.

Cantona was offended by his coach's opinion that he wasn't a 'modern' striker. His performances for the national side ensured he was still considered at club level, but those opportunities became rarer. Cantona became frustrated, leading to confrontations between player and manager. The forward knew his future lay elsewhere. Provincial club Nîmes had hired Michel Mézy as their coach; Mézy had been Montpellier manager during Cantona's loan there. Tapie asked for approximately £1m, and the Nîmes chairman, who was also the town mayor, released public funds to finance the transfer. Cantona had been happy to leave Marseille due to the political controversy there and wasn't enamoured at being involved in this sort of issue; he was, however, keen to play for the club.

He was made captain but Nîmes struggled, and to compound matters, seemed to look better when Eric wasn't in the side. Cantona scored only twice, with his lack of form attributed to a thigh injury and a lack of quality around him. Still, he appeared to be warming to the task, and some of the younger players seemed to have an affection for their skipper. However, as was par for the course with Cantona in French football, one thing got on top of another until it all came to a head.

Eric was struggling to cope with the death of his grandfather when Nîmes played St Etienne on 7th December 1991. The game was coasting to an unremarkable 1-1 draw when Cantona finally snapped at the referee's failure to award him free-kicks for a succession of heavy challenges. In the face of this perceived injustice, Cantona grabbed the match ball and threw it at the referee. He was halfway to the dressing room before the official had a chance to brandish a red card.

The disciplinary committee suspended him for four matches, taking into account his poor disciplinary record. He took great exception when he felt the panel were unfairly dealing with him. The panel leader told him: "You can't be judged like any other player. Behind you there is a trail of the smell of sulphur. You can expect anything from an individualist like you."

Cantona promptly addressed each member of the panel individually and called them an idiot. The four-match ban was extended to two months. On Thursday 12th December 1991, Eric Cantona announced to the football world that he would retire from the sport altogether. As we know, of course, this end was merely a new beginning.

# A Winter's Tale

**E**ric Cantona's road to Manchester came via detours through Sheffield and Leeds but it isn't a giant leap to say he almost ended up in Liverpool. Eric had dreamed of playing in England, partly thanks to his memorable brace at Arsenal that the French press dubbed "the miracle of Highbury". When it came to moving abroad, if it wasn't going to be Cruyff's Barcelona, then where better than the north of England, with plenty of clubs with a romantic history?

On 6th November 1991, Liverpool played Auxerre in their second round UEFA Cup tie. French manager Michel Platini was in attendance and met with Anfield boss Graeme Souness afterwards. "He said he had a player – a problem boy but a proper player. Cantona," Souness told the *Daily Mail* in December 2016. "I said the last thing I needed was another problem player. I didn't need more hassle. I said no thanks."

Platini felt strongly enough about Cantona's future that he was trying to facilitate a move across the Channel, urging his assistant Gerard Houllier (who had studied in Liverpool) to go through his contacts in England.

Cantona and Nîmes agreed his three-year contract would be terminated, on the condition that if he did come out of retirement, it would be to play for Nîmes. Certainly, it seemed his career was over, *The Guardian*'s footballing obit reflecting: "It was a firecracker of a career, marked by brilliant moments, unpredictable turns and a series of explosions."

Indeed, the press coverage concentrated on reminiscing rather than predicting a return. One reporter quoted Eric's mother, who said: "When he was a small child, he could not bear the slightest injustice. He was different from other kids."

Platini failed to convince Cantona to reverse his decision, but persevered with the England idea. Houllier contacted Dennis Roach, an agent who had masterminded transfers including Trevor Francis' landmark £1m move to Nottingham Forest. Francis was now manager of Sheffield Wednesday. Houllier made a call to propose the signing of Cantona. The Owls boss sought the advice of former England team-mate Glenn Hoddle, who said: "If you get the chance, go and get him."

What followed was a saga which played out over little under three weeks and yet was so significant that entire alternate timelines have been theorised in the intervening years.

Sheffield Wednesday had just lost embarrassingly at home, 6-1 to Yorkshire rivals Leeds. Cantona was scheduled to arrive the next day but there were issues with his contract, with Nîmes perturbed that their star man was set to release himself from his self-imposed exile after just four weeks.

"Cantona's scored 14 goals in 20 games for France and if he's not playing club football then his chances of playing in the

European Championship are severely handicapped," Francis told reporters on Wednesday 22nd January. "He was due here last Sunday and he has still not arrived. There are one or two technical points still to be put right. A fee has been agreed if we want to buy him at the end of the season."

Jean-Jacques Bertrand, Cantona's lawyer, had told reporters Cantona had agreed to pay Nîmes £700,000 to release him from the contract, but that he couldn't afford it, so it was in the club's interests to reach an agreement. Wednesday had made two offers – £600,000 for a straight transfer, or £100,000 for a loan until the end of the season. Nîmes wanted approximately double in both respects.

Negotiations continued until the end of the week and Graham Mackrell, the Wednesday secretary, flew to Paris to sort it out. "If he likes us and we like him, then we'll sign an agreement for him to stay on loan until the end of the season when we'll have an option to buy him," Mackrell told *The Guardian* after a five-hour meeting on Saturday 25th January 1992. "He's looking forward to coming here very much."

The clubs reached an agreement and Cantona travelled on the Sunday. Unfortunately, the weather in Sheffield was dreadful, causing Trevor Francis to make alternative training arrangements for a week that was already disrupted due to a six-a-side tournament at the Sheffield Arena.

Francis arranged sessions in the indoor gym at Hillsborough Leisure Centre and the all-weather Aurora training complex on Bawtry Road, just off the M1. Neither the club's training ground at Middlewood, or their Hillsborough stadium, had undersoil heating at the time.

Francis had lofty ambitions for Sheffield Wednesday and the bold move for Cantona brought a great deal of local attention.

Television cameras were present for the player's first day in South Yorkshire.

"It takes me back to my first day in Italy, when I couldn't speak Italian, and it's similar to Eric, he can't speak a word of English," Francis told local news in an interview televised from the Hillsborough Leisure Centre on Monday 27th January. "But he's a good player, it's given a buzz to the place as well, the interest that it's generated over the last few days, we've never had so many people at the training session...."

Through an interpreter, Cantona said: "I wanted to play in England, the opportunity of Sheffield came and I'm very happy to be here. I met a lot of sympathetic people, the club is a very old one and I'm very happy to be here."

On Tuesday, a team was sent down from Oldham Athletic to face a Wednesday team with Cantona in it on the artificial turf pitch at Aurora. In the 90-minute practice match, Cantona scored a hat-trick. The location of the complex is interesting as its proximity to the motorway meant it had been used, on occasion, by Leeds United.

The following day Wednesday had a double training session at Aurora. After the first session, Danny Wilson, the former Wednesday striker, claims Cantona ordered steak and chips for lunch. "I remember saying to him, 'Woah, what are you doing? We're training this afternoon'," said Wilson to *The Times* in 2017. " He replied: 'Well, you might be, but I'm not.'"

The former Northern Ireland international insisted that was the height of Cantona's idiosyncrasies during his brief time in Sheffield. "We'd been reading articles about him and what he did in France, but he was no problem at all," Wilson said. "He didn't want to run in behind people, so if you played that kind of ball, he would just look at you with disdain."

That morning, Cantona had been introduced to dressing room banter, England style. Cantona had arrived in cowboy boots, and the mainly-Yorkshire contingent in the Wednesday squad saw a chance to have a bit of fun at their new colleague's expense, tying his boots to the ceiling. Cantona saw the funny side and seemed to be part of the group in an impressive public showing at the Sheffield Arena that evening.

Some 8,206 were in attendance to witness Wednesday get humbled 8-3 by the Baltimore Blast; Cantona's reputation only grew despite the defeat, with *The Guardian* reporting that he "produced some elegant skills".

On Thursday 30th January, Francis met Cantona's lawyer – the meeting, in Cantona's mind, was to sign the contract. The Wednesday boss had other ideas and wanted to extend the trial period. The reasons have been debated time and again and we will explore them but it is perhaps most convenient to refer to this contemporaneous report from *The Guardian*.

"His lawyer told me he is a big star in France and that he would lose face if he stayed for another week on trial," Francis told them on Friday 31st (published 1st February 1992). "If he wants to come back he is very welcome. The last time I saw Eric was at Sheffield Arena on Wednesday night. I met his lawyer and union official on Thursday and requested that he stayed a further week. The next thing I received a fax from Eric saying he had enjoyed his time here and was going home.

"Even the greatest manager in the world would not have been able to make a decision on a player after seeing him in two training sessions on an artificial pitch and once indoors. I couldn't commit us after only three days to a substantial fee and wages for the loan."

In Philippe Auclair's seminal book *Cantona: The Rebel Who Would Be King*, Dennis Roach said: "The contract was supposed to be signed on the 30th January. Trevor was a very good footballer but, as a manager, he hadn't yet learnt to make quick decisions… so he hummed and ahhed, and in the end, I got a phone call from Howard Wilkinson at Leeds."

Wilkinson told a Leeds United fans forum that Wednesday full-back Nigel Worthington had tipped him off about Cantona's location – though he said it was "the tiniest room of the Holiday Inn", the player was in fact staying at the Swallow Hotel just outside the city centre. The Leeds boss had returned a call to Gerard Houllier – Houllier had been informed by Roach of the issue, and implored Wilkinson to sign him. Wilkinson's own research on the player had been fairly intensive as he sought an extra dimension to his frontline for their championship charge against Manchester United.

Francis responded by telling reporters: "I made a reasonable request, to ask him to stay for this week in the hope the weather would improve and he could train on grass. He rejected my request and he's gone to Leeds… it's a great move for him and I wish him the very best. He was absolutely first class, he conducted himself very well and I'm pleased he's got the chance to stay in English football."

Cantona's version of events? "He didn't invite me for a trial. I was there for a week and I thought I was there to sign," the Frenchman told *FourFourTwo*. "My lawyer was there and he spoke to try and find a way with my contract. I trained and played in a friendly game. We won 4-3. I scored three goals.

"After one week, he asked me to spend one more week on trial. There weren't a lot of foreigners in England then, maybe some from the north of Europe but not many from the south.

"Maybe they were suspicious, but I was a France international and Sheffield Wednesday wanted more time to decide about me. That was not a very good way to go about things."

In 2012 Francis talked to *The Yorkshire Post* about the saga, and there were a few new additions to the story. "I was doing a favour for Dennis Roach," said Francis. "He approached me with Michel Platini – he had already asked Graeme Souness – and asked me if I would do a favour to Platini. He was very keen to get Eric Cantona back playing and wondered if I would have a look at him. I said, 'I'm not in need of another centre-forward, but as a favour, I will do it'.

"It was built up as if I was looking to sign Eric Cantona which was never, ever a consideration. He was here to do a few days training, putting himself in the shop window. It took me by surprise the entourage he arrived with. At the time, we were in the midst of some pretty bad Yorkshire weather. We weren't able to get on the grass. We went onto an astroturf and had a little kickaround. Then there was an indoor tournament.

"After those two days, it was put to me are you going to sign him and I said, 'I don't think so. We would like him to stay for a few more days training'. I think his manager took that as an insult. I don't know if it was a breakdown in translation but they regarded it as he was Eric Cantona and he was not going to be on trial. The whole thing got a bit messy and he said to me, 'I have got a chance to go to Leeds', so he had my blessing.

"We had only just come into the top league and the majority of our players were on Championship (Division Two) contracts. To even contemplate getting Cantona into our 'little' Sheffield Wednesday team was never really a starter. There was never a realistic chance that Wednesday would sign him.

"He went to Leeds and did okay. I became very friendly

with Howard Wilkinson and in the year that Leeds won the championship, Howard couldn't find a regular place for Cantona. I don't think Howard was too perturbed when he received a million pounds for him."

In his 2019 autobiography, Francis added: "People still ask, 'How did you miss out on Eric Cantona?' I already had my players in forward areas. The kind of contract he would have wanted would have killed my whole budget. Hopefully this puts to bed the Cantona story – another myth!"

Unwittingly, in attempting to flee a controversial past, Cantona's first days in the UK had been the talk of the sport for all the wrong reasons. He hadn't even kicked a ball in anger. Sheffield Wednesday's role, and Trevor Francis' come to that, in Cantona's journey to Manchester United wasn't yet over. The decision to rebuff a Sir Alex Ferguson bid for David Hirst would have significant implications down the line.

Naturally, Wednesday fans consider this time a 'What if?' period of their own past, with the idea that Cantona's arrival on a permanent basis would have seen them, and not Leeds, lift the title that season. Wednesday finished third, seven points behind champions Leeds. Seven points is too big a gap to seriously consider what ifs, but close enough that supporters can't help but wonder anyway. *The Sheffield Star* described the episode as the 'biggest what if' in the club's history.

Cantona later insisted he "loved those few days in Sheffield" but he was at Elland Road to see his new club take on Notts County instead of playing for the Owls at Hillsborough against Luton.

# Brush With Glory

The tone in the reporting of Eric Cantona's move to Leeds United was altogether much more serious than it had been for Sheffield Wednesday. Perhaps that had something to do with the ambitions of Leeds under Howard Wilkinson – the club were challenging for the league title. Wilkinson's time at Elland Road had been an unqualified success; he'd instilled drive and commitment into a workmanlike squad, before adding quality components to make them one of the best teams in the country. His reputation for discipline had earned him the nickname 'Sergeant Wilko'; an affectionate moniker which his old players often still refer to him by.

Manchester United believed they had emerged as the best team in the country following their 1991 triumphs over Barcelona and Red Star, and their January successes over Leeds in the domestic cups emphasised that belief. Under Wilkinson, Leeds had established themselves as the worthiest of contenders to Alex Ferguson's team, ahead of

Arsenal and Liverpool, who were on downward trajectories.

There were similarities in the work being done at Old Trafford and Elland Road. Experienced players such as John Lukic, Gordon Strachan and Gary McAllister were complemented by bright young talent including Gary Speed, Gary Kelly, Jamie Forrester, Mark Ford and Noel Whelan – a crop of players whose reputation was not, at the time, too dissimilar to Ferguson's Class of '92, who were about to enjoy their FA Youth Cup triumph.

There was a vibrancy to Leeds' play, making them more attractive than Wilkinson's reputation would suggest. Despite concerns about how Cantona would adapt to his manager's disciplined approach, the Frenchman told reporters through an interpreter: "It's normal that a trainer wants discipline and there will be no problems about it."

Leeds defeated Notts County 3-0, with Cantona watching from the stands, and all the talk after was of the man soon to bolster Wilkinson's attack. "Eric has taken a cut, but we have put some big incentives into the arrangement which he likes the look of," Wilkinson said. "I have never signed a player without seeing him in the flesh, but I've seen enough of Eric on video. As far as I'm concerned he doesn't have a reputation because I don't believe everything I read in the press."

Cantona later revealed more of the initial conversations that took place. "My new manager invited me to watch the match between Leeds United and Notts County," he told reporters in February 1992. "Our conversation lasted a little more than an hour. No contract had been signed, but we knew a mutual adventure would soon be bringing us together. There would be no question of a trial period. My examination would take place on the field. Howard Wilkinson was convinced that I could rapidly impose myself on Leeds United, but he also let me understand that he didn't want to push me too quickly.

"English clubs display a certain distrust of foreign players. Their football is made out of aerial duels, of hard running and of tackles which cannot be endured unless a player's physical condition is almost perfect. The British establishment also thinks that while a footballer who comes from the south of Europe may have irreproachable technical skills, his body will be unable to stand up to the strains of the northern football.

"And here I can better appreciate the judgements of Michel Platini and Gerard Houllier, who helped me cross the Channel. They knew my heart and my legs were made to get on with British football."

The Frenchman was asked what he knew about Leeds. "They beat Sheffield 6-1, and a long time before that they played Bayern Munich in a European Cup final in Paris," he said. "I've always admired the English game. It's spectacular, with big crowds, and I like the rapport between players and fans... Everything is beautiful. The stadiums are beautiful, the atmosphere, the cops on horseback are beautiful. The crowds respect you."

Cantona's assessment of how the British public perceived him may well have been accurate. His reputation for technical prowess preceded him and Leeds fans were immediately taken by their enigmatic new star. Before he had even kicked a ball, the fans had a chant for him and felt his arrival would propel them to another level. Yet that excitement wasn't immediately felt in the Leeds dressing room, and, despite the furore around Cantona, it says much about the coverage of football in those days that for some, the Sheffield Wednesday story seemed to pass them by before this strange, tall, Gallic man turned up for training on the Monday after the Notts County game.

"I knew nothing of him prior to him coming in, I didn't even know about what had happened with Wednesday," Jon Newsome, the then-Leeds centre-half, told me. "You might have two or three times a season when a player would come on trial and we initially felt Eric was one of those."

Over time, Cantona's reputation as a first-class trainer was one that several Manchester United players became inspired by. In February 1992, it seemed the player was finding his feet. "Eric was really quiet, maybe because of his lack of English," Newsome recalls. "The first thing that struck me about him was that he was a proper athlete. At Leeds, Howard had a huge emphasis on fitness work, strength and conditioning, and Eric fit into that with ease… You could see in the first training session at Fullerton Road, our training ground.

"It wasn't the best surface, it was a bit muddy. There was no easing him in, balls were being pelted into him and his touch was immaculate. A few of the lads were surprised; I remember Gary McAllister commenting on how good he looked."

Tony Dorigo recalled one standout incident. "He was one amazing player," he said. "In his second training session, we were playing with goals pushed up to the 18-yard line. John Lukic threw the ball out to Eric Cantona. He was on the halfway line; the ball was falling over his shoulder. Eric volleyed it first time, right-footed into the top corner 40 yards away."

Despite the language barrier, Cantona made an immediate

attempt to integrate. "He did try and fit in. In those days the lads went out for a drink or a meal, and while he was quiet, he did come along. He never shied away from any occasions with us," said Newsome.

So Cantona was now an official member of the Leeds squad, but the controversy over his move raged on as Trevor Francis was quoted as saying he expected the player to have a second week at Wednesday; the implication being it was Cantona who broke the agreement early. Cantona responded "my behaviour has been irreproachable and entirely honourable" while his lawyer, Jean-Jacques Bertrand, added: "We knew nothing about a trial. We thought we had come to sign a loan contract. We did not have permission from Nîmes to stay at Wednesday for another week without a decision."

The week ended on a happier note. Cantona knew he was in the squad to play at Oldham on 8th February and on the morning of the game he woke to the news he had been called back into the French squad by Michel Platini, to face England at Wembley. "He is so important that I would pick him even if Leeds did not," Platini insisted.

"He sees things others cannot see. He can score or provide goals and often will prefer to make a beautiful assist than score an ugly goal. I try to tell him there is no such thing as a bad goal! But he has his own opinion."

Boundary Park in Oldham may not strike the general football fan as a venue that would be of particular interest for the French public, but the Latics game with Leeds was screened live on television in Cantona's homeland. The thousands of pairs of eyes had to make do with a cameo appearance from the new man, unable to make an impact as Leeds lost 2-0. "English defenders are very determined but always fair," Cantona said afterwards. "I didn't really enjoy that. It was very fast, too fast for me at times, physical, but not dirty."

It was Wembley next for Cantona to play his first full match in England. Eric lined up alongside Jean-Pierre Papin but the game was decided by goals from Alan Shearer and Gary Lineker. Afterwards, he explained he was still getting used to the speed of the game.

Cantona was selected for his first start, wearing number nine (replacing the absent Lee Chapman) at Goodison Park against Everton. It was a quiet performance in a 1-1 draw though after the game Howard Wilkinson did stress Cantona would quickly adapt to the physical demands of the English game.

The Leeds fans wouldn't have to wait too much longer to begin to see what the fuss was all about. However, with Chapman back for the visit of Luton Town, Wilkinson put Cantona back on the bench.

The signing had brought a tactical headache of where to play him. Wilkinson was playing a 4-3-3/4-5-1 with Chapman serving as the figurehead, while Cantona's best form had come playing in a deeper role. This much was obvious to all, even to those who only had a limited time with him, such as Danny Wilson at Sheffield Wednesday, who had noted Eric would not be the type of striker to make runs behind defenders.

This made him different to the likes of Rod Wallace, a more nimble player, who had something in his locker that Cantona chose not to have. And chose has to be the right term here, for there was no doubting Cantona possessed the speed to run past opponents, if that took his fancy. There are rare instances of that occurring throughout his career, usually as moments of surprise. Also within his capability but not his natural game was the role of a traditional target man, filled by Chapman.

Cantona's ideal position was not a role the Leeds United team had for him, so his most likely place would be one of the wide forwards. Cantona would attempt to play in the narrower pockets between the full-back and the centre-half, rather than wide on the touchline. This was where he found his greatest success in a Leeds shirt, anyway.

In the first half against Luton, Wilkinson was forced into a reshuffle when Tony Dorigo was injured. Cantona came on and played just off Chapman, registering his first goal for the club when Gary McAllister's lay-off presented him with an empty net. Five minutes from the end, Eric turned provider, intercepting the goalkeeper's clearance to head towards Chapman, who secured a crucial three points. It had been a mixed game for Cantona, though the tactical reshuffle which accompanied his introduction hadn't helped.

"It's trench warfare out there and it helps if you know when to duck," Wilkinson said. "Eric is going to take time to adapt to a totally different environment and a more frantic style of football and we have a bit of a communication problem. By the time you shout 'Duck', he's dead. We are a team who shout a lot and Eric is not getting all the messages yet. He's an excellent player. It's just a shame he wasn't born in Barnsley."

Cantona, meanwhile, was able to convey one message: "I'm very happy for the goal. Leeds are a very good team."

Lee Chapman, standing alongside Eric on the Elland Road pitch after the game, told reporters: "Eric doesn't speak the language. It's very difficult for him, it will take time, but he's a good player and good players don't need to talk the same language and I thought today we fitted in very well together. Eric was getting my flick ons and he looked lively."

In his 1993 book *My Story*, Cantona was more verbose about

his first strike: "There is nothing more paradoxical nor more breathtaking than a goal in front of a crowd which is waiting for it," he recalled. "At that exact moment when the ball went into the net, thousands of supporters behind the goal seemed to plunge towards the turf. In scoring this goal at the Kop End I became seduced. I had met, it seemed, my new family."

Cantona was back on the bench two weeks later as Leeds travelled to play Tottenham Hotspur. With 15 minutes left he came on with the visitors leading 2-1. Within seconds, he had set up a goal for Gary McAllister to secure the points and settle the nerves. Leeds were top, after a four-game wobble. It was one of their most significant results of the season.

There was one goal for Cantona in March, in a 5-1 win over Wimbledon when he took to the field in the number 3 shirt. He was, however, playing up front, and was able to mostly play in the hole behind Chapman. It was a thrilling performance and Cantona's goal, after he had run the entirety of the Wimbledon half with the ball, was most certainly the highlight. A 1-1 draw at Arsenal strengthened Leeds' position, but a 4-0 drubbing at Manchester City did the Blues' neighbours United a favour to send them back top.

City did at least return the favour a few days later by getting a 1-1 draw at Old Trafford. Alex Ferguson's team were two points clear with a game in hand and heavy favourites to win their first league title in 25 years. However, an unavoidable obstacle laid in wait for the Manchester club; the poor winter and their cup form had come at a significant cost, with a number of league games rescheduled. They would play Southampton at home, Luton Town away, Nottingham Forest at home and West Ham away with just 48 hours between each game.

Then, just ten days after the Southampton game, this hellish run of fixtures would conclude with a trip to Anfield. Leeds would have their own trip to Liverpool and the congested Easter schedule of two games in three days but other than that, had a good amount of space between each match.

United full-back Clayton Blackmore would later lament his own role in proceedings; his excellent goal at Elland Road that eliminated Leeds from the League Cup contributed to the respective fixture schedules. Mark Hughes had also scored to knock Wilkinson's side out of the FA Cup, though, at the time, it wasn't seen as the blessing in disguise it would turn out to be for the Leeds players.

"It didn't cross our mind," Jon Newsome says. "We felt disappointment to be eliminated from the cups. Particularly in those days, it was a big disappointment... yes, it's true we could concentrate on the league, but that wasn't even something we spoke about. Only in the last half dozen games, that's when we discussed the title. Howard kept telling us to carry on and play our football. Manchester United were an outstanding side. But we had a great side, and a great youth side too, so there was every reason to believe we were on a level playing field."

One of those games was Chelsea, though Leeds did enough to establish a 1-0 lead against them, with a goal from Rod Wallace, who was brought off for Eric late on. Cantona made a sensational cameo here, which undoubtedly ranks highest when Leeds supporters look back at his contribution to their title-winning campaign. He was provider first, setting up

Chapman to secure the points, before scoring a remarkable third goal to leave the home fans bewildered at the stardust they had just witnessed. He ran on to a throw-in down the right channel, already having the bouncing ball under his control. Here he was closed down by Chelsea defender Paul Elliott, seen of as one of the most intelligent minds in the game. Elliot, however, was unable to prevent Cantona bamboozling him, as the Frenchman outrageously flicked the ball over his head, once to the left, and once more, before the ball had even bounced again, to the right. It presented the opportunity for a shot at goal, which Cantona took emphatically, smashing the ball into the top corner. Gary McAllister later said: "It was a privilege to be on the pitch when it went in."

Leeds were back on top, but all that anyone was talking about after the game was this moment of magic. Elliot magnanimously compared Cantona to Marco van Basten; English football suddenly had every reason to understand the hype.

Cantona later described the goal: "In three touches I deceived the defenders, without the ball touching the ground and then finally placed the ball in the far corner of the net. The fans stood up in the stands, singing and chanting. It was a very moving and extraordinary experience."

Surprisingly, this moment of magic also presented the first murmurings of discontent. Gordon Strachan, whose throw technically counted as the 'assist', dismissed the quality of the goal by saying, "It came when the game was already won." Not exactly a scathing criticism, but laced with enough subtext to suggest some didn't want their own contributions overlooked.

Of course there are moments in football which stand alone within bigger storylines and the goal was certainly one of those. It was said the moment finally convinced Wilkinson to make Cantona's move permanent. But there were reports on 10th April, the day before the Chelsea game, that it was Leeds' intention to do so before the deadline of 15th April which had been imposed by Nîmes. Leeds had paid £100,000 with a further £800,000 due if the move was made permanent. Wilkinson had waited until the last minute, as Cantona's wage of £7,000 per week would be a big commitment.

In 2019, Wilkinson used a different line – that the move was almost certain to not be made permanent. "We had an understanding that if we wanted him after a certain date we had to pay," Wilkinson told the *Daily Mail*. "We expected him to go back but then we're in the title race, and Chapman got a serious facial injury. We were playing Chelsea and Cantona scored a goal where the ball came in the box, he flicked it over his head, over the centre half's head and volleyed it in and the Kop went crazy. The chairman is sat next to me. He digs me with his elbow and says, 'That's just cost me a million quid'."

No more goals followed that season but Cantona continued to make a significant impact. After coming off the bench at Coventry, he won a penalty almost immediately, which Gary McAllister scored to secure a 2-0 win. It was the defining moment. Manchester United were in freefall, with injuries costing them dearly in defeats to Forest and West Ham.

It set up a huge day where Leeds would play at Sheffield United and Manchester United would go to Liverpool. In the week before these games, Cantona was named in the French squad for the European Championship that summer.

Leeds played their game first, on the 26th April, and looked nervous to begin with. A fortuitous Rod Wallace goal just on half-time drew them level. Jon Newsome then headed the visitors into the lead before a scrambled equaliser from the

Blades. Then, under pressure from Cantona, home defender Brian Gayle headed over his own keeper and into the net. Leeds had one hand on the Championship trophy and would have both if United failed to win at Liverpool. Which is precisely what happened.

The days which followed were of understandable jubilation. After an open-top bus parade to the City Hall, Cantona looked out over the thousands of supporters in the street and told them in his broken English: "Why I love you? I don't know why, but I love you."

On the last day of the season, an interview with David Hopps, titled 'The Frenchman who made champs of Leeds' was printed in *The Guardian*. "I lived in France with the same pressures as Paul Gascoigne suffered here," Eric told Hopps. "My passion for the game was far outweighed by the problems. Football is my life but I needed to live a normal existence outside the game. I decided never to play football anywhere in the world except England. I'm scared to sound like a hypocrite but the way I've been received has been exceptional. It would be an advantage to speak more English, but football is a language and I'm a Frenchman; I can speak with my hands. The fact that spectators are excited by the way I play is one of my greatest sources of pride. I have always played football for pleasure."

Cantona, by his own admission, had struggled to sleep over the week between the penultimate and final fixture of the season through the adrenalin. In something of a reversal of the trend, he started the game against Norwich and was brought off with 15 minutes to go, to rapturous applause.

Gary McAllister described Cantona's influence in the title race as "vital", and Tony Dorigo said "he was important to us" but not everyone sees it that way. "He contributed, but I would say he played a small part in it," says Jon Newsome. "You've got to be careful to give the praise fairly – it would be unfair to the lads who played 40-odd games to give all the praise to Eric.

"He did his bit, he scored some great goals, important goals, but then you could say that about many of the players in that run-in. Maybe it gets attached to him more because of what happened when he went to Manchester United."

It is true that Cantona's contribution of three goals in 15 appearances is perhaps embellished but, as with everything associated with him, his influence transcended mere numbers, as well as the conventional standard of appraisal for footballers.

They were hardly a team in trouble without him, but Cantona's arrival gave Leeds an extra presence in attack, with a few crucial assists in there as well as goals, and that certain sense of *je ne sais quoi*. The Yorkshire club were suddenly far more multi-dimensional and cosmopolitan, with Eric's presence transforming them from a conventional attacking outlet into an unpredictable menace. The goal scored against Chelsea was the sort you just couldn't imagine anyone else in the British game having the skill to execute.

Newsome is right to say that Eric's contribution is overstated because over time it occasionally is misrepresented as a suggestion that Cantona single-handedly won the league for Leeds. That wasn't true, and it is a disservice to all who did contribute so much. However, it is not an exaggeration to say he made a crucial, or even the crucial, difference.

There was much to look forward to for the Frenchman and Leeds. A three-year deal was on the table and he had found an adoring support in his adopted home. However, things were about to take a familiar turn in the eventful life of Eric Cantona.

# Leader or Follower?

I t was clear that a major reason behind Eric Cantona's winter U-turn was the forthcoming European Championship and an assurance from Michel Platini that he would be selected for the squad. France had failed to qualify for the 1990 World Cup and this was Eric's first opportunity to play in a major international tournament.

Perhaps this also goes some way to explaining his decision to follow Platini's suggested path to England. If that choice was made with Sweden 1992 in mind then the experience of the tournament was an undoubted disappointment.

The competition started brightly enough and Eric was named alongside Jean-Pierre Papin up front for their first game. Platini changed his own 4-3-3 system to accommodate Cantona, but the Leeds forward's only contribution of note was a booking. Papin grabbed France's equaliser in a 1-1 draw against Sweden. Cantona and Papin played together for the full 90 minutes in the next game, too, a dull goalless draw with England. Both of these sides were eliminated before the knock-out stages, with England losing 2-1 to the host nation and France going down by the same score to eventual winners Denmark. In his 1993 book *My Story*, Cantona described the tournament as a "great anti-climax."

If there was a trend amidst the transience of Cantona's career, then it was probably how his fortunes tended to change once he worked with a manager he didn't get on with. So when Michel Platini left the France post after the summer of 1992, Cantona's relationship with the national team became more complex. "It took me some time to get over the disappointment of Platini's departure, to whom I owe so much," Cantona said. "I would have wished that he had left with the victory which his stature and talent merited."

With Eric being such a complex personality, there was perhaps a certain inevitability of a polarising period awaiting him back at Elland Road. Partly subdued due to France's failure, Cantona should have felt optimism back in Yorkshire. He certainly seemed ready for the rigours of the English league and spoke positively about his staggered integration.

There was always the reality, though, that Leeds had overperformed in 1992, and their mean league position was, to be blunt, lower than first. Liverpool had been the last club to retain the title in 1984. Leeds' victory was not quite the underdog story of a Leicester City in 2016 but nor were they favourites to win the first Premier League title. That distinction went to Arsenal. Of course, in Eric, Leeds had an ace who could make the difference, but by the time the new season rolled around, the atmosphere at Elland Road was markedly different.

Resentment may not quite fit, because Cantona was almost as popular with his team-mates as the Leeds fans, but there was a certain dissatisfaction about the perceived dispropor-tionate nature of the contribution attributed to the Frenchman in Leeds' title win. Worse still, that stemmed from the top.

In Philippe Auclair's book on Cantona, the author intimates Wilkinson was "puzzled" by the plaudits given to Eric, and felt the forward was "stealing his thunder". It's a theory that holds more water when you consider the acrimony which was to follow, and also Wilkinson's admission that until the goal against Chelsea, there hadn't been an intention to make Cantona's move permanent. Still, the decision had been made, and 'Sergeant Wilko' now had a reason to force Cantona to conform. In the hard days of a pre-season, that approach may not have been surprising. After all, this was Cantona's first summer in England, and he welcomed the physical test.

It was natural that everyone wanted to see if there was sustenance in Cantona's form or if he was merely capable of these rare moments of gold dust. Damagingly, though, the eagerness to test Cantona appeared to extend to within Elland Road. Where once his individual ways had been embraced, they would quickly be seen as rebellious. Wilkinson, having now committed to Cantona for the long haul, sought to impose his own standards on the player.

Another word relevant to the debate was accommodation. The connotations of this word often reflect badly upon any footballer because should they require accommodation then the first question is usually: Isn't that player good enough to fit in? The rebuttal, more often than not, is that it not about the player, it is about the team, and allowances cannot be made. The Uniteds of Leeds and Manchester were about to provide two very interesting case studies in accommodation.

After a pre-season which didn't seem to suggest Cantona

would be an automatic first choice, the player started against Liverpool in the Charity Shield. And, for the first time, he would wear the number seven shirt. This, though, was still in the days before names were put on numbers to 'own' them (that was the following season). Times were indeed changing and another new development was the 'no-backpass' rule. Many teams suffered drastically from this new law and Leeds were one of the victims, as John Lukic struggled to adapt.

The champions would concede four goals on six separate occasions in the league and four times before Christmas. They also conceded three to Liverpool at Wembley, but luckily Cantona made history by becoming the first foreigner to score a hat-trick at England's most famous stadium. Leeds won 4-3, a red herring that positive days were to come that season.

"Despite enjoying cult status at Elland Road, he was little more than a peripheral figure as Leeds won the title, but he is said to have benefited greatly from Wilkinson's arduous pre-season regime, and certainly looked both fitter and sharper," wrote Joe Lovejoy in *The Independent*.

"If he can sustain form and enthusiasm, he will be a snip at £900,000 – a quarter of what Blackburn Rovers have paid for the less gifted Alan Shearer... if the Frenchman applies himself he should be much the better player. As ever with the flair merchants, it is a question of attitude rather than aptitude."

Howard Wilkinson insisted his own influence had facilitated the great performance. "He's better now than he was six months ago," the Leeds boss told reporters. "He has benefited from pre-season training, but he's still learning. When I say nice things to him, he understands me very well. When I suggest he works harder, he finds it more difficult."

Cantona later described the hat-trick in "the temple of

football" as "one of the best days in my career". In the week between the Charity Shield and League opener, he told *L'Equipe* that he felt "more open" in England than in France. "It is not that I have changed, I am the same," he said. "It is rather as if I am now the son of the person I used to be."

In the season opener on 15th August, and the first ever Premier League game at Elland Road, Leeds played Wimbledon. In their match programme, season-ticket holder Terry French had written a poem entitled *Ode to Eric*; on the pitch, Cantona created the winning goal for Lee Chapman.

A draw at Aston Villa followed before a 4-1 capitulation at Middlesbrough; Cantona scoring Leeds' consolation, and emerging as the only player with any credit. Eric's supreme consistency was the only sure thing from an erratic Leeds side who followed that Boro humbling by trouncing Tottenham 5-0. Cantona scored another hat-trick, and created a goal for Lee Chapman. Absurdly, Wilkinson still seemed to believe the Frenchman was the reason for the sudden dysfunction.

Both Wilkinson and Cantona were bemused by Gerard Houllier's decision to name Eric in his first France squad, for a friendly against Brazil in Paris the day after the Spurs game (Houllier having been named as Platini's replacement). Cantona travelled, despite everyone knowing he couldn't play.

Having missed a day with Leeds in the build-up to a huge game against Liverpool, Cantona was livid and announced to *L'Equipe* that he was "done" with the national team. It would only be temporary, but Houllier told reporters that Cantona had requested to not be selected for the World Cup qualifier against Bulgaria in September. "Eric told me he didn't feel mentally ready to play for France," Houllier said.

Cantona was the subject of attention for the build-up to the weekend's big game. Liverpool defender David Burrows spoke about their recent Wembley encounter. "Cantona has a vast amount of flair and quality and an eye for goal," he said. "I couldn't get near him that day. If you give an international player like him space he's going to show his quality."

Cantona returned to England and played well again against Liverpool and then scored both goals in the 2-2 draw at Oldham. With nine goals in seven games, the striker had started the campaign in blistering fashion and was the centre of attention as Leeds travelled to Old Trafford.

This was no top of the table encounter, though. Alex Ferguson's side had lost two of their first three games of the season and had also suffered the blow of an injury to striker Dion Dublin. The former Cambridge man had arrived for £1m after Ferguson had failed to sign Alan Shearer from Southampton and David Hirst from Sheffield Wednesday. But Dublin broke his leg, leaving United short up front. It was sixth vs eighth in front of the Sky television cameras.

In his column for *The Guardian* that day, Lee Chapman spoke about Cantona's issues with the language barrier and his own experiences playing in France: "A significant part of any footballer's life is his involvement in dressing-room banter. To listen to this day after day without understanding a word leaves you feeling very frustrated. Life on the field for Eric could not have contrasted more vividly with his experience in France. Instead of the slow build-up game favoured by French teams he found himself trying to come to terms with the frenetic pace of the English First Division.

"It was no surprise he looked at his best coming on as a substitute, when we witnessed the flashes of brilliance that proved to be a taste of things to come... Eric's ability to run at players and create situations out of nothing has given our attack an extra dimension. It has also encouraged those around him to be more adventurous. He is competent in the air and is not found wanting on the physical side. His recent decision to stop playing for France is a sign of further commitment to Leeds. Today, in front of a live TV audience, Eric can display just exactly what France will be missing."

Cantona was subjected to pantomime booing from the United fans. He was playing on the left of a front three after tactical switches by both managers had created a bizarre pattern of play. Cantona had been tipped to play on the right, in front of Jon Newsome and David Batty. But Newsome was moved to centre-half and Chris Fairclough was given the task of marking Ryan Giggs. Only one issue; Giggs and Kanchelskis switched places, and United also had two-footed full backs in Denis Irwin and Clayton Blackmore, which threw Leeds' balance off and helped to create the opening goal, made by Giggs for Kanchelskis. Ferguson's team were 2-0 up at the break after an error from John Lukic allowed Steve Bruce to score. The visitors were unable to make an impression but Cantona came closest with an acrobatic overhead kick, having escaped the attention of Gary Pallister and Steve Bruce.

The following week, there were renewed hopes of Cantona turning out for France when he was paid a visit by Gerard Houllier. "We spoke of my son's drawing, of the child's imaginary world, of life, of Leeds, which is a nice town,"

Cantona told Canal Plus TV. Would he return to the national side? "If they need me." That time would come very soon.

The timing of Houllier's visit would turn out to be crucial. Already, tensions between Cantona and Wilkinson were growing as the Leeds boss pressed back against the conventional wisdom of not upsetting your star man.

"I began to have increasing difficulty in decoding the language used by my manager," Cantona said in *My Story*. "His comments were strange and incoherent. One moment he would tell me I owe everything to him, that I was a Frenchman lost in the English league and at other times he would say that without me the team is nothing and that I am the essential piece. I do not understand such contradictory messages.

"If you look at the statistics of my contribution to the team, he had no reason to reproach me for anything. He was unable to criticise my attitude to training or my relations with my team-mates. I discussed these problems with my family, but I was at a loss to understand. What did he want from me? I was adored by the Leeds fans, I was working as hard as ever. But our relationship continued to get worse."

One of the common criticisms of Cantona was related to his performances in the European Cup. Those began from his very first game in the competition for Leeds, at Stuttgart. Cantona had lost possession in the build-up to Stuttgart's first goal in Germany in a 3-0 loss. He had pulled his hamstring in the process but was set to play in the return.

On the eve of the second leg, Wilkinson had heralded Cantona as possibly the greatest signing in the club's history – considering this was the club who had bought the great John Charles, it was quite a statement. "I had resigned myself to

Eric missing the second leg," he told reporters ahead of the game. "He made a crucial error which might have had the effect of prolonging his injury, but he has been nurturing a wish to make amends."

The press conference came on the same day that Wilkinson's autobiography, *Managing to Succeed*, was published, with the headline being that he had rated Cantona's chances of making a long-term impression in England as "less than even".

For Leeds to have any hope of qualification then an early goal seemed necessary. Just before the 20th minute, Cantona's fantastic cushioned header into the path of Gary Speed got the comeback started.

Stuttgart equalised in the 34th minute. Within five minutes a penalty for Leeds restored their advantage on the night but they had to wait until midway through the second half to revive genuine hope. Cantona got between two defenders and flicked the ball over the goalkeeper. Leeds were in front 3-1 and even got a fourth through Chapman. They could have completed the most unlikely of turnarounds when Cantona was presented with an opportunity to make it five. His chip went over; Leeds were eliminated. Or so they thought.

In the 83rd minute Stuttgart brought on defender Jovica Simanić. There was just one problem. Simanić was from Yugoslavia, and the German team already had three foreign players on the field – the limit as permitted for the competition. The German side were punished with a 0-3 scoreline, on this occasion precisely the outcome needed for Leeds to draw the tie. Although they argued their opponents should have been disqualified, a play-off game in Barcelona was arranged.

In that game, Cantona struggled and was brought off with the game tied at 1-1. Within a minute, his replacement, Carl

Shutt, had scored to earn a place in the next round against Glasgow Rangers.

Having been allowed to delay joining up with the international squad to play in that game in Spain, Cantona had a star turn as France defeated Austria 2-0; he set up the first and scored the second. He explained his absence from the previous game as trying to ensure his wife and son were settled in Yorkshire. Additionally, Cantona had felt devastated by Platini's departure, and clearly Houllier's September intervention had been warranted. "It seemed to me difficult to live without him, and it was," Cantona said of Platini to *L'Equipe*. "It's like a woman you love who goes away. Every one you meet after seems faded. Even the most beautiful."

So much of the subtext of Cantona's psyche seemed to revolve around loyalty and fairness. There could be no doubting of his commitment to the Leeds cause in his time there; even putting his international career at risk to benefit his club. But Leeds' ambitions for the 1992/93 season needed hasty revision. Three defeats before the October international break tempered hopes of retaining the title, but there was a European tie against Rangers, dubbed 'The Battle of Britain'.

It certainly was a battle for Eric in the first leg as he dealt with some aggressive attention at Ibrox. Leeds lost 2-1 and towards the end of the game, Cantona was substituted for Rod Wallace. He headed straight down the tunnel.

Gerard Houllier travelled to Leeds to watch the return leg, and before the game met Howard Wilkinson. The Leeds boss showed Houllier a tape of the Rangers game, specifically Cantona's reaction to being brought off. Houllier tried to explain that in France, players would often do that late in games, but Wilkinson insisted it was an act of disrespect.

In Philippe Auclair's book on Cantona, Houllier – who had also been at Ibrox, where he was sitting next to none other than Alex Ferguson – told the author he recalled saying to Ferguson: "Maybe I'll have to find another club for him."

Leeds' hopes of making an early impression in that return were dashed when their visitors did instead; Mark Hateley's sensational goal gave them a strong advantage. It was apparent in games such as these, where Leeds were underdogs, that there was perhaps a greater incompatibility with their style and Cantona's. Against Rangers it seemed to be a game plan that balls would be played behind the defence for Cantona to run onto. Though he was no slouch, that did not seem to be a tactic which worked to Cantona's strengths. He preferred the ball to him, so he could paint the picture in front of him. He wanted to play in front of his opponent.

It wouldn't be the last time this discussion would be held in Cantona's career, but the reality was nothing to do with his ability to perform against continental opposition, rather, a basic matter of where he was asked to play.

Leeds went 2-0 down on the night, and 4-1 down on aggregate, when Ally McCoist headed home. The English champions now needed four goals, or further administration errors, to rescue them. Cantona did have the final word on Leeds' European campaign when he scored in the 86th minute, volleying in from a Chapman knockdown, as Leeds threw everyone forward.

However, as friction between player and manager increased, they were about to reach a stage where the relationship would break down rapidly and irretrievably...

# Creative Differences

The morning after the European Cup exit, Howard Wilkinson tried to pick his team up for the away game against QPR in two days' time. That courtesy of a morale-boosting exercise did not extend to Cantona, who travelled with the team to London ahead of an agreed period of leave in France for a couple of days, only to be given his passport in front of his team-mates and told unceremoniously "Off you go!" by Wilkinson. The Leeds players were speechless.

The matter had been compounded by a personal meeting the evening before where Wilkinson had informed Cantona that he wouldn't be playing because his style was incompatible with what the manager wanted. It was suggested by some in the press that Cantona had even walked out on the club.

In his 1993 book *More Than A Match*, Lee Chapman recalled the episode: "Eric's departure took most people by surprise, even though the players had realised his days were numbered. After our defeat by Rangers, Eric was dropped for the game against QPR but the team was not announced until the morning of the match, when we gathered to rehearse our set-pieces. Those not in the starting line-up are handed red bibs and required to act as the opposition; quite often the first a player knows of [being dropped] is when the coach, Mick Hennigan, thrusts the dreaded bib in his direction.

"To say Eric was not thrilled would be an understatement. On our return to the hotel he ignored two attempts at conversation by the manager. He also failed to turn up for the pre-match meal and arrived late for the team meeting wearing the kind of clothes I knew would antagonise the manager.

"Eric was given a public dressing-down and told to make his journey to Paris immediately. I knew from that moment Eric would leave sooner rather than later. There can be no doubt Eric's sublime talent was not suited to Leeds' more direct style. His inclusion demanded compromises from both player and team, and neither was best served."

Bizarrely, that was not the end of Cantona at Elland Road. Once he had returned from France, Eric maintained his professionalism for a time. "He was a very good trainer," Tony Dorigo told the *Mail* in 2017. "We had no problems with that. There were no doubts over his ability.

"I remember one time in training he scored this incredible goal, and anyone else would have gone absolutely crazy and run around like a lunatic. He just jogged back to the halfway line and was like, 'Let's start again, that's what I do.' We stood there thinking, 'Okay, we've got this now.'

"You could see the player. When he left, I felt we lost something. He could give us something a bit different. Our strength was team spirit and the boss felt it didn't work. Howard was very demanding of people to do certain things and Eric didn't do everything. We also didn't play to his strengths. He had to fit into how we wanted to play."

It wasn't working. Leeds were eliminated from the League Cup by Watford with Cantona putting in possibly his poorest showing for the club. Recalling the chain of events which led to Cantona leaving, former Leeds chief executive Bill Fotherby said in 2017: "All the conversations with Howard were, 'If you can get Cantona out of Leeds, get him out.'

"On our training ground they would go through set-plays and moves. Howard was very strict. He would say, 'You, Cantona, you stand in front of the centre-half.' Cantona would reply, 'I don't do this' (and then spit). He wouldn't stand there and head the ball. He walked off. He was causing a little bit of friction."

Following a temporary reprieve on international duty – where Cantona scored in a 2-1 win over Finland – things finally came to a head as Leeds prepared to face Arsenal.

"The gaffer announced the team on the Thursday – Eric wasn't in it – and we went out to train," remembers Jon Newsome. "Within five minutes Eric said he had torn his thigh, so the gaffer sent him to see the physio. After training, Howard went to the treatment room where he was told Eric hadn't been in. He'd walked off the training ground, had a shower and gone home. So on Friday we had a team meeting and Eric turned up late. We had club suits on and he turned up in jeans. A few words were spoken. The following week he was gone."

The journalist David Walker corroborated that story to the *Mirror* in 2017. "Cantona shirked responsibility on defending at corners and free-kicks and, on one occasion, walked off the training ground claiming he had a muscle injury," Walker said. "I've never met a Leeds player from 1992 who felt Wilkinson made the wrong call by selling Cantona. They all knew how

Eric's previous club careers invariably ended in tears, tantrums and walk-outs. They couldn't trust him. He had to go."

Indeed, a furious Cantona refused to report for training the following week – and, in his place, a transfer request arrived instead. The faxed request included the enigmatic line: "The salmon that idles its way downstream will never leap the waterfall", according to Paddy Barclay's *Football – Bloody Hell!* biography of Alex Ferguson. Whether idling or leaping, Leeds United had just won 3-0 against Arsenal in a rare victory that seemed to justify Wilkinson's decision.

In May 2017, Wilkinson recalled: "I left him out against QPR and that didn't go down well. He went back to France. We got a transfer request a week later that said he wanted to go to Manchester United, Liverpool or Arsenal. It was out there on the football radar. We couldn't hide the fact that he was in the squad for the QPR game and then on the Saturday lunchtime he'd gone. People knew he'd disappeared."

"For me it was ridiculous and it was obvious he couldn't stay at the club," says Newsome. "Eric wasn't toeing the line. He'd burned his bridges with the gaffer."

Gordon Strachan – of course, a prior critic of Eric's – later insisted it wasn't just the manager the Frenchman had fallen out with. "Eric had made up his mind that he couldn't relate to big Lee Chapman as a player," said Strachan. "He found it hard to understand how Chappy played and Chappy found it difficult to understand him. We had to play a different style... we didn't have megabucks to change the whole side just to suit Eric Cantona. Hard work made us tick – and no lack of skill, but sometimes when we went away from home, Eric just couldn't understand what we were at. It frustrated him. When we went to Rangers, he just didn't produce a performance. We needed a bit of help He had made up his mind he wanted to leave. Nobody had anything against him personally. ."

Cantona's transfer request stated, strangely, that he wanted to move to one of three clubs – Arsenal, Liverpool or Manchester United. Most reports of his eventual transfer refer to it as a bolt from the blue; an accident which only happened because of a phone call made about another player. It seems a coincidence that a transfer request can be made, specifically mentioning a football club, on 24th November, and a speculative enquiry from said football club can be made in the other direction on the same day, with the deal being concluded the following day.

And yet a coincidence it appears to be; and if time has presented the deal harshly in the perspective of Leeds, let us at least remember there was little chance of the relationship between Eric Cantona and Howard Wilkinson improving.

Instead, it was heading towards implosion, and far from them feeling like they lost out by selling him so cheaply, Leeds United may have found themselves paying the price of a hefty three-year contract to get the player off their books, on top of the £1m they had paid Nîmes. There was also the matter of a £500,000 bonus Leeds had agreed to pay Cantona if he stayed for a certain length of time.

The story of Cantona's move to Manchester is instigated by a phone call from Bill Fotherby, so his account is probably the best to begin with.

"I rang United about Denis Irwin, who had been at Leeds as

a young boy," Fotherby told *The Independent*. "Martin Edwards said there was no chance but I asked him to at least speak to Alex (Ferguson). Normally, I wouldn't have expected him to ring back. This time he did, offering me a different player I knew Howard would not be interested in. It was then he asked about Eric. I said no way and that it was impossible.

"But I knew what Howard felt about him, and I knew this additional payment was due. Martin asked if I would talk to Howard. Howard was out house-hunting in Leeds, so the only person I spoke to was Mick Hennigan. I said, 'I can't believe it. Guess what has come out of the blue. Howard will absolutely love it'. I left it a couple of hours, rang Martin and said, 'I can't believe this but Howard is willing to let the boy go'."

In 2019, Martin Edwards' version of the story was as follows: "I was in my office one afternoon when I got a call from Bill Fotherby. He said, 'Martin, Howard quite fancies Denis Irwin, would you be prepared to sell him?' I said I didn't think so, I would ask Alex but I doubted it.

"But then something suddenly came to mind. I was friends with Irving Scholar, the former Tottenham Hotspur chairman who lived in Monaco. Whenever we talked he would rave about this lad Cantona. 'He's made for you, he's a player made for United,' he would say. 'His style of play is suited to United. I can see him in that red and white strip.'

"Having read about the falling out between Howard and Eric, I remembered how important he'd been to Leeds' title win. If he hadn't gone there, I am sure we would have won it. He kept on scoring important goals and had crucial contributions, and then he scored that hat-trick against Liverpool in the Charity Shield, when he was magnificent.

"I told Bill, 'I'll find out about Denis, but would you be

prepared to sell Cantona?' Bill was almost too honest for his own good. 'You know, that's not as daft as it sounds,' he said. So I called Alex and told him of Bill's enquiry. He said no, as I expected. And then I said, 'Would you take Cantona if I could get him?' Alex said, 'Too bloody right I would!'

"Bill called to follow up about Irwin. I told him Alex wasn't having that, but we'd take Cantona off his hands, almost as if we were doing him a favour! Bill said, 'We're open to selling him, but we have one problem at our end. He's very popular. The crowd love him. We'll get slaughtered. Howard will do it, but only if we do it very quickly. I said that was no problem."

The consequential negotiation over the fee reads almost like a sitcom exchange.

Edwards: "What do you want for him?"

Fotherby: "£1.6m."

Edwards: "I won't pay that. But we'll take him off your hands for a million."

Fotherby: "I can't do a million! I told you I'd get slaughtered. I'd get lynched at that price. £1.5m… what about £1.4m? I can't go any lower than £1.2m."

Edwards: "Bill, I'll give you a million."

Fotherby: "Well, can I say it's £1.2m?"

Edwards: "You can say what you like."

"I called Alex to tell him and he couldn't believe it," Edwards says. "I know there are many variations of the story but I hadn't ever had a conversation with him about Cantona before that."

Sir Alex's recollection of the story famously differs from Edwards' but is presented here in the interest of completion: the Manchester United manager says he was in Edwards' office at the time the call was made from Fotherby, and that he wrote Cantona's name down on a sheet of paper to raise the question. Ferguson says the phone call had occurred during a conversation where chairman and manager were discussing signing Peter Beardsley to replace the injured Dublin.

Whatever the intricacies of how events unfolded, Cantona and Bertrand travelled to the Midland Hotel in Manchester to meet Ferguson and Edwards on Wednesday 26th November. The agreement for him to sign for Manchester United was a formality. Ferguson had hoped to rush the transfer through so Cantona could play at Arsenal on Saturday, but was unable to.

There was a little more information in Ferguson's post-retirement book *Leading*: "After a game against Leeds United... I was in the bath with the players, listening to their analysis of the match. Steve Bruce and Gary Pallister were raving about Eric Cantona... Bruce was particularly complimentary...

"Even as we signed Eric Cantona, I sought advice from people I trusted. I chatted with Gerard Houllier and the French sports journalist Erik Bielderman. I also spoke to Michel Platini who said, 'You should sign him, his character is underestimated, he just needs a bit of understanding.'"

Ferguson also described how unusual the negotiation had been: "I've never seen a deal done as quickly as Eric Cantona's. We met at a hotel in Manchester. He came with Jean-Jacques Bertrand from the PFA in France. So we had a cup of tea there, and Jean-Jacques went to the table with the chairman. The chairman got his calculator out and said, 'We'll do that.' Eric and I were just having a cup of tea. Eric doesn't speak much English, and I was practising my French.

And the chairman said, 'Right, can we shake on that?'

Jean-Jacques said, 'Yes!'

'Eric, you haven't told Eric,' I said.

And Jean-Jacques never even asked Eric if he was happy

with it. Eric always trusts him to do the deal. But that must have all been done in half an hour."

The United boss described the press interest on the Thursday and Friday as "incredible". The Old Trafford club had long been the most popular club in the country. They had even drawn the highest crowds in the country, on average, in their season in the Second Division in the 1970s. Despite their quarter-century of underachievement, there was a fascination with recapturing the glory of the Sir Matt Busby era.

In 1992, they came as close as they ever had to regaining the title, and Eric Cantona was perceived as a last throw of the dice by Ferguson. His team had just won against Oldham Athletic but that was preceded by seven league games without a win which had left them in 10th place. Goals were a problem, with United failing to score in a third of their games. The pressure was building and so to bring in Cantona was a bold move.

In 2016, the transfer of Paul Pogba back to Manchester United from Juventus was launched with a promotional video by adidas posted on social media, with the midfielder posing alongside grime artist Stormzy. The announcement sent the sporting world into a frenzy. It was a world away from how most United fans learned about Eric Cantona signing for the club, which was either on the late news or via Teletext.

"We're pleased to announce we have agreed terms with Leeds United for the transfer of Eric Cantona and he's agreed a new three-and-a half-year contract to take him through to the end of June 1996," Martin Edwards said at a press conference on Friday November 27th as he sat flanked by Cantona and Alex Ferguson.

"I see Eric as a Manchester United player, the kind we want at this club," Ferguson said. "He has style, he has class and this club will suit him. His goalscoring was instrumental in the success of Leeds. I am happy to bring another striker to the club, one who won't be overawed by playing at Old Trafford."

"I wouldn't say I was shocked, but I was surprised," Ferguson admitted, referring to how easily the transfer was conducted. "It's strange how things develop."

It was put to the United boss that it surely couldn't have just happened through a chance phone call the other way. "More or less," he said with a poker face.

On the player's short temper and his own, Ferguson smiled: "Well, the French and Scots have a great old alliance if you know your history, I'm hoping this is part of a new alliance! It will be a new experience, and a challenge for me too... he's got all the assets of the top players in the world. Leeds United are a fabulous, big club, but I think he'll find that Manchester United is even bigger and that's maybe the stage he needs. There was no hesitation. I'm glad he could join us."

"Obviously arriving here in Manchester, I hope this is for a long time," Cantona said via an interpreter. "I'm here first of all to win my place in the team, I've got a duty to score goals... we will all have the aim of winning honours for Manchester United. In any walk of life, whatever the job, I feel that you learn things, and the day I stop learning, that's the day I will retire from the game."

The player insisted he had not let Leeds' fans down: "We are in a country which is free, democratic and not a dictatorship, so I am free to make the decision I wish to make... My working relationship with Leeds didn't break down. My few months there were among the best I've ever had from the point of view of the manager, players and fans.

"It might seem unthinkable to some people at Leeds for

me to come to Manchester United, but I see it as a positive move. I can understand that some Leeds fans may feel I have let them down. But in no way do I feel that. I hope I have reached my spiritual home. I have to score goals for United but I am also here to work for the team and win honours for the club."

So Ferguson was off to a good start already, introducing Cantona not only without mentioning the prior indiscretions but instead pointedly referenced his ability as a footballer with that "good reputation" remark.

There was the question of what Eric's new team-mates might make of the signing. Centre-back Gary Pallister (who, of course, had lobbied for the move!) was caught on the hop by a journalist who knew before him and made him guess. "I was stunned," Pallister said. "I went through a long list of goalscorers but never mentioned Cantona because I just never expected Leeds would sell him. There was such a rivalry between the two clubs I never for one minute thought they'd let a player of that class move to us."

Disbelief was a way of describing Lee Sharpe's reaction: "Yeah, right, absolutely no chance," he thought when he heard. There was a greater apprehension in the reaction of Bryan Robson, the incumbent of the number seven shirt Cantona would inherit. "The players weren't convinced at the time that it was such a good signing," Robson said in his autobiography *Robbo*. "Eric had a reputation for flitting from club to club. Now Leeds wanted to get rid of him. We had a great set of lads and we didn't want anyone upsetting things."

Steve Bruce was equally taken aback: "I was absolutely flabbergasted. At the time, I did not realise just how accomplished a player he is. I had seen him at Leeds and knew he was good, but I did not appreciate what an influence he could exert on the rest of the team."

"When I heard the news it wasn't necessarily a case of 'wow'," Paul Parker says. "There wasn't the coverage that there is now so we didn't know a lot about him... I missed the game against them but I can remember Brucey and Pallister raving about Eric. I think that's what sold it to the boss. It was a case of wait and see for us. We'd heard the stories about him...

"What he did for Leeds was give them the difference," Parker later added. "We needed a difference at that time, as good as we were. Eric was definitely that on and off the park."

Ferguson had dealt with big characters but none came with the sort of baggage the Frenchman was arriving with. Almost every spell at every club had ended badly. Hindsight has proven all the predictions of the transfer going horribly wrong to be hilariously misjudged but those pundits were merely hedging on what they felt to be a safe bet.

Take Liverpool legend Emlyn Hughes, who dismissed Cantona as a "flashy foreigner" in the *Mirror* on Saturday 28th November 1992. "A masterstroke... Me? I say it's a panic buy," Hughes said. "One last frantic roll of the dice to see if the Frenchman can hit the jackpot for Alex Ferguson. It could either win him something, or cost him his job. Break the bank – or bust him. And I'll admit when I heard the news I was simply staggered. Cantona looks the business, but in my opinion he's a flashy foreigner. He'll score goals for United... when they are two up. But don't look for him to get in there when it hurts, or to decide a game and be a matchwinner.

"Ferguson is becoming desperate to win the league, but his side can't score goals. I'm certain Cantona is not going to put that problem right. I cannot see him being the man who'll either get goals or start Mark Hughes scoring. Shearer was his man and Fergie is now getting stick for missing him. Now he is forced to go clutching at straws. If United win the league it will prove to be the best buy of all, but if they don't..."

The prevailing thought at the time was that Leeds United had done best out of the deal. Cantona would become embroiled in a public war of words with Howard Wilkinson, with the Leeds boss getting in first. "This move gives Eric a better chance of first-team football than he would have had at Leeds," Wilkinson said on 27th November, before telling reporters the day after: "It is easy to do that which is popular, but it is not necessarily right in the long run. I can tell all the fans that what happened was in the best interests of Leeds United. I hope that people don't allow themselves to be whipped up and forced into saying silly things."

His words did little to appease Leeds fans, who rung up the club, radio stations and the *Yorkshire Evening Post* in droves to complain. And while hindsight has made it look like a great deal for Ferguson and United, it is worth pointing out there was no logical solution that saw Leeds United and Eric Cantona together for very long. If not Old Trafford, Cantona was on his way anyway; he had requested to leave, and the biggest headache at Elland Road was how they were going to convince someone else to buy him.

There was no way that Fotherby would have sacked Wilkinson, the manager who brought him a league title, in order to appease Cantona, but even if he had, there is no guarantee that a successor would have done any better. There would have more likely been a revolt from the players, who would have all backed the manager over the player; the bubbling resentment of the perception of Cantona's contribution, mixed in with what most felt to be indiscipline on the player's part, gives us enough weight to justify that theory.

Certainly, that's what former Leeds defender Jon Newsome believes. "I can imagine Howard having this issue with Eric, wondering how he was going to solve it, and then all of a sudden somebody wanted to give him a million quid," he says. "In Howard's defence he probably thought it was okay. In hindsight, people look at it differently. Hindsight is wonderful. But I would bet good money that nothing good would have come out of Eric staying at Leeds because his relationship with Howard had totally broken down."

And so it wasn't ever a case of Leeds keeping Cantona, but more a case of where could he go? Getting back what they paid for him was good business. What about the other clubs on the player's wish list? Liverpool had already said no and it's difficult to envisage a scenario at Arsenal where he would have succeeded under the defensive George Graham.

So it was Manchester United for Eric Cantona; and a platform upon which he would reinvent and redefine both himself and the club he was representing.

# A Blank Canvas

E ric Cantona's first step towards reinvention was in challenging those preconceptions held by his new Manchester United team-mates, a journey which began on day one. The Frenchman travelled with the team to London as they prepared to face Arsenal; at 9.30am on the morning of the game, Brian Kidd knocked at Alex Ferguson's hotel room and informed him that Cantona had asked if he could train.

The pair weren't back by midday, when the rest of the team had gone down for lunch – Kidd informed Ferguson that Eric had worked intensely. Ferguson would observe this personally when, on the Monday, Cantona stayed behind on the training pitch after the morning session and asked his boss if he could be assisted by two young team-mates for further practice.

So, the influence provided by Cantona was immediate, even if the change in attitude at the club took a little longer to catch on. Ferguson was in love. In his 1999 autobiography he wrote: "I had resolved I would ignore all past attempts to present him as an *enfant terrible*, I would judge him on what he was like in his dealings with me, making my aim to communicate with him regularly and to try and understand him."

It was obvious early on just how taken the United boss was with his new player. "The boss absolutely idolised Eric," Paul Parker says. "It didn't bother us because we knew what he was giving us. So too did the boss. There was a lot of pressure on him for taking that on because it can't have been easy. He was almost putting all of his eggs in that basket."

Cantona was making an instant impression on his new team-mates, coming in early as well as staying late. "He would come in at half past nine in the morning, an hour before us lot, do his own warm-up and practise his skills and his touches," Paul Ince said. "He just had that aura and presence… He took responsibility away from us. It was like he said, 'I'm Eric, and I'm here to win the title for you'."

"He was nothing like the guy we feared he'd be," admitted Mark Hughes, his new strike partner. Hughes was the goalscorer in United's 1-0 win at Arsenal. Having left Leeds just as they defeated the Gunners 3-0, Cantona could have been forgiven for thinking a place in the team might have been hard to come by as he watched from the directors box.

That was the impression given by watching United legend George Best, who observed: "Cantona must be worrying how he is going to get in in front of anyone the way United are playing."

Even Ferguson joked that it might be the case: "I'm panicking a bit now. I honestly don't know how I can fit in Eric next Sunday." He did, however, emphasise it was tongue-in-cheek. "I have no doubts or fears about this player," the United boss added. "Eric will have seen how difficult it is going to be to get into the side. What I have tried to do is bring an international player to our club and create a competitive edge up front."

There would be a more straightforward chance to introduce him into the first team without upsetting anyone. United travelled to Lisbon to play Benfica at their famous Stadium of Light in a friendly to commemorate Eusébio's 50th birthday.

On the day of the game, *L'Equipe* ran an interview with Cantona, which would cause ripples back in the UK. "I never had any problems with anyone at Leeds," he said. "Everything was fine and, if there hadn't been this offer, I would have stayed. [Wilkinson] accuses me now. But you only have to look at my performances for Leeds to be convinced I was worth my place. Eight goals – I was a hit with everyone. I had become the leader. [Leeds fans] have smashed windows and had a go at the chairman. Wilkinson does not know how to get out of it, so he accuses me. I like changes. I need them more than most people. Now it's up to me to prove what I can do."

Ferguson, too, was talking to the press, adding: "We're not even thinking about all the innuendo about Eric – this man can become a giant at Old Trafford. All that matters is what happens on the pitch. Let Eric enjoy playing for Manchester United and all the peripheral things won't matter. He's now a United player. The business is done."

Cantona started against Benfica, wearing the number 10 shirt, and attracting most of the attention. Paul Parker soon became aware his new team-mate's high standards. "Eric wanted the ball and he would demand it even if there were three players around him," Parker remembers. "I can remember once not passing and the look I got from him… all I knew is that if I was in that situation again, I was definitely going to give him the ball. I never wanted him to look at me like that again!"

There was no question of a rift, though, despite United losing the game 1-0. Portugal had been a bonding experience. "It was a valuable getting-to-know-you exercise," Ryan Giggs recalled in his autobiography. "Four or five days away with the lads helped him no end. We all went out to a casino for a few beers and he seemed to be at home straight away – nothing like the aloof figure of legend."

"People talk about how a foreign player comes over and brings their own style and influences others but Eric quickly became one of us," Parker adds.

With some differences, one might add. Cantona, a peacock in need of a stage, found it at Old Trafford. He was far from the first big name forward to arrive at the club tasked with turning around their fortunes but he was perhaps the first in some time to be enamoured by the romance instead of being dogged by the weight of expectation.

"Before starting my first training session with Alex Ferguson, two images came clearly to my mind," Cantona recalled in his book *My Story*. "My father had told me how Bobby Charlton scored a goal against the great AC Milan… Charlton is still working for Manchester United. He has come to symbolise the club, just like the other heroes of those unforgettable times – George Best, Denis Law and others. They are real, living legends who ensure the prestige and grandeur of Manchester United will continue. These icons from the past come now to watch us play and they speak to us in the dressing rooms…

"The other impression I had of the club was more recent. The players whom I was joining had won the Cup Winners' Cup in 1991, beating Barcelona 2-1. This was no mean exploit – it showed the club was capable of competing with the very best."

Alex Ferguson's famous quote sums it up perfectly: "He swaggered in. He stuck his chest out, raised his head and surveyed everything as though he were asking, 'I'm Cantona. How big are you?'"

Old Trafford was an experience to be enjoyed, not endured; another subtle shift which would help other talented attackers yet to show their best. Andrei Kanchelskis was struggling and had considered a move back home a year after signing for United. "I had to change my attitude and my performance if I was to have a future at Old Trafford," the winger admitted, referring to his experience before Cantona arrived.

"Defenders were becoming used to my moves… In my six weeks out of the side I thought Ferguson had made up his mind about me. I would turn up for training, do what was asked of me and go home."

Ryan Giggs, meanwhile, was shouldering a lot of responsibility for a teenager. In Kanchelskis' spells out of the team, Giggs would often play on the right, with Lee Sharpe on the left. It was Giggs who helped Cantona settle quickly; Eric stayed at the Novotel in Worsley due to its proximity to his family in Leeds. Giggs would pick him up for training and games.

Upon the return to England, Cantona learned he would be on the bench against Manchester City on Sunday 6th December. He also returned to a great deal of controversy as Leeds United manager Howard Wilkinson had reacted angrily to the comments he had heard about in *L'Equipe*.

Wilkinson made his programme notes for that Saturday's game against Nottingham Forest all about Eric (and shared them in advance with the *Yorkshire Evening Post*), blasting "Eric Cantona left because he wanted to go" and elaborating: "He wasn't prepared to abide by the rules. I have categoric proof of that… The easy way to avoid disappointing his fans would have been to stay here working within the rules of the club, but he felt he couldn't do that. So be it. He can't have his cake and eat it."

Wilkinson wasn't finished there. He took the unusual step of addressing the Elland Road crowd of 29,364 with a pre-match statement over the PA system. "Trust me, I think I've done reasonably well here with two championships in three seasons," he declared, which elicited applause. Wilkinson then said Cantona had wanted to leave because he was frustrated at not being in the team. "There's only one Sergeant Wilko!" rang around Elland Road.

After 67 minutes they might not have been so rapturous in their appraisal; relegation-threatened Nottingham Forest were 4-0 up, with Roy Keane scoring twice. The Leeds manager said afterwards: "It was so bad that maybe people will spend all week talking about that and not Eric Cantona."

There was more positive press to be found that day, with Alex Ferguson telling reporters Cantona had "tremendous ability".

That much had already been acknowledged by his new club mates. "Straight away you could see the flamboyance and the flair," Paul Parker remembers. "His ability was easy to see, he had that arrogance and belief in himself."

Ryan Giggs concurred. "I realised immediately what a good player Eric was – how strong and quick he was," he said. "I couldn't believe a big man could have such pace. Once he got going, nobody could outrun him. He was one of those guys whose speed is deceptive."

The United players were now seeing his ability at close quarters. There was now the small matter of translating that onto the pitch. Having helped him get to the ground, Ryan Giggs also accommodated Cantona's arrival into the team as the Welshman was withdrawn at half-time in the Manchester derby at Old Trafford following a broken toe suffered from a challenge by Steve McMahon. The ex-Liverpool man then set his attention (not for the last time) on Cantona. It was a quiet debut for the Frenchman, but a thunderous shot from Mark Hughes earned United a 2-1 win.

"The winner I got against Arsenal last week probably gave me just as much pleasure," Hughes said. "Eric Cantona is a very good player. I wouldn't say his signing had resulted in any more effort from the strikers – you have to play for United at full revs every week anyway."

Ferguson gave a low-key assessment of Cantona's debut. "Anyone coming into a derby finds it hard," he sympathised. "Eric showed some great touches and two or three great crosses, but he will be glad to get that one over."

Hughes was the match-winner again the following week, as Cantona started his first game. On this occasion, he wore the number seven shirt, in place of the injured Bryan Robson. This low-key moment was effectively a passing of the torch, although Robson would wear his famous number one more time, in the last game of the season.

The 1-0 win against leaders Norwich City in early December 1992 was fairly laborious and there was no immediate sign of the glorious things to come. There was no question of incompatibility, more an issue of where best to play the new forward.

Against the Canaries, Cantona played behind Hughes, inter-changing in the 'hole' with Brian McClair.

This was to the chagrin of Paul Ince, ostensibly Eric's partner in midfield and instructed to rein in his own attacking instincts for one afternoon. "It's all very well doing the flicks when you're winning, but when you are losing, it's more important for someone to put their foot in," Ince complained.

Alex Ferguson did praise Cantona's vision, saying he "starts attacks out of nothing", but this was a subdued start. "His first pass was only six yards but it opened up the whole game. He does simple things like that," Ferguson said.

Giggs and Robson were missing for the trip to Chelsea the week before Christmas; Cantona would be under added pressure to deliver his first meaningful contribution in a red shirt. In *The Guardian* on the morning of the game, there was a feature on George Scanlan, the former Everton player who was now an interpreter and helped foreign players settle in Britain. One of those players, of course, had been Eric Cantona. On the Frenchman, Scanlan said: "He's a delightful bloke. He looks rather taciturn but he is very sensitive, kind and courteous. I think he plays his football that way too."

At Stamford Bridge, there appeared to be a little more structure to United's formation, with McClair lining up alongside Ince, allowing Cantona a clearer sense of his own responsibilities. It was a scrappy game and midway through the second half the home crowd took great delight in seeing Eddie Newton side-step Cantona. That loud cheer was followed moments later by a roar, as David Lee scored a fortuitous deflected goal from distance.

Three minutes later, though, United were level, with Cantona exacting a little bit of revenge on the crowd. Lee Sharpe's cross was nudged into the forward's path by Mike Phelan, and Cantona showed fine awareness to turn and volley into the far corner. It was by no means as magical as his last goal against this opponent, but was arguably more important, earning United a crucial point to keep their momentum going.

In these early days it was natural to consider that Cantona was indeed a lucky charm (rather than the leading figure), the man with the Midas touch whose mere presence coincided with an upturn in fortunes. In his report for *The Guardian*, Paddy Barclay wrote: "The lesson seems to be: sign an individualistic foreigner and take the title. United's form since Cantona arrived at Old Trafford suggests they might be capable of following suit, though until yesterday the resurgent flow of goals from Hughes had been more influential than his new partner, perhaps the most enigmatic of all imports.

"Cantona's inconsistency has long been discussed in France, where a prevalent opinion was that he required an extra spurt of pace to become as good a player as he thought he was. We were grateful enough for his first-half contribution, without which United would have created nothing."

Hughes' upturn in form was plain to see, and although this may have been of a coincidence rather than a consequence of Cantona's arrival, there were promising signs of the pair working together. There was certainly none of the abrasion most had predicted between these two firebrand stars.

"Everyone had told me that our temperaments would clash," Cantona said. "The reply to that came on the pitch, in the dressing room and on the training field… When I came to Manchester in November 1992, the club undoubtedly had the best defence in the league – but not the best attack, scoring just 18 goals in 17 games."

Of course, Eric Cantona had joined a team that was excellent and potentially exceptional. Their all-British and Irish defence had international calibre players with their three first-choice English players unfortunate to have relatively quiet international careers due to a golden age in England defenders.

The attacking figures Cantona quoted were also true, but overstated. Any side that had Hughes and McClair up front, with Giggs, Sharpe and Kanchelskis supplying the bullets, were not short of quality. They were however short on confidence, with Hughes never being the prolific goalscorer Ferguson hoped to get in a Shearer or a Hirst, and McClair slowly evolving to become more of an all-rounder.

Cantona was not a 30-goal a season man either but Ferguson now had five or six players capable of getting up to 15 goals each. A year before, the United boss had watched his team plunder 19 goals in the six games before New Year. In the second half of the season, they scored 27 goals in 28 games, drawing a blank on eight separate occasions.

On Boxing Day 1992, Eric gave the first indication of his truly transformational potential. Inside six minutes United were two goals down at Hillsborough, with David Hirst (who else) giving Sheffield Wednesday an early lead. There was certainly no sign of a resolute defence. The visitors piled forward, coming agonisingly close a few times through McClair, before Cantona finally beat Chris Woods only to see his effort cleared off the line. The gung-ho approach was punished when the Owls grabbed a third on the hour-mark. 3-0, and Trevor Francis in the home dugout was probably relieved to feel he would be dodging questions about Cantona.

Only it wasn't going to end that way. Just as at Stamford Bridge, the jeering home fans were about to be given a bitter pill to swallow. United's luck finally turned when Paul Parker found Lee Sharpe, whose cross was headed in – finally – by McClair. The Scot's own redemption was complete when he made it 2-3, heading in another Sharpe cross. It was Cantona who had the final say; Sharpe again the provider, with the Frenchman pushing the ball over the line to equalise.

Some United fans had found their way into the lower section of the Leppings Lane stand and Cantona rushed over to celebrate with them, much to the annoyance of the home supporters. "I think I showed I can score from close range as well as the more spectacular efforts," Cantona told reporters afterwards. "Goals like that are just as important as the beautiful ones. I feel I can fill any role Manchester United want from me whether it's a playmaker or defender or finishing off chances. It all comes easy to me. I'm sure that goal delighted our fans."

"It was this reversal of the situation which clearly illustrated our determination to believe that we were not beaten, even when all the evidence seemed to point that way," the forward later said. "It was to be one of the keys to our success."

Forty-eight hours later and Cantona's influence was evident as United hammered Coventry 5-0. The forward showed intelligent link-up play with Sharpe and Giggs; he was scorer and creator in the second half, netting a penalty and laying a goal on for Sharpe. United ended 1992 in first place in the Premier League, the first time they'd been top all season.

# KING ERIC 7

## Taste of Perfection

**E**ric Cantona had scored in his last three league games of 1992 and while the contribution was not insignificant, it was fair to say that the Frenchman's new club were waiting for the kind of statement that he had made at Leeds.

Howard Wilkinson had pointed out in his *Yorkshire Post* columns that none of Cantona's three league goals in the old First Division were crucial, insomuch as they did not influence the result. It was a simplistic assessment that ignored the numerous assists and contributions which did influence results, but it was convenient in its cold truth. Without Cantona's goals, Leeds would have had the same number of wins and the same number of points, and, crucially to the entire argument, the same trophy at the end of the season.

The same dismissal could not be made of Cantona's short time at Old Trafford, with two of his three goals being equalisers to rescue points. You can't understate the importance of those goals, but they were not in the same class as some of his strikes for Leeds. Manchester United fans were still waiting for that big moment.

His impact in Manchester had been considerable enough to have journalist Paddy Barclay pondering if lightning might strike twice as far as Cantona's fortunes on a title-chasing team were concerned, and on 3rd January the writer spoke to a couple of club stalwarts about the Frenchman.

Paddy Crerand opined that the style of play was possibly more important than winning the league that season: "United were top of the league a year ago – and there wasn't the buzz you feel now. More than at any time since I was playing, the club is alive. The 3-3 with Sheffield Wednesday was magnificent too.

"It's as if the good old days were back and the major factor is the Frenchman. Eric Cantona is so clever it's untrue and the lovely thing about special players is they're infectious. The things he tries, the others try, and it's the way the team are playing that's got middle-aged fans jumping about like two-year-olds."

Reserve team manager Jim Ryan told Barclay: "People talk about him as if he dwells on the ball, but what I've seen is one and two-touch stuff and movement, with the likes of Mark Hughes and Brian McClair following suit so the whole movement of the side becomes quicker. Coventry were pulled every which way. This was what the crowd here want to see – visitors getting a real pasting from start to finish."

A straightforward win over Bury in the FA Cup opened the year, before Tottenham travelled to Old Trafford. Cantona – who had scored that hat-trick against the same opponent earlier in the campaign – hoped to find Spurs equally pliable this time around. Alex Ferguson's team broke the deadlock just before the break. Denis Irwin's cross from the left was met by a majestically leaping Cantona at the back post. His body was almost perfectly straight as he met the ball, looping a header over Erik Thorstvedt in the Spurs goal.

"It always stood out to me how he would stand so upright," remembers Paul Parker. "He never bent over. God knows how he tied his laces. His stature was incredible – he always had that manner where he kept his frame so straight."

In the context of footballers in general, it was extraordinary technique. In the context of Eric Cantona's catalogue of goals, it is almost forgotten when people remember this game. That's because Cantona's moment of arrival at Manchester United, his statement of intent, finally came in the 52nd minute.

His team were attacking a corner. Spurs cleared, but Irwin collected the ball from Hughes on the left. For the next five seconds Old Trafford was witness to a cerebral passage of play, a seminal moment which defined a major shift in the culture of the team. Irwin played the ball inside to Cantona, who instinctively stabbed his foot into the ground, generating back-spin on the return pass. Irwin demonstrated fine anticipation, automatically moving into position despite the plethora of bodies in-between. The weight of the pass was perfect and provoked a roar as great as the goal which followed, as the full-back slammed the ball into the net to make it 2-0.

"This man is playing a game of his own!" remarked John Motson on *Match of the Day*. United won 4-1, although Cantona was withdrawn late on with a hamstring issue.

"The second goal was absolutely magnificent," purred Ferguson. "He's brought something extra to our team. Eric has lifted everyone round about him."

United legend George Best had said earlier in the season that Ferguson might struggle to fit his new player in the team.

Having witnessed the moment of magic, Best was happy to revise his opinion. "I didn't think Cantona would fit in here, but after seeing him today I think he's the best £1 million signing Alex Ferguson has made," he said. "That was the most stylish performance I've seen from United this season."

Cantona himself tried to play it down: "I don't think I played badly, but the team's personality is more important. If I wanted a lot of personal attention I'd have taken up tennis… or found myself a nice girl to play mixed doubles with. We started to score goals but that is why they bought me. I came here to make the difference. The style of play suits me."

Yet it could not be denied that the former Leeds man was having a big influence on his new team and its personality. Now settled in that deep-lying forward role, it hadn't taken Ferguson long to identify the area that best suited Cantona and the team. It seemed almost too easy, too perfect.

Observations about changes to this system will follow later, but be it by choice or force, tinkering with it adversely affected the performances of the individuals and the team. In the week after that performance against Spurs, Paddy Barclay grabbed an exclusive interview with Cantona.

"Whenever I have joined a club, it is with the intention of staying," Eric told Barclay. "Although my ambition is to develop by following my instincts, it's important to stress this must be within a team framework. I most admired Brazil in 1982, because the affinity between excellent players meant no one stood out. Yet they could all play naturally. They were not forced into a system. At United I have good players around me, and the liberty to play as I wish. The ball is passed through defence and midfield, which is the game I am used to.

"At Leeds I was dissatisfied because the style was more direct.

Now at United we can dream, even if we cannot celebrate until the championship is won. Maybe it will be here I find stability. Maybe not. It is not something I look for. Maybe I'll want it when I'm older. The main thing is to live for pleasure."

The forward rubbished the idea he would move to Italy: "The spectacle there is in the stands. On the field, the result is everything. Of course, the result is important, but so is beauty and natural expression. In France, too, that is being lost. I cannot think of anywhere except England where it still thrives. I always felt a need to come here."

Barclay also put Michel Platini's 'beautiful goal' quote to Cantona. Eric smiled: "Did you see my goal against Sheffield Wednesday. Was that not ugly enough? I'm making progress."

But Ferguson's team were making progress of their own and they were playing more beautiful football, with some beautiful goals – Cantona didn't travel to London as United beat QPR with some style. He also sat out the FA Cup fourth round tie against Brighton, and returned for the visit of Nottingham Forest. Eric was provider in this game, with an impressive cushioned pass on the volley for a late Mark Hughes goal to seal the points in a 2-0 win.

He set up a goal for Brian McClair in the next game, though this time he tasted defeat for the first time in a United shirt; Ipswich Town's 2-1 win putting the Reds down into second place (Ipswich's neighbours, Norwich City, were back on top).

Before the next game, an alleged interview was published in *L'Equipe* where Cantona declared he would leave Old Trafford in the summer of 1994. "If we win the title and France qualify for the World Cup, I'd like to stop in 1994," he was quoted as saying. "But we must have both results. It won't be easy, but it's possible. I'm very proud to play for Manchester United. I want to win and to give my contribution." It also included this quote of Eric's, referring to his time in Manchester: "I'm passing by."

*The Guardian* reached out to Cantona's interpreter for clarification – he was "highly sceptical" about the comments."

Back in M16, the quotes were taken with a pinch of salt and Cantona took to the field against Sheffield United on the 35th anniversary of the Munich Air Disaster. In a reflection of changing attitudes in the intervening years, neither side even wore black armbands on the day. The Blades – who had inflicted an opening day defeat on Ferguson's side – grabbed an early lead, and appeared they might frustrate the Reds again.

It seemed to be an off-day for Cantona, until the 65th minute, when United finally drew level as the Frenchman created a goal for McClair from a Denis Irwin cross.

Sheffield United were pinned back and when defender Mitch Ward could only slice a clearance, Cantona was there to control and half-volley into the near side of the goal. A winner with ten minutes left, having created the equaliser, but visiting boss Dave Bassett was not impressed after the game. "Eric Cantona's nothing special," he said. "Cantona is no more difficult to play against than any of their players. If I had the chance I'd buy some of the other players before him."

It was perhaps a bit of bitter bluster from the coach who would later say it was "no coincidence" that United were fighting for the title since they signed Cantona (and even attributed his team's own win in the FA Cup soon after to

Cantona's absence). It was probably asking too much for a similar revision of opinions up at Elland Road, the venue of Manchester United's next game, and a first return to his old ground for Eric Cantona. The team coach arrived, 'greeted' by a few hundred Leeds fans screaming 'Judas' at their old striker.

The game was screened live on Sky and so the whole nation (well, the whole subscribing nation) tuned in to see Cantona looking fairly nervous, shocked by the animosity. "I knew I was going to get a hot reception… if I was a Leeds fan I would have reacted the same way," he said, though he later described it as an "atrocious atmosphere" that had been "orchestrated".

"Like all great clubs, Manchester United is venerated and detested, feared and envied. But with Leeds fans there is a quite distinctive and special hostility… The Leeds fans had drawn aeroplanes with 6th February 1958 written on them (what a sense of humour!) to try to goad the Manchester supporters who, in return, shouted back at them, 'Thanks very much for selling Eric to us'!" Cantona later recalled in *My Story*.

United defender Steve Bruce remembered the toxicity of the welcome. "Those Leeds fans who only a few months previously had been chanting 'Ooh, aah, Cantona' had changed their tune," Bruce said. "From worshipping the ground he walked on, they now showed no hesitation in spitting where he walked, and even spat at him as we got off the coach."

Cantona's former colleague Jon Newsome was in the Leeds team. "I was given the task of man-marking him," Newsome says. "The Leeds fans were baying for his blood. Eric tried to elbow me and got a yellow card; for me it was a matter of staying as close as I could for 90 minutes and kicking him whenever I could."

Job done; Cantona had a quiet game and United were

relieved to leave with a goalless draw. Only that wasn't quite the end of the unpleasantness; as the teams left the field, Leeds fans claimed Cantona had spat at them as he went down the tunnel. He was charged by the FA though he strongly denied it; he admitting to spitting, but insisted it was on the tunnel wall. Police could find no evidence to support the claim, but on the announcement of this, Leeds fan Mark Edwards came forward and claimed to have been hit by the spit.

One policeman did provide a written statement supporting the fan's claim, and this persuaded the FA to make a charge of misconduct. Cantona was warned about his future conduct and fined £1,000; the relatively lenient punishment considering the severity of the alleged crime attributed to the provocation the player had suffered.

"I'm glad the truth is out, people kept asking me if I had made it up," Mark Edwards told the press. "But there were a lot of witnesses. Everybody loved him at Leeds. He was under pressure when he came back, but there was no excuse for what happened. I still think he is one of the best players in the league. I only wanted an apology."

Cantona – who did not contest the charge – continued to maintain his innocence. This was one battle not worth fighting. "There were those who suggested I was showing contempt for the fans who had been cheering me a few months before," Cantona said. "Given the collective hysteria that reigned that day, the incident was quite laughable."

As United prepared to face Middlesbrough shortly afterwards, Cantona lined up against Chris Kamara. The two had not played together as Kamara had left Leeds two months before Cantona arrived, but the Boro player insisted there was some familiarity with their common ground. "Eric

Cantona told before the game how disappointed he was with the crowd's reaction to his return there," Kamara said.

"But at Leeds the fans are worth a goal start. There is so much expectation around Old Trafford, it seems to get to the crowd. They need something special to get them going."

Cantona was on the scoresheet in a routine 3-0 victory over Boro; as well as all the goals that are included in his classics collection, there are so many that miss out because of the ever-so-slight imperfection of the final execution. This was one such goal, which saw him twist and turn past his marker in the box. But his first shot was saved, with the rebound converted, taking some of the gloss away.

"Cantona will never look natural in English football," Michael Henderson wrote in *The Guardian*. "There is something of the poet in his disdain for the clutter around him, and he is selfless enough to furnish others with many of his best lines... No ball is too difficult to stun or to lay off, so he is an ideal conduit for others to play through, seeing the possibilities earlier than they do and having the facility to achieve these aims."

Eric was also booked in the game, earning him a two-match ban; at first, his team-mates did not appear to miss him, as they won 2-1 at Anfield to exact some revenge for the loss there the year before. But defeat to Oldham made the home game against Aston Villa vital. United led Villa by a point but Ron Atkinson's side had a game in hand; should they win in Manchester, then they could have a five-point advantage with nine games to play.

It was a fantastic game, with both sides going all-out for the win. When Steve Staunton scored in the second half, it seemed United would be haunted by their old boys; Atkinson, of course, their former manager (who had already tasted success against his former employers in the 1991 League Cup final) and Paul McGrath, their legendary ex-defender, putting in the kind of shift that had commentators questioning Ferguson's judgement. The margins between success and failure were narrow, but there would be little sympathy if the United boss was unable to deliver a league title this time around.

But his team's response was instant; their frenetic pace did not let up, and United quickly grabbed an equaliser. It was another crucial contribution from Cantona, who headed an Irwin cross back for Hughes to power home. This potential decider ended in a stalemate – as you were.

Ferguson was keen to see it as a point gained. "In the modern trend of football my United are a breath of fresh air," he said. "Cantona has such vision. I'd pay to see him play."

The following week, United were in an identical situation at Maine Road, and this time it was Cantona who headed in an equaliser. The Frenchman then came the closest to getting all three points in a tight game against Arsenal that finished goalless. After four matches without a win, United had slipped to third in the table, two points behind Norwich (who they faced at Carrow Road in their next game) and one point behind Aston Villa.

There is a more famous moment that people identify as the turning point in the 1992/93 season but the likelihood is that the pivotal moment came five days earlier. I'm referring of course to Steve Bruce's double against Sheffield Wednesday, but the game at Carrow Road saw United put on their first genuinely breathtaking display of football since Eric Cantona's arrival. Indeed, it was an eight-minute passage of play that still gets talked about today; it was one of those periods where everything seems to align – the two teams fighting for the title, the sense of occasion due to United's generational struggles and the identity of the main protagonist.

It was Cantona, of course, who got the ball rolling. Having received a pass from Lee Sharpe, the forward took a touch to control. The ball was still bouncing when he spotted the right pass; the type of pass that gravity would make awkward for even the most technically proficient. Cantona made it look easy, with the weight perfect for Ryan Giggs to race on to. In truth, it was such a magnificent pass which caught the Norwich defence flat-footed that both Sharpe and Paul Ince had also run into great positions. Giggs rounded Canaries goalkeeper Bryan Gunn to score.

Cantona was not involved in the second goal which came seven minutes later through Andrei Kanchelskis, but rarely has a player's influence been more felt. The flicks and back heels between Ince, Giggs and Kanchelskis were outstanding and representative of the respective ability of those three magnificent players; and yet, that style of play was conspicuous by its absence in the pre-Cantona days.

United were running riot. Less than 60 seconds later it was 3-0, with the hosts caught on the counter again. Paul Ince rampaged past three, drawing out Gunn and then rolling the ball casually across to Cantona who accepted the gift.

Norwich pulled one back but lost 3-1; it was one of those rare games where every player had put in an exceptional shift, and yet Alex Ferguson was still keen to reserve special praise for Cantona, who he described as "quite marvellous".

"That was the turning point," Cantona later said. "We played the perfect game. We played perfect football."

# The Wait Is Over

After a run-in with many crucial, potentially defining moments, when Manchester United finally did win the English league championship after a wait of more than a quarter of a century, they did it without kicking a ball.

As the 1992/93 season reached its conclusion, there was an absurdly-scheduled World Cup qualifier round, and Eric Cantona was called up by France to play against Sweden on 28th April. Sweden went ahead in Paris before the hosts were awarded a fortuitous penalty.

"The penalty kick is the most fearsome of actions, but it is easy to execute," Cantona said later. "I enjoy this moment that holds all those who are watching in suspense. It's terrible, with the executioner face to face with his victim. Fifteen seconds punctuated by a flash of lightning. The crowd explodes or crumbles. The penalty is either happiness or sadness, nothing else. I put the ball on the spot and scored. Then, in the 85th minute, I discovered that discreet charm enjoyed by goal poachers. A moment's inattention by the man marking me and I dive in and the score eloquently tells the story: 2-1 in our favour."

Eric said "a greater pleasure" than scoring two goals "came from the huge stands from which the fans shouted my name." Cantona celebrated with team-mates until 2am before catching a 7am flight back to Manchester. With United not playing until Monday 3rd May, he had a longer weekend to recover than normal. But this was not a normal weekend.

On Sunday 2nd May, Cantona was relaxing at the Novotel in Worsley. Aston Villa were playing Oldham Athletic. The maths were simple – if Villa defeated Oldham, a United win over Blackburn Rovers would earn them the Premier League trophy. Perhaps that was a big ask, because Rovers were flying high and would be committed to stopping United (particularly as they were coached by Liverpool legend Kenny Dalglish), but then Alex Ferguson's side had won their last five games.

They would be right to feel that destiny was on their side, particularly after they followed up their fantastic win at Carrow Road with a performance which showed another side to their character. Before that fateful game with Sheffield Wednesday on 10th April, Cantona had once more featured in the press. He appeared keen to rubbish those reports about leaving Old Trafford in 1994.

"When I give an interview the quotes that are used aren't the ones I would like them to use," he said: "Life is like a woman. You weary of some women, but some always find something new – every day, every evening in their dress, their conversation, the way they behave… Leaving a club is like leaving a woman. When you have nothing left to say, you go."

Early on against the Owls, Cantona suffered a wrist fracture.

John Sheridan then scored a penalty in the second half to give the visitors the lead. There was a growing anxiety until Bryan Robson was introduced as substitute; the midfielder calmed things down and helped his team-mates get back to basics.

There was still an element of fortune, however; earlier in the second half, linesman John Hilditch had become the referee after Michael Peck was injured. Alex Ferguson had been complaining to Hilditch at half-time about interruptions and how there ought to be lengthy stoppage time.

United drew level with five minutes to go, with Steve Bruce heading in from a corner. It was a body blow for Trevor Francis' team, who had played at Wembley the week before in an energy-sapping game against rivals Sheffield United. Ferguson learned Aston Villa had been held to a goalless draw and tried to get the message to his team. He wanted them to calm down and not risk losing by chasing the win.

However, the raucous atmosphere inside Old Trafford made it impossible for the manager to get his message across, and the inspired United players, galvanised by this momentum, charged forward for a winner. It arrived four minutes into stoppage time when Wednesday failed to clear a corner and Gary Pallister crossed for Bruce to thunder home a header.

A beaten Francis moaned to Ferguson, and to reporters, that United's winner was so late it was "in the second leg"; both Bruce and Ferguson claimed there should have been an extra few minutes added on!

Cantona played on despite the fracture, wearing a protective splint on his wrist. With Robson having performed so well against Wednesday, he was expected to replace Cantona at Highfield Road just two days later. Ferguson planned to do just that; but Robson, in a remarkable and yet utterly characteristic show of sportsmanship, urged his manager to keep Cantona in the side, because the team's fluency was more important.

Cantona was immensely respectful of this gesture he called "the final sacrifice"; that respect was most certainly mutual. "Eric was a great professional and not just a natural talent," Robson said in his autobiography *Robbo*. "He was terrific with the fans. On the pitch he gave them what they wanted and off it he always had time to sign autographs and pose for pictures. He loved the adulation. Unlike some showmen who don't contribute to their team, Eric gave us an awful lot."

United won 1-0 at Coventry, though Eric came off for Robson in the second half. He had been refused painkillers before and could not continue; he was, however, back in his number seven shirt as his team gave a more comprehensive destruction of Chelsea at Old Trafford. It was 2-0 at half-time and Cantona sealed the victory when Hughes and Giggs combined, the latter floating a ball to the far post, and Eric reaching highest to head it in.

"Eric has taken a lot of the weight off me," Mark Hughes said afterwards. "He likes to receive the ball so we can share the workload." Asked about the language barrier, the Welshman stressed the universal language of the sport: "It's nods and winks and a bit of arm-waving. I enjoy playing with Eric. He is always looking to thread things into me. He also enjoys knocking one-twos. It is a joy to play in this side."

It was now a two-horse race for the title, as Norwich had fallen out of the running. Aston Villa were second on 74 points, and United had a point more, with a superior goal difference. Each game was crucial. United played at Crystal Palace, with Villa at Blackburn, on the evening of 21st April 1993. Of the 30,115 supporters at Selhurst Park, it is estimated more than half were United fans. The atmosphere was frenzied; with most having that peculiar feeling of anxiety and expectation. Palace, struggling against relegation, were giving a good account of themselves. United's players seemed to have their minds on events at Ewood Park. At half-time they were given the most incredible boost – Villa had collapsed and were 3-0 down.

Buoyant, United were immediately more composed. Just after the hour, a Palace goal kick was thumped back by a powerful Bruce header. The ball found Cantona on the left, and the home defenders backed off. His fine pass across the box was volleyed home by Mark Hughes.

In the last minute, Cantona played a ball across the pitch to Paul Ince; the England midfielder used his body to shield the ball across him. He pushed into the box and drove home. 2-0, and a four-point gap with just two games left. One win from either of those games would mean Manchester United were champions of England for the first time since 1967.

An Aston Villa defeat would bring the same result. In the 29th minute of their game against Oldham, Liverpool-born Latics midfielder Nick Henry converted. Oldham had conceded three goals or more on eight separate occasions in the league, including their last game at Spurs, and yet held resolute at Villa Park. Atkinson's team looked deflated as their second half efforts amounted to nought. The referee added just 72 seconds of injury time before blowing the whistle.

In the Novotel, Cantona had the television on to catch the result on the news. The Frenchman received numerous phone calls to his room that afternoon, all of congratulations. The last, at 9pm, came from Steve Bruce, who implored Eric to jump in a taxi to get to his house in Bramhall.

"When I arrived at Steve Bruce's house, *We Are The*

*Champions* was playing," Cantona remembered. "We will hear the voice of Freddie Mercury again some hours later and his song will be taken up by over 40,000 spectators. In the room which opens onto the garden there is a celebration. Everyone's there, all my team-mates from United. Obviously, I can't swear eternal fidelity and loyalty but, as long as we stay together, I am convinced we will be able to move mountains…

"Steve Bruce had just put dozens of beers and as many bottles of champagne on his bar when, just after midnight, Kanchelskis arrived. Finally, the full team is there. What price would our supporters have paid just to be with us at our improvised celebration? In one movement we were all drinking to the victory. A page of history in British football had just been made."

The Bruce house was also a convenient place for journalists to congregate and get all their quotes for the morning papers.

"I am overjoyed, and feeling wonderful," Cantona told the *Daily Mirror*. "I have got what I wanted after leaving Leeds, and that makes it all even more special for me."

A couple of the players were keen to reserve special praise for their new(ish) striker. "There have been two main differences this year," said Peter Schmeichel. "The first is we knew what to expect this time – the second was the arrival of Eric Cantona."

Eric's strike partner agreed. "Eric Cantona has been a massive factor for us," Mark Hughes said. "His flicks and shimmies have inspired us."

There could be no questioning his contribution to Manchester United's title challenge. His goals had been crucial in four games (in that they had been the decisive winning goal or equaliser) with numerous assists to boot.

When trawling through the list of platitudes given to Cantona, it's possibly best to begin with the more reserved. For example, while Clayton Blackmore said that United's fortunes had been changed by the arrival of Gary Pallister, he added of Cantona: "I don't think anyone realised how good he was until we saw him up close. His touch was exceptional, he had wonderful composure and could be clinical in front of goal.

"I think he made Mark Hughes a better player, too. Sparky would always hit the ball with power, but after training with Eric and observing the care with which he would move the ball, he adapted his own game."

In his own autobiography, Pallister emphasised it was a team game. "Sometimes I listen to pundits who give the impression that Eric won everything by himself," he said. "In fact, he needed nine fellow outfielders who would graft their hearts out to provide a platform for his creativity. That was a service he had never enjoyed on a consistent basis. So while I would agree that Eric was blessed with a talent supreme and that United were fortunate to find him when they did, equally I believe that he was fortunate to find United."

Nonetheless, Pallister does not hold back in his praise for Cantona's ability: "When he arrived we could see straight away that he was a showman, in that he needed to express himself through his football. He was always trying things in training, astonishing little flicks and touches that the rest of us wouldn't dream about, and we loved that flair.

"He had a unique aura, a certain arrogance, so that when he

walked in his chest was always puffed out. I suppose it could have upset some people, but it didn't upset us. We'd heard he was a difficult character, that you couldn't rely on him, but we were determined to take him as we found him and welcomed him to the club as we would have done any other player."

It is perhaps one of the most telling signs of the enigma Cantona was that even the two players who had encouraged their manager to sign him were ultimately left stunned by how good he was. But even if some were keen to remind everyone of the great team Cantona had joined, none of his new colleagues would try to downplay his contribution.

"In some clubs there is resentment when a new player arrives," said Steve Bruce. "Problems of this nature do not tend to occur at Old Trafford. It says a lot for the spirit of the club that I have never seen any resentment towards new players."

No one was closer to Eric in his first season than Peter Schmeichel; the pair roomed together on away trips, and the giant Dane was certainly not shy about expressing the significant contribution Cantona had made. "By means of his own mental energy – and his ingenious footballing skills – he gave Manchester United an extra five per cent," the goalkeeper said. "Manchester United's style of play changed. Our leader had arrived, the uncrowned king of the team was in our midst, and he carried himself accordingly. Not because he was in any way stuck-up, snobbish or aloof; in fact, quite the opposite was the case: he was a highly intelligent man, both on and off the field, and an immensely nice bloke…

"Acting as a link between the midfield and the front runners, he was often brilliant, constantly feeding his team-mates with inventive ideas and moves which were executed with technical skill and delicate style. Cantona was a two-footed player.

Strong as an ox, he could leap prodigiously with two defenders on his back, bring the ball under control with his chest and slip it through openings that no one else had realised were there…

"Eric Cantona's importance should not be measured solely by his exploits on the pitch, but also on the basis of his innate ability to inspire and the desire for experimentation he instilled on the training ground… His play became fluent, magical and surprising, filled with elegance; I used to stand in my goal and delight in the way in which the thrill of a successfully executed move would transfuse itself into the whole team and strengthen us – and, we often felt, make us almost invincible."

Right-back Paul Parker is even more straightforward. "I would say that him coming gave us the league title," he says. "He was the missing piece that we didn't even know we needed. He came from nowhere. What we got was a player who could do anything with the ball and it suddenly opened up so many new options for us. It got the best out of other players. Kanchelskis and Giggs were suddenly able to take their game to another level. His ability was easy to see, he had that arrogance and belief in himself. We were a close squad, we'd been through the torment of losing that title, and people were beginning to question us. But the story really began when Eric came.

"All of a sudden we were winning games more comfortably. He could turn a poor performance into a good win, even if he wasn't playing the best game himself. He could win a game with a good pass or a goal. We appreciated that. The Leeds players perhaps had a different mentality. Maybe they were a bit jealous because he was the one getting all the accolades, but all I can say is that I was doing my bit defensively and he was a player who was laying on the goals or scoring them."

Bruce concurs with Parker: "Opponents never knew from

which direction the goals were going to come. Eric helped to create this situation by his vision; you only had to see the goals he scored himself and those with which he was involved to understand what I mean: a back-heel here, a switch of play there. Fabulous stuff that gave our whole play a new dimension."

In Cantona, Ferguson had found a player that was truly one-of-a-kind. The Frenchman was a once-in-a-generation talent, the kind who transcend convention, and it made him all the more mysterious because that description perfectly summed up his personality too. Here was a man who read and wrote poetry, who painted and drew, who studied philosophy; a man who would have a pint of beer, but would usually drink champagne even when in a bar with the other players.

He was a man who happened to play football and enjoyed it because of the ability to express himself. It stands to reason that the occasions such as the penalty for France against Sweden evoked such vivid feelings in him; he was curious about the human condition.

Within the constraints of football's tactical system, Cantona was as free a spirit as could be. It stands to reason that there was such doubt over the compatibility of Hughes and Cantona. But it did ignore one basic principle of football – that good footballers can find a way, and if they do, it can rip up the blueprint of convention.

The stars had aligned for Cantona in Manchester for much deeper-rooted reasons than most consider. There had been a time in France where Cantona appeared to flirt with the idea of moving to Barcelona. It was no surprise one of Cantona's idols was Johan Cruyff. Cruyff had worked with Rinus Michels and the pair were probably the most famous exponents of the 'Total Football' philosophy. Of course, Pep Guardiola is renowned for adopting the same approach with Barcelona.

It was this philosophy of expression Cantona loved and of course the Netherlands, Ajax and Barcelona were the teams most associated with that style of play. However, there are links tying this style to Manchester United long before Guardiola was born, and long enough ago to provide a satisfactory explanation for why this free-spirited Frenchman found such a fitting stage to play his football in the early '90s.

Cruyff, like Michels, were students of Jimmy Hogan, the British coach responsible for the 'Hungarian revolution' which transformed continental football. This chain of command had started with Hogan and had been passed down, first through Josef Blum, who coached Karl Humenberger at French side Strasbourg. Humenberger – who said Blum "opened my eyes to a style of football I hadn't considered before" – implemented that style when he became Ajax manager in 1954. Michels played under Humenberger to continue the chain.

Lancashire-born Hogan was a coach in the 1910s who decided the future of the game lay in improved technical ability. In Britain, physical strength and stamina were the preferred attributes and Hogan's visions were met with resistance. When he was part of a Bolton Wanderers team that travelled to the Netherlands, a seed had been planted for Hogan, and he soon returned there as a coach. Ironically, his Britishness, and their recent superiority, meant less resistance from the Europeans, and so an extraordinary journey began. Simply speaking,

Hogan favoured a 4-2-4 system and freedom of expression, encouraging players to be inventive without disregarding the core values of hard work.

So what does this history lesson have to do with Cantona and Manchester United? Jimmy Murphy, the assistant to Sir Matt Busby, was influenced by Hogan's thinking, and when he was given carte blanche to instill his own style on the youth and reserve set-up at Old Trafford, it was a version of this style he went with. Some players over the generational gap – bridging from the '50s right through to the '90s – would speak of learning a 'position and a half' to cover a team-mate if they were out of position.

Liverpool famously had their own system throughout the club that could be described as homogenous. The United players had a different term for it – robotic. They would not develop players in the same way as at Old Trafford, but they would sign players at a young enough age to run through a year or two in the reserve side to become identikit versions of the first team. Former United defender Graeme Hogg once said: "They looked and moved the same by position. Some of them even looked the same. It was uncanny."

United's own system was more fluid and personal, adaptable to the individual. In the mid-1950s, before the Munich disaster, United had a prolific conveyor belt of talent; while they could change players with ease, these players brought their own personality into proceedings while maintaining the core values of working hard, covering a team-mate and trying to entertain the crowd.

The game evolved with the introduction of the *catenaccio* style. With British teams now competing in Europe, it made sense for them to adopt these sensibilities too, and so four man defences with conventional full-backs became the norm. By the time George Best, United's next great maverick talent, came through the ranks the greater structure to defending meant the freedom enjoyed by more cavalier players was more restricted to the forward areas.

The Munich disaster coincided with this change and so United's next great team was more conventional and less fluid. Whilst it might be a stretch to suggest Manchester United deserve inclusion when the conversation of 'Total Football' is brought up, it is not too big a jump to say Jimmy Murphy's own variation of what Hogan was doing was no less a personal take than that of Michels or Cruyff.

Incidentally, in 1947, Hogan became youth coach at Celtic, where he taught the game to Tommy Docherty, and then even later still, he worked in a similar capacity at Aston Villa, where he taught the game to none other than Ron Atkinson. Docherty and Atkinson implemented their own 4-2-4 styles at Old Trafford in the 70s and 80s. United fans loved it. Any reference to those teams is generally supported by the belief that this is the way United are supposed to play.

Two former United players, Sammy McIlroy and Brian Greenhoff compared the style under Docherty to the style played by Barcelona – Greenhoff saying in 2012 their game was a "prototype of the pressing game Barcelona and Spain have perfected… we were ahead of our time in many respects." It was easy to raise an eyebrow at such a lofty statement then, but perhaps Greenhoff was more right than he even knew.

Alex Ferguson was also a clear advocate for a 4-4-2 or 4-2-4 formation, and in his early days at Old Trafford he sought the advice of Jimmy Murphy as he rebuilt the youth infrastructure at the club. Ferguson employed Brian Kidd and Nobby Stiles

– students of Murphy, of course – to work alongside Eric Harrison (hired by Atkinson!) to oversee that process. The gradual integration of those young players into the United team in the mid-'90s would bring the club as close as they ever had been to the early to mid-'50s.

This all gives a genuine gravitas to that supposedly intangible feeling that Cantona had found his 'spiritual home'. In fact, the relatively unknown links to the teachings of Hogan and its association with all that Cantona loved about the game almost make it feel as if the magic is finally explained. If Cantona couldn't play at Barcelona, or at Ajax, then the only natural place for him to be was Manchester United.

Cantona stands alongside George Best and Cristiano Ronaldo as a trio of players who had a majesty and aura that no other player did, yes in the history of Manchester United but also arguably in British football. But Cantona was unlike Best and Ronaldo. The latter pair were possibly more alike with each other; they would play in any number of positions in the front line and would, on occasion, frustrate even their team-mates with their individuality. There was (rarely) the same level of frustration with Cantona.

The Frenchman also had his own area of the pitch; the 30 yards between the halfway line and the opponent's penalty area were of his command. Here he could dictate the play, either as conductor, freeing his speedy team-mates towards goal, or as predator, waiting with perfect timing.

Always with his head up, back straight, bravely facing forward, bravely wanting the ball in front of the opponent and daring, just daring, them to try and stop him. He knew he was better. He had an almost ethereal quality which permeated through his team-mates, making each of them better, almost by osmosis. His confidence became theirs. His personality became theirs, became the club's.

You can almost read that in the subtext of Gary Pallister's description of how the team felt as they prepared to face Blackburn Rovers on the night Old Trafford celebrated the championship. "Walking out on the pitch was quite incredible," he said. "Banners, flags, scarves, everything was waving, it seemed the very stands were waving. There was just so much deep, deep emotion, and we were bursting with pride. It was like 11 Eric Cantonas going out there with our chests puffed out, we were on top of the world, an indescribable feeling."

Ferguson's team played with an incredible swagger to recover from an early goal conceded and win 3-1. The United boss was keen to shine a spotlight on his star man's contribution: "Cantona has illuminated the stadium, he brought imagination to our game that only great players bring. Players respond to that, they were magnetised by him, they couldn't give him the ball quickly enough. He created a flair and chemistry that United followers understand."

Emotion and pride is present in Cantona's recollection of the game: "Paul Ince, who has no equal in causing havoc, is everywhere. Giggs, bristling with insolence, takes on his man down the line, juggling the ball. Lee Sharpe, still only 21, shows his nonchalance as he creates so many holes in the Blackburn defence... As for Steve Bruce, our heroic captain, the fact that he'd acted as wine waiter for us the night before didn't stop him in any way from getting hold of the ball or hitting some excellent long passes. Bruce is happy. I am enjoying myself."

On 3rd May 1993, Eric Cantona and Manchester United became as one.

ﷲ

# Stylishly Attired

**M**anchester United's only ever league visit to the County Ground in Swindon was also the scene of Eric Cantona's first 'eruption' in English football. Within days he would be accused of not only disgracing the club he represented, but the country in which he plied his trade. The 1993/94 season had resembled a fuse slowly burning away and in March it finally ignited. The only surprise was that it took so long.

A sign of things to come awaited Cantona before the final whistle had been blown on the previous season. United still had the small matter of their last game at Wimbledon, and a swift return to Selhurst Park after their recent win over Crystal Palace. Cantona – wearing 11, as Bryan Robson was starting – played his part in another win but was subjected to some roughhouse treatment from the notoriously physical Dons. On one occasion, Vinnie Jones, who as this story unfolds would himself go on to have a close encounter with Cantona, applauded a robust challenge on Eric from John Fashanu. The crowd was much more accommodating, though, with the capacity attendance once more majority Red, and as soon as the whistle went, supporters raced on to the pitch to celebrate. Cantona was accosted, and when he was able to emerge from the melée, it was without his shirt.

During an international game for France over the summer, Eric suffered a hamstring injury. As a precaution, he remained in France, and even did a bit of catwalk modelling for Paco Rabanne, instead of travelling with United on their pre-season tour to South Africa. He took his place in the starting line up against Arsenal in the Charity Shield, with United boosted by the arrival of record signing Roy Keane from Nottingham Forest. There seemed no early concerns about Eric's condition as he marvellously controlled and crossed a ball to Mark Hughes to volley in the opener in the eighth minute.

Arsenal equalised and the game went to penalties; Cantona taking United's fifth, with Arsenal leading 4-3, and scoring it. Ian Wright missed his, and United won. A victory, but the decision to play Cantona had backfired, as his hamstring issue would keep him out of United's opening four league fixtures.

Ferguson's team started the season in imperious form, defeating Norwich 2-0 at Carrow Road and then cruising past Sheffield United 3-0. A 1-1 draw against Newcastle United denied the Red Devils a tenth consecutive league win, but their place at the top of the table was consolidated with a magnificent 2-1 win over Aston Villa at Villa Park.

Perhaps there was a little more substance to the theory that United were a great team with or without Cantona? Leeds boss Howard Wilkinson might have felt vindicated by Ferguson's side's form, especially after he had once again been asked about

Cantona's contribution to United. "He does what he does well, but he does it best in a winning team. People say he won us the championship last season, but I didn't play him in any of the last crucial matches," said Wilkinson, although Cantona did in fact play a part in each of Leeds' last 15 league games.

Still, the form of Andrei Kanchelskis, Lee Sharpe, Ryan Giggs and Roy Keane was strong enough to suggest *The Guardian*'s pre-season prediction of a second-place finish was a little pessimistic. The question was put to the manager – would he have a problem finding a place for Eric again? The answer came before the game against Southampton, as Cantona was put straight back into the team.

"I always think with Eric playing the team is going to win the game," Ferguson told reporters before the game. "He either scores or a goal or makes one."

Kanchelskis was the man to make way. There was no disruption to United's free-flowing style and after just four minutes, Sharpe justified his own inclusion with an acrobatic volley. Southampton equalised, but by the 17th minute, United were back in front, and there was no prize for guessing the identity of the goalscorer.

The Saints thought they were on a counter attack but Paul Ince robbed Neil Maddison just outside the penalty area. The ball rolled gently into the path of Cantona on the left-hand side of the box, and the Southampton defenders quickly turned on their heels to try and intercept. Even home goalkeeper Tim Flowers had a moment where he was caught in two minds – should he try and close the forward down, or stay on his line.

The Frenchman showed magnificent anticipation and the utmost composure to assess the situation, dismiss all the frantic panic of his opponents and chip the ball with his first touch into the far corner. The defenders were too late. Flowers was not so far off his line to be exposed, but had been punished nonetheless for a split-second of hesitation.

"There were glimpses of what could be achieved this season: the awesome potential of perhaps the greatest champions we have seen in more than ten years," said *The Sun*'s report. "United's potential is the second goal by Cantona – the brilliant chip that could close the goal of the season competition after just three Saturdays."

Denis Irwin scored early in the second half to secure the points, allowing Ferguson to make a couple of changes. One of them was Ryan Giggs. Ferguson couldn't help but sense an opportunity to educate the youngster about the brilliance of Cantona's goal: "I told Ryan Giggs, 'When you reach that level of accuracy you can call yourself a player.' I told him he was watching a master at work."

Cantona was on the scoresheet again four days later against West Ham, but it was his bewitching performance rather than the quality of his goal (a penalty) that caught the eye in a 3-0 win. "The cavalier Cantona, the craziest of Ferguson's footballing magicians, was simply awesome, even in the midst of so many gifted, supremely-skilled footballers," said *The Sun*.

The September international break did nothing to interrupt Cantona's flow, as a win over Finland put France on the brink of World Cup qualification. As he resumed club duties at Stamford Bridge, he almost scored one of the most incredible goals in British history. Chelsea 'keeper Dmitri Kharine came out of his goal to head a long ball away; he was only successful in clearing it to Hughes. The Welshman headed it to Cantona, who, at 40 yards from goal, was still – surely – a safe enough distance away. As it transpired, only just. The Frenchman's ingenuity brought gasps as he demonstrated the agility for which he was now renowned, arching his body, on the turn, quickly enough to generate the requisite power in a half volley to send the ball back towards goal.

The ball went over Kharine, but bounced up and hit the crossbar, rebounding into the stopper's hands. There was relief for the home fans who still applauded the outrageous effort. It was as close as Ferguson's team would get – Gavin Peacock scored the only goal to inflict the first defeat of the season.

It was not the ideal way to prepare for a tricky trip to Hungary to face Kispest Honved in United's first game in the European Cup (now rebranded as the Champions League) since 1969. At this point, the Champions League could only be entered by domestic champions, while clubs could only field three foreign players, plus two players who were assimilated – these players must have spent some time in the club's youth system.

Manchester United, then, were hit hard by this complication, as the countries within the UK were treated as 'foreign'. Welsh trio Ryan Giggs, Clayton Blackmore and Mark Hughes, as players developed by the club, were assimilated. Denis Irwin and Roy Keane, being from the Republic of Ireland, were of course foreign (though Irwin was assimilated due to his tenure in England), as was Scottish Brian McClair. Then there was Peter Schmeichel, Andrei Kanchelskis and Eric Cantona.

For Ferguson, it was impossible to field his first-choice team of Schmeichel, Parker, Bruce, Pallister, Irwin, Kanchelskis,

Keane, Ince, Giggs, Cantona and Hughes. That would include four foreigners and three assimilated players. Two would always have to miss out.

In Honved, the United boss decided to play a 4-3-3. Ryan Giggs would play from the right and Lee Sharpe from the left, with Robson, Ince and Keane providing thrust from midfield and Cantona up front. United scored three goals in the first half, Cantona getting the last one, and secured a 3-2 win. It was not quite the fluent football United fans had been used to, but the high-scoring encounter gave them cause for optimism.

The following weekend, Arsenal were the visitors to Old Trafford. With seven minutes to go in the first half, United were awarded a free-kick in a promising area. Ryan Giggs looked interested but Cantona and Irwin claimed seniority. Irwin's style of taking set pieces from this distance was to strike the dead ball, but he stood off this time. Paul Ince tapped it into the path of Cantona, who, from 25 yards, unleashed a blockbuster of a strike that gave David Seaman no chance.

It left a bitter taste for visiting boss George Graham, who had tipped Cantona to be a one-season wonder at United. "I still think Cantona will let you down at the very highest level," the Arsenal boss had said weeks earlier. "In the big games, against Inter Milan or whoever, I think Cantona will go missing. He's a cry-babe when the going gets tough."

But Cantona was the man for all occasions; he was rested for the Coca-Cola Cup defeat at Stoke City, but recalled to face Swindon Town at Old Trafford. The newly-promoted Robins were already rock bottom but seemed optimistic of an upset on such a grand stage. Those hopes were dashed in the first five minutes when Cantona set Kanchelskis away to score the opener. Cantona then showed his own clinical edge to make it

2-0. Mark Hughes made it 3-0 and it was all too easy for the league leaders. So much so, in fact, that they became sloppy, and Swindon hit two late goals. United killed the game off in injury time, but Hughes' muted celebration for his second was possibly reflective of the knowledge that he and his team-mates were about to get a rollocking from their manager.

"Games like this don't turn our players on and sometimes they leave you speechless," Ferguson said. "If we'd dropped a point, I'd have been glad. It would have taught us a lesson."

*The Independent*, though, agreed with the general consensus that there was one player exempt from such criticism, saying Cantona was "merely brilliant".

There was definitely a more concentrated edge to United's next performance as they navigated their home leg against Honved with ease. Ferguson opted to drop Roy Keane and recall Hughes to play in the more familiar shape, though Giggs again played from the right. The 2-1 win set United up for a second round clash with Turkish champions Galatasaray. Clearly the first leg advantage had afforded Ferguson the luxury of playing his usual shape at home, but as the first game against Galatasaray would be played at Old Trafford, he would have a difficult decision to make.

Before the October international break, United beat Sheffield Wednesday 3-2 at Hillsborough, and then rested Cantona in the League Cup return leg against Stoke City.

Most of the United players would be returning to Old Trafford in despondent mood after the break. England had suffered defeat to Holland and were all but out of contention for the World Cup. Cantona's France, meanwhile, had qualification in their hands, but lost at home to Israel despite leading 2-1. They would have to wait until November's home game with Bulgaria to hopefully seal their place in the United States.

Back on club duty, Cantona played a crucial part in both of United's goals in their win over Tottenham, but Spurs boss Ossie Ardiles predicted Ferguson's side would struggle in their next European game because of their lack of killer instinct.

Against Galatasaray, the United boss went with a strong line-up with the emphasis on attack. Denis Irwin was dropped and Lee Sharpe played at left-back, with Lee Martin in at right-back as Paul Parker was injured. It meant Ferguson could play Keane, with Cantona and Giggs wide of Hughes. The element of surprise seemed to work, and United were 2-0 up within 13 minutes.

Call it complacency, unfamiliarity or inexperience; the performance of the English champions inexplicably fell apart and by the 62nd minute, they were 3-2 down and staring down the barrel of the club's first ever home defeat in Europe. Galatasaray were better than anyone had anticipated but this was nonetheless a huge potential embarrassment.

Ferguson acted swiftly, bringing off Robson for full-back Phelan, restoring Sharpe to the wing and ordering his team to play in their usual shape, albeit with Giggs on the right. With nine minutes remaining, Keane's lofted ball into the box was met on the volley by Cantona at the back post. 3-3, and United's blushes just about spared. *The Independent* said Cantona's contribution had been "priceless" and the *Mail* said his goal "saved (United) from the worst of embarrassments".

Alex Ferguson was not looking at the positives. "After we lost that lead I kept thinking about what Ossie said," he explained. "There have been plenty of signs recently. They get in front and it becomes a carnival. Two or three players start treating it as a one-man show and start running with the ball. When you're

2-0 up and you think what's at stake, the progress in the cup has been risked by a lack of team play."

This was not vintage Manchester United. It was arguably the first grumblings of a sticky spell which would really surface in the early spring. However, the response to that draw was three consecutive domestic wins. A victory at Everton was achieved through United's only shot on target, though what a shot – Lee Sharpe connecting with an excellent volley. A League Cup demolition of Leicester City was followed by another subdued home performance in the league against QPR. The visitors scored early on and United's response was dreadful.

It took a half-time hairdryer from Ferguson to get his team going again, the equaliser coming though Cantona. He picked up the ball in his own half, evading Alan McDonald before approaching the opponent's goal. The defenders backed off him, frightened to commit. When it came to Cantona, he could make either decision look foolish. This time he took advantage of the space and drilled in a fabulous shot from 20 yards. Five minutes later, United had scored again through Hughes to complete the turnaround. This 2-1 win left United 11 points clear after just 13 games. Even when not at their best, they were too good for domestic opponents.

Some sensed a growing complacency within the ranks; that without the need to raise their game, when it finally came time to do so in Europe, they found they were unable to flick the switch. There was also some frustration that in most games they were being pulled into aggressive battles.

Hopes that European football might provide the platform for that expressive football had been hampered by the enforced changes and Ferguson was once more made to tinker in the away game against Galatasaray. It was a trip that had a terrible atmosphere as soon as the team stepped off the plane, where home 'supporters' greeted them with banners that said, amongst other things "Welcome to Hell", "This is the end of the road" and "You will die", and chanting "NO WAY OUT, NO WAY OUT." Nothing was lost in translation. Alex Ferguson tried to put on a brave face while he sat on the coach and a flag with a skull was held up to him outside of the window.

Armed police led the team into the Ali Sami Yen stadium; home fans had been in the stadium for hours. The atmosphere was one of pure hatred. The United boss fielded a 4-5-1 formation with the front six the same as against Honved away. Cantona had United's only real chance just after half-time, but isolated, and with Galatasaray players keen to throw themselves to the ground, the Frenchman grew frustrated.

On one occasion, he tried to retrieve the ball from one of the home players, only for his opponent to throw himself to the ground theatrically. To everyone's bewilderment, referee Karl Rothlisberger blew right on 90 minutes (it's fair to say United probably did not have a goal in them anyway), and Cantona, incensed, went to remonstrate with the official. Despite the game being over, Rothlisberger quickly pulled out a red card and pointed it in Cantona's direction as the teams were shielded off the field and towards the dressing rooms.

In the tunnel, there was a huge altercation with Cantona and Bryan Robson in the middle of it. In a scuffle with police, both players were hurt. "At the end of one tunnel was the sanctuary of our dressing room, but before we could reach it, I saw a policeman punch Eric Cantona in the back of the head," said Steve Bruce. They were pushed back into the away dressing room but the war was far from over.

"In the dressing room Eric went crazy," Roy Keane

remembered. "He was determined to go back outside to sort out the rogue cop who'd been wielding his truncheon. Eric was a big, strong lad. He was serious. He insisted he was going to kill 'that fucker'. It took the combined efforts of the manager, Brian Kidd, and a few of the players to restrain him. Normally I wouldn't have backed off a fight, but even I wasn't up for this one. There were a lot of Turks out there!"

Cantona was publicly vociferous in his demand for the truth. "I was punched on the back of the head and it's a great scandal," he said to press. On what he said to referee Karl Rothlisberger: "I just told him he was a bad referee."

Cantona later told *L'Equipe* it was "one of the biggest scandals I have seen in my life" and "I am certain that referees have been bought in the European Cup and I ask myself whether Mr Rothlisberger had not also been bought." On being knocked out, he said: "Galatasaray is a little team but today so were Manchester United."

When later retelling the story in *My Story*, Cantona said he did not in fact speak to the referee. "I simply went up to shake his hand and indicated with my fingers that his rating for the match was zero," Cantona said. "What annoyed me most is that I was hit on the head with a truncheon by a policeman, the sort of fellow who sends you to prison for being out of work, or when you are hungry and you go and steal a bar of chocolate from the supermarket. He was the sort of bloke who thinks the world revolves around him when he's in uniform. Even dressed up like that, he has not the courage to act face-to-face.

"Of course, I was upset at being knocked out of the European Cup, at the spoiling tactics of the opponents, at the fact that no stoppage time was added, and by being given the red card after the game had ended. But, above all, I had been hit from behind by that shit of a Turkish policeman. Maybe we'll bump into each other again some time!"

Alex Ferguson could barely believe it. "We did not play well and when desperation crept in, the whole thing became a shambles," he said. "The guy with whom Cantona clashed over-reacted. The lad was desperate to do well but frustration crept into our game. Eric complained about no time being added on; there was hardly a minute extra. Then a policeman punched Cantona. We have filmed evidence of that."

On Cantona's performance, the *Express* were particularly critical. "Cantona, the touch player, couldn't touch the high-notes when asked to go solo," read their report.

It was true that Cantona was ineffectual, but we have to consider mitigating circumstances. After all, if there is such a great mystery about 'why Cantona underperformed in Europe', we at least owe it to that discussion to consider why. Certainly in 1993, the foreigner rule was a handicap. It forced Ferguson to prioritise.

One must have sympathy with the United boss but in all of the variations of line-ups, not once did he go with Kanchelskis, Giggs and Cantona, either as a trio of front players or as a trio behind Hughes. Irwin would have had to be sacrificed, and so too would Keane or Schmeichel. But Lee Sharpe and Bryan Robson were adequate replacements, who had been used in those positions. There was a chance to use United's best attacking options but it wasn't taken. Consequently, it seems harsh to be too critical of Cantona's performances when the team was never set up to get the best from him. This subject would come up again, but in November 1993 most people were focussed on the controversy with officials and police.

One person not duly concerned about Cantona's actions in

Turkey was chairman Martin Edwards. "It wasn't just him, there was Robson who was involved in the scuffle in the tunnel, so it wasn't necessarily the same as his previous problems," Edwards said in an interview for this book in 2019. "We knew what we were getting, we knew he flared up at times. But his value to the team meant it was worth putting up with it."

In the days following the match, the newspapers across Europe carried the "scandal" quotes from Cantona as well as those quotes about the referee being "bought". UEFA president Lennart Johansson weighed in on the matter: "If these reports about what Cantona said are true, he is in big trouble with our disciplinary committee. Mr Cantona should know better than to make remarks about referees."

Jean-Jacques Bertrand, Cantona's lawyer, denied Cantona had said anything after the game to Rothlisberger. The official was later banned for life after allegations of match fixing in the 1996 Champions League (he had also been involved in a controversial incident at the 1994 World Cup). There was never an investigation into his performance in Turkey.

Next up for United was the small matter of the Manchester derby; although the occasion was at least one Ferguson knew his players would have to be up for. Following this first real moment of difficulty with Cantona, Maine Road would prove a test of character.

The derby on 7th November is significant for another reason; it was the first time Cantona played with his collar up, a trademark that would come to be associated with him as vividly as the number seven shirt. Cantona was superstitious as many other footballers were, and on this occasion, it is said that after feeling a twinge of sciatica, he decided to wear the collar up, possibly to remind him of the importance of that famous posture. Clearly a placebo effect, but clearly effective, and so indelibly Eric Cantona. It became iconic partly because of its evocative imagery, easily associated with another cocksure, enigmatic legend in Elvis Presley.

Yet one wonders if, in his own superstitious way, this was Cantona's way of calming that fire inside him after the trip to Turkey, a way to focus his thoughts on moving forward.

As Eric and his team-mates entered the pitch, the City fans attempted to generate hostility. Some home fans close to the tunnel had bought boxes of Turkish Delight and threw them at the United players. The atmosphere was white-hot while City boss Brian Horton sprung a formation change, playing with a sweeper and hoping to catch United on the counter-attack.

In the early stages it seemed as if United were fired up to exact revenge on those closest to them. In the 21st minute, though, the hosts found a way through, exploiting the mismatch in height between Paul Parker and Niall Quinn at the far post – 1-0. Ten minutes later it was two, as Steve McMahon whipped it in for Quinn, who got there ahead of Schmeichel.

United were rocking. Half-time was as welcome as the bell at the end of a round for a struggling boxer. So often, Alex Ferguson is credited with the turnaround of his team's fortunes. While he certainly deserved credit for what was about to happen, the events of the next 45 minutes owed much to the brilliance of Cantona. His approach had always been one of bravery and it was that trait which appeared to prevail here. The Frenchman dropped deeper, almost as an auxiliary midfield player, helping United flood that area. City were left with an extra defender but considering the purpose of that player was to prevent United's star man getting on the ball, it left Horton's team desperately trying to find an answer. At 2-0, they had an extra concern of how they should approach the game, with their primary mandate to protect the lead.

Cantona crossed from his new deep position but Gary Pallister was unable to get a clear connection. From the goal-kick, United skipper Steve Bruce thumped it back upfield; Michel Vonk chose what he felt was the safe option, heading the ball back to Tony Coton. Only now, Cantona had found a pocket of space behind the three defenders, around five yards in front of the nearest blue shirt. Eric, with time and space, made it 1-2. It provoked greater concentration from the home team. They would not switch off again, and so it would need something clever to get through for an equaliser.

Andrei Kanchelskis then broke through, but was thwarted as Coton smothered. Kanchelskis was taken off for Ryan Giggs and it was a magical combination between the Welshman and Cantona which finally brought the leveller 12 minutes from time. Cantona collected a clearance, took it down on his chest and juggled the ball with not only magnificent control, moving from right, to left, to right, back to left foot, but also a level of composure and arrogance that barely seemed to belong in the circumstances. He found Hughes, who found Keane, who found Giggs on the right. Giggs' first-time ball lacerated the City defence and Eric was at the back post to put the most stunning end to a brilliant move.

United piled forward. There was barely a question of if they would score again; rather when. That moment arrived three minutes from time, when Keane stabbed in a dramatic winner. Eric later described the match: "It came only days after we had lost out to Galatasaray and the press had been quick to suggest our golden run might be over. But the spirit in the team is magnificent. We were to need it, because we go in at half time 2-0 down. I play much deeper in the second half, and we begin to play much better. We are sweeping forward. We will not be stopped. I score two goals to draw us level. I run to the fans massed behind the goal to celebrate. They sense we will win and they are happy because it is worse to lose to City than anyone else. They are right… We had proved that we could recover from the disappointments of Europe."

Alex Ferguson was again in awe of his striker's contribution. "Eric's performance showed the sheer intelligence of the man," he said. "He knew exactly what was needed to cope with City's sweeper system and came up with two goals as well."

Even Horton was sporting in his assessment. "Cantona caused us all sorts of problems going deep – that shows what a good soccer brain he possesses," the City boss lamented.

This was the tone in the press as well. The *Manchester Evening News* concluded: "The Reds pulled out something special, but I doubt they would have managed it without Cantona's instinctive decision to drop deep to confuse City's sweeper system."

And the *Star*: "Forget Istanbul! Eric Cantona is back on his throne as the King of Football and Manchester United are back in business."

The upturned collar would remain.

# KING ERIC 10

ŴÝ

# Fire and Fury

In the wake of these derby heroics, Cantona now joined up with the French team for their final World Cup qualifier against Bulgaria. He was cleared to play in that game but the UEFA commission had banned him for four club European matches, although they accepted he hadn't questioned the integrity of the referee.

World Cup qualification was on Eric's mind as he went to Paris. All France needed was to avoid defeat. The early tension was interrupted by the light-hearted sight of a chicken strutting on to the pitch. The bird showed fleet of foot to evade attempts at capture and left the field to huge cheers. You can insert your own joke about egos, strutting cocks and chickens, but it seemed a perfect prelude to what followed.

Before the game, there had been an altercation following comments David Ginola, the then-PSG winger in the French squad, had made about some of his compatriots lacking character. Cantona was infuriated, feeling Ginola had pointed a finger at him and Jean-Pierre Papin.

Certainly nobody could accuse Cantona of lacking character and he took centre stage shortly after the feathered friend had left, volleying in fantastically from a Papin knock-down. Bulgaria levelled before half-time. The hosts were still masters of their own destiny. In the second half, Ginola came on for Papin, as Gerard Houllier attempted to close the game out.

With 15 seconds of normal time remaining, Ginola had the ball high up in the right-hand corner; the optimum position for wasting time. Instead, the winger hit a cross for Cantona, but it was too high and ended up in the right wing-back area for Bulgaria to counter. Emil Kostadinov strode forward and smashed a sensational shot in off the bar as the clock ticked to 90. Such was the shock that when the game restarted, a French TV network displayed the incorrect score graphic of "France 2 Bulgaria 1". That was corrected on full-time – nobody was left in any doubt of what had just taken place.

Houllier was livid and accused Ginola of "committing a crime" against the team. In a book, *Secrets de Coachs*, published in 2011, Houllier claimed Ginola had insisted Cantona and Papin should be dropped due to their history with Marseille: "PSG play at the Parc des Princes. PSG's enemy is Marseille. When he says that Papin and Cantona should not play and that he should play instead... he is a bastard because every time Papin or Cantona touched the ball, they were booed."

Ginola threatened to sue Houllier for defamation, while Cantona kept somewhat quiet about the episode, speaking only to *France Football* where he accused the winger of being "too weak" despite having the technical ability to succeed.

Houllier was soon gone as France manager. His successor,

previous assistant Aime Jacquet, held meetings with the senior players, with Cantona's bullishness about qualification for the European Championship in England in 1996 impressing the new boss, who named the United man captain.

England and Wales had also failed to qualify for the World Cup, while due to an issue with the Russia manager, Andrei Kanchelskis would not be going to the US. It was a glittering roll call of players in the Cliff dressing room who wouldn't be appearing – Peter Schmeichel, Paul Parker, Steve Bruce, Gary Pallister, Paul Ince, Bryan Robson, Kanchelskis, Cantona, Ryan Giggs, Mark Hughes and Brian McClair. In fact, Roy Keane and Denis Irwin were the lucky ones. It was a downbeat mood Cantona was returning to but there was no time to rest on any laurels, as the next opponents were Wimbledon.

The Dons' physical threat was something United had been getting used to from other teams, and over the winter it would reach boiling point. "The rough-house battles between the Crazy Gang and the aristocrats were infamous," read the match report in the *Star*. "The Dons just loved kicking the mighty Reds off their perch. John Fashanu pinpointed the difference from a year ago. United don't cry now, can't be intimidated and they kick back just as hard."

United won 3-1, with Cantona setting up two goals. It was a statement of intent from the Reds, who laid down their own marker – the visitors only committed one foul, as opposed to United's four. The number seven had once more been the instrumental figure, as noted in *The Observer*'s report: "Pallister and Hughes supplied the first two goals, the Welshman's effort a quite stunning strike courtesy of the endlessly creative Cantona, who competed as if determined to be noticed."

Eric was certainly noticed in the week that marked the

one-year anniversary of his move to Old Trafford. The club released a commemorative video, *Eric The King*, in which he said: "I have a kind of fire inside me which demands to be let out. Releasing it is what fuels my success… I couldn't possibly have that fire without accepting that sometimes it wants to come out and do harm. It is harmful. I do myself harm."

If Manchester United had seen anything of that temper so far, it had been brief, in Turkey, and with some mitigation. Eric Cantona may have come with a reputation, but the extenuating circumstances gave cause for the club to give their talisman the benefit of the doubt. The wild-eyed fury that had taken even Roy Keane aback seemed to have had some justification.

United struggled to get going in their next game, Ipswich showing defensive discipline to get a goalless draw at Old Trafford. So it was on to Highfield Road and Coventry City where Cantona's anniversary was marked in style, with the match-winner on 60 minutes. It was another tough game and this time it was Peter Schmeichel who earned most praise afterwards, repelling the Sky Blues on a number of occasions.

"Teams have always raised their game against us but now that we are champions they lift themselves even more and it makes it difficult to sustain our performance," Schmeichel said afterwards. "We have to contain them until they cannot stand the pace any more, then hit back."

Just like the game against Ipswich, though, these were the sort of matches United would have to get used to. "Football is all about opportunities – Coventry had enough of them but they didn't take then, Eric took his chance well – defenders often take their eyes off him when he drops into midfield," explained Alex Ferguson. "He can be the fulcrum of our passing game and then suddenly be up there, back in the attack."

Both Schmeichel and Cantona were influential again as United won in the League Cup at Goodison Park, the Dane saving a late penalty and the Frenchman instrumental in the only goal. Qualification for the quarter-final was straight-forward, and at the end of November it appeared the defence of the league title would be, too. After just 17 games United had amassed a 14-point lead over Leeds United in second.

Following that win at Coventry, Paddy Barclay had referred to Cantona's signing in *The Guardian*: "We all swallowed the tale of how Cantona came to cross the Pennines from Leeds – Howard Wilkinson rang Alex Ferguson to ask about Irwin; Ferguson countered with an inquiry about Cantona and was pleasantly surprised by the response – but in fact United's manager had been nudged in the right direction by a Frenchman who insists on anonymity."

We know that Ferguson did speak to a few Frenchmen, though the specific one in this case was Gerard Houllier, who with his Merseyside connections and ambitions of one day managing at Anfield, did not want to be seen as having encouraged this seminal transfer.

The request for anonymity was not made on the impulse of his departure from the French national team. In fact, it stemmed as far back as March that year, going by this otherwise meaningless line from a Barclay piece: "Ferguson was tipped off by a French friend that Cantona wanted to leave Leeds."

The anniversary had given United cause for celebration, especially considering the way things were going in the league. Usually dropping points at home would be seen as a setback, but a 2-2 draw against Norwich City on the first Saturday of December was a footballing celebration. Cantona set up both goals, for Ryan Giggs and Brian McClair.

"From the timeless talent of Eric Cantona... here was a match to dispose all concern about the custody of the game," said the *Mail*. "It is not a matter of surprise even to those paddling canoes up the Zambezi that Manchester United once again played football of sublimity in the second half."

A 3-0 win over Sheffield United that week caused one bookmaker to stop taking bets on Ferguson's side winning the league. That victory was secured by a stunning third where Cantona played the role of rapid forward. He had been defending a corner, which Schmeichel punched clear, and the Frenchman nodded to Lee Sharpe. Sharpe played the ball up to Ryan Giggs on the halfway line, who casually flicked the ball up and passed it into a space inside the centre-circle. Demonstrating surprising speed, Cantona's every touch was majestically controlled as he advanced into the penalty area and drilled in with his left foot via the near post. From his headed clearance, to his finish, was a little under eleven seconds.

A draw with Newcastle United had Magpies boss Kevin Keegan praising the adventurous style of Ferguson's side. "It's a shame they are not still in Europe because they could have had the nation backing them," Keegan said. "Look at their game. Look at their front line. What excitement."

There was one person who was tasked with getting a closer look – Aston Villa's Earl Barrett was instructed to man-mark Cantona in the last game before Christmas at Old Trafford.

The two encounters between these sides in 1993 had been

**Treble chance:** Cantona scores a hat-trick for Leeds against Spurs in the early part of the 1992/93 season, but it isn't enough to persuade his manager Howard Wilkinson that his enigmatic French striker is worth persevering with.

**National pride:** Eric wearing the colours of the French team, for whom he showed glimpses of his abundant natural ability.

**Spiritual home:** The Frenchman would soon find himself somewhere he'd be more appreciated. November 1992 sees him sign for Manchester United, brought in by a manager happy to accommodate his new striker's individualistic streak...

**Trophy time:** Cantona is the catalyst for United in 1992/93, sparking an upturn in fortunes that sees the club claim their first league title since the halcyon days of 1967.

**Turk war:** The Frenchman sees red following United's European exit against Galatasaray in Istanbul, before a tunnel brawl involving baton-wielding Turkish policemen.

**Neighbours collared:** Eric inspires United to a scintillating derby fightback against City at Maine Road, scoring twice in a 3-2 victory and orchestrating the Reds from a deep position – a game which also sees him turn up his collar for the first time...

**Studs-up:** Cantona lunges in on Norwich's Jeremy Goss during an FA Cup tie at Carrow Road in 1994. He escapes a red card, but it serves notice of the Frenchman's propensity for a rush of blood to the head...

**Long shot:** Cantona shows immaculate technique to cushion and then volley home against Wimbledon in a 1994 FA Cup tie – one of his finest goals in a United shirt during an epochal victory for Alex Ferguson's side.

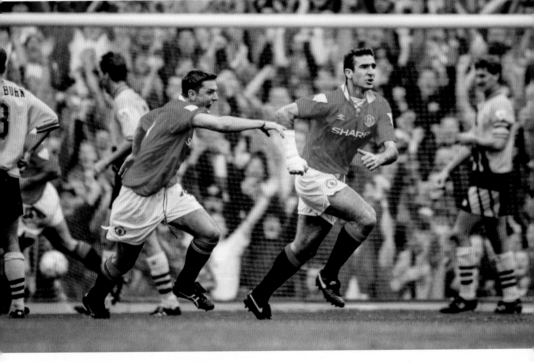

**Power points:** Another Cantona classic in the 1993/94 season – this time a strike of sheer venom to beat Arsenal as the Reds chase a domestic double and a second successive league title.

**Paying the penalty:** Eric sends Chelsea's Dmitri Kharine the wrong way for a second time as United win the FA Cup, before United's penalty hero celebrates with room-mate Peter Schmeichel on the sodden Wembley turf.

**Bets off:** Dennis Wise's attempts to put off Cantona include offering him an impromptu wager ahead of his penalty effort. The Chelsea man would soon find himself out of pocket.

**Sealed with a kiss:** The Frenchman is fast becoming United's talisman, and here he toasts FA Cup victory as the Reds complete a glorious domestic Double to conclude the 1993/94 campaign.

**Crowd scene:** Cantona gets his marching orders against Crystal Palace for lashing out at Richard Shaw, before a walk down the Selhurst Park touchline that would have a seismic impact on English football.

thrilling and this third was a fitting final act. Despite the close attention, Cantona was once more United's best player, scoring twice in a 3-1 win. United were deserved victors and had Ron Atkinson saying the only way they could be caught is if every rival was now given six points for a win.

"It was the team that sparkled," Cantona said, shrugging off the personal praise. "This is the best team I've played for… It was an honour to be so closely marked. It is the first time I have been man-for-man marked in this country. It happens in Europe and it's all the same to me. I'll change my game to counter it. Today it worked for me, maybe next time it won't."

Over Christmas, newspapers ran yearly review pieces and inevitably most of the focus on Manchester United was on the difference one man had made.

"We're just very grateful he's here," said club legend Bobby Charlton. "He's such a great player. I'm still pinching myself. A player like that only comes along once or twice in a lifetime. You respect his skill. Eric is the brainiest player I've ever seen, he sees such a lot when he has the ball. He slows us down and stops us wasting good positions. We finish almost every move with an effort on goal. The other thing is his ability to release players, even when the pass doesn't look on. If you make the run Eric will probably get you the ball."

United's manager and chairman were both asked how long they might expect Cantona to stick around.

Ferguson: "If he is here today, tremendous, but if he is gone tomorrow we just say, 'Good luck, Eric, thanks for playing for us, you were brilliant'." Edwards: "I don't think contracts mean anything to Eric. If he wants to walk out he probably will do."

The joyous romps of the festive football ground to a halt against Blackburn on Boxing Day. Rovers were now emerging as the most credible challengers to United. Having got an early lead, Rovers turned the game into a physical encounter, with Colin Hendry, David Batty and Alan Shearer all booked. "Eric Cantona, United's glorious match-winner so often this season, was kept in check and the Frenchman showed flashes of his infamous temperament," said the *Star*.

Those flashes would become prominent in the following weeks, but first, a flash of brilliance, as United salvaged a 1-1 draw against Blackburn. Paul Ince was the beneficiary of chaos in the box when Peter Schmeichel headed up for a late corner.

It was not the most fitting way to mark the news that Cantona had been named in third place in the 1993 *Ballon d'Or*, behind Roberto Baggio and Dennis Bergkamp.

He was in more familiar form in United's last game of 1993, creating the first and scoring the second in a 5-2 win at Oldham. It gave Alex Ferguson the opportunity to rest Cantona as he was substituted with 25 minutes to go. The win marked 100 points earned, and 100 goals scored, over the calendar year.

Leeds were the visitors to Old Trafford on New Year's Day and Ferguson's team struggled, for once, with the intensity of the occasion, hampered by Ince and Hughes' absence.

"Eric has changed us from possible winners into definite winners. He is playing some fantastic stuff," the United boss said before the game, but afterwards, he conceded that Howard Wilkinson's side had contained him. "Chris Fairclough did a very good job on Eric Cantona, but Eric still showed a great awareness and was always ready to receive the ball."

Fairclough had been given the Earl Barrett job, only this one was more personal. United were held to a 0-0 draw and Cantona was almost constantly held by the Leeds defender. Eventually frustration boiled over and Cantona was booked for a foul on Gary McAllister (ironically his closest friend at Leeds). On one occasion, Cantona appeared to stamp on Fairclough, and referee David Elleray gave Eric one or two lengthy dressing-downs as opposed to sending him off.

The ineffectual display gave Wilkinson an apparent justification to dismiss the events of the previous year: "He is the same player on a different stage, in different circumstances. When he was on my stage, we were losing matches. Those were not performances conducive to the way he played, so I left him out, he didn't like it, and he asked to go."

The implication was obvious but suggested Wilkinson must not have seen Cantona's December performances, where he'd performed exceptionally when repeatedly physically tested.

However, Ferguson was still keen to give his talisman a rest. He had done so against Oldham but couldn't against Leeds, due to the size of the game, and this was the case again against Liverpool three days later. Cantona created an early goal for Steve Bruce and United raced into a 3-0 lead at Anfield before throwing it away to draw 3-3.

Cantona couldn't be dropped from the following weekend's game against Sheffield United in the FA Cup; the Blades having disposed of United with Cantona absent in 1993. The Frenchman played his part in a 1-0 win in more ways than one. He was involved in the build-up for the goal, but it was the execution of the strike that had his fingerprints all over it.

It was scored by Mark Hughes, who exchanged passes with Cantona, Keane and Ince before converting; but it was the sort of deft, one-touch play that you would not have considered United capable of prior to November 1992. It is true that Alex Ferguson encouraged creativity in his team but players can be just as influential as coaches. This Manchester United side were characterised by the speed of their wingers, the strength of their core and the skill and imagination of their number seven. As Clayton Blackmore had observed, Cantona made players around him better.

A Coca-Cola Cup quarter-final at home to Portsmouth finally provided Ferguson with a chance to rest his talisman. It didn't go to plan; the United boss tried to explain to Cantona why he was making that decision, but changed his mind when he saw Eric's reaction. "If I left him out, I would probably never see him again," Ferguson recounted.

Predictably, Cantona made a crucial contribution in a 2-2 draw, the Frenchman getting his team's second goal. "Cometh the hour, cometh Cantona," concluded *The Guardian*.

Next up in the frantic schedule was Tottenham at White Hart Lane. Another game Cantona would be needed for. However, Spurs were a more accommodating opponent, keen to play their own football; this provided Cantona with the platform to have one of his best games for weeks as United won 1-0. Hughes scored the goal but Cantona got the praise, tipped by *The Times* to become the player of the year.

"I've been looking to give him a break but he doesn't want it and it seems he doesn't need it," Ferguson said. "He has showed he has the resilience to cope with the unique demands of the English game… he just wants to keep on playing and playing!"

There was at least a full week between games before Manchester United took on Everton, but the physical duress was replaced by an emotional one two days before the game when Sir Matt Busby, then the most successful manager in the club's history, died aged 84.

"Nobody can ever write about Manchester United without mentioning his name," Cantona reflected. "You sense his blood runs through every vein of the club's body. His name is engraved in the hearts of all those who love beautiful football. His kindness, courage, gentility and resilience serve as an inspiration to everybody. His legacy of playing with style will be preserved. His ideals, principles and beliefs will not be forgotten. I am pleased that I played in front of him."

The game against Everton became an emotionally charged affair, contested in marvellous spirit. Cantona was exceptional. *The Times* described United's performance as "spellbindingly entertaining"; the number seven must have thought there was some magic force preventing him from getting on the scoresheet. He was denied by a great save from Neville Southall and then saw a header cleared off the line before Ryan Giggs met Roy Keane's cross to head home.

In the second half, Cantona took a pass from Giggs down on his chest magnificently, and turned whilst still in the air to connect on the volley. Agonisingly, it thundered back off the post to deny Old Trafford a goal fit for the occasion. Eric shook his head in disbelief. Later, both Giggs and Cantona performed elaborate back-heels to set up Pallister, who could only screw his shot wide. The 1-0 victory was not reflective of the entertaining show Cantona had given the supporters.

After Cantona helped his team navigate the replay against Portsmouth and get through to the semi-final in the League Cup (he set up the winner for Brian McClair), it was time for another cup game and another testing afternoon.

Norwich City, under new boss John Deehan, adopted a more defensive approach than earlier in the season, with the aim to frustrate the Reds. That meant more man-marking treatment for Cantona, who had John Polston as a shadow at Carrow Road. Polston did not even give his opposite number a moment's peace when his own side were attacking.

United scored in the 18th minute through Roy Keane. Cantona had managed some good moments, exciting the travelling fans with his fine passing. Eventually, though, the personal attention triggered a reaction. The Frenchman went in heavily on Jeremy Goss, who jumped up and tried to retrieve the ball. Then Cantona launched himself into a two-footed tackle not dissimilar to the one which had caused all that controversy against Nantes player Michel Der Zakarian. Referee Paul Durkin deemed it a yellow card, to the bewilderment of all inside Carrow Road.

More insult to injury was to follow for the home side. Cantona scored United's second in the 73rd minute, and less than five minutes was involved in another altercation, this time with Polston. One reporter said Eric had "backheeled the defender in the shoulder".

The report in the *Express* described the good and bad of United's controversial star: "In a contentious tie Cantona emerged as a man prepared to let his boots do some pretty bad talking when the chips are down... but it was perhaps typical that Cantona, who committed two of the worst fouls of the fourth round, should also sew up this tie with a supreme example of his strength and skill under pressure."

The match was screened live on BBC One, and host Jimmy Hill described Cantona's behaviour as "despicable".

Questioned afterwards, Ferguson leapt to his player's defence. "The Cantona incidents were a result of his frustrations – he wears his heart on his sleeve and if he is provoked by sneaky opponents he'll do something about it," he said, before turning his attention to Jimmy Hill. "If there is a prat going about in this world he is the prat. I'm not interested in Jimmy Hill, neither are my players. He writes us off in the warm-up – that's how much he knows about the game.

"The BBC are dying for us to lose. Everyone is from Liverpool with a supporter's badge. They will be at our games every week until we lose, that mob, Bob, Barry, Hansen. That's what will drive us on. Eric probably reacted to a bit of off-the-ball intimidation. You can't take the law into your own hands, but some of his passing was incredible."

By all accounts, Eric Cantona already received preferential treatment. Ferguson knew he had a player, a person, who was different to any he had managed before. There was no point trying to pretend otherwise. "I did things for Eric and for the really special players that I did not do for others, but I don't think this was resented, because the players understood the exceptional talents had qualities they did not possess," he said. "My relationship with Eric might also have been helped by the fact neither of us were English and, to some degree, we considered ourselves outsiders."

Nonetheless, there were occasions where the United boss had to make a stand. The Norwich incident was one of many that could be cited as examples of his excellent management. "For public consumption, the gaffer called Jimmy a prat, but privately he wasn't impressed by what Eric had done, and let him know in no uncertain terms," remembered Ryan Giggs.

The result saw United qualify for the fifth round, where

they would meet Wimbledon at Selhurst Park. Before then, games against QPR and Sheffield Wednesday were settled by magnificent solo efforts from Giggs, taking some of the spotlight away from Cantona (though Eric did score at Loftus Road in a 3-2 win).

Ahead of that Wimbledon game, Joe Kinnear made his intentions perfectly clear when it came to Eric Cantona. "We are going to tie him up and gag him," the Dons boss said. Just 20 minutes were on the clock when Vinnie Jones scissor-tackled Cantona at a little over knee height. It should have been a red card.

David Elleray, the referee, waved only yellow. In the context of recent events, United could scarcely complain. They would have to get on with it and provide another answer.

Their response was to put on a spectacle which was arguably the best from a Manchester United team under Alex Ferguson since he had become manager seven-and-a-half years previously. Instead of getting involved in a battle as Wimbledon wanted, Cantona simply walked away from the crowd assembled around the referee.

Less than three minutes later, Jones clattered into Paul Parker in another potential red card offence. Elleray told Jones he was on his last chance. The tactic from Wimbledon had been to try and provoke a reaction early on and now instead they had set themselves out as the aggressors.

The tone shifted. United felt capable of playing their football knowing that Elleray would have to take a harder line the next time a rough tackle came in. The Reds pressed high and enjoyed long spells of possession. It became a matter of when, and that moment arrived just before half-time in spectacular fashion. From a Schmeichel goal-kick, Hughes held the ball up on his chest magnificently, and played the ball to Irwin on the halfway line.

The full-back played a cross-field pass towards Andrei Kanchelskis. Gary Elkins anticipated, stepping in front to head clear. Or so he thought. His clearance went straight to Eric Cantona. Words barely do justice to what followed. Eric controlled the ball with his right foot, flicking the ball upwards. Before letting the ball bounce, he showed tremendous technique to take the effort on the volley. The ball flew over the despairing dive of Hans Segers, into the top corner.

In his magnificent book on Cantona, Philippe Auclair described the goal with the melancholic lament that he felt surely dogged the player in such moments; that no matter how much one might try to make it so, a sport like football, with all of the unpredictabilities, can never be received or explained as art in the same way that music or painting can.

Anyone compelled to write about Eric Cantona inevitably arrives at this topic. Auclair insists sport is competition and of course he is not wrong. But if art is subjective, in that its beauty is defined by the recipient, then the form in which art is presented, and found, and created, can surely also be subjective?

Just as one can often remember the same way they felt when they first heard a song, or saw a painting or a movie, so too can the memory of a goal, or a piece of skill that thrills you so much you just want to watch it time and again, or even get a football and try it yourself, just as you might be inspired to pick up a guitar, write a song or make your own movie.

Back at Selhurst Park, Segers stood motionless, hands on his hips, for a couple of seconds. If Elkins' clearance had landed at the feet of any other attacker in the country, it would have probably been a safe one. Even players who could consider themselves peers of Cantona would not think of doing something as audacious. Anyone who has ever played football appreciates the challenge presented by gravity. The pass from Irwin was looping downwards and the header from Elkins had surely killed the momentum of the ball. It was a celebration of everything Cantona; his balance and posture, delicacy of touch and speed of thought. To do what he did, to get the power just right, both his touch and his finish had to be timed to absolute perfection. They were.

Wimbledon, despite being at home, were wearing their lucky red away kit. United were dressed in their green and gold Newton Heath commemorative strip, making the memories of Cantona's strike that bit more vivid. That could be said for many of United's great moments that season – for the first time, they had an all-black strip, and the sight of Cantona slaying opponents in this shirt with a big yellow seven on his back was seared into the minds of supporters.

There was nothing lucky for Wimbledon on this occasion as the second half saw them toyed with as if they were docile mice instead of the Rottweilers they were often portrayed as.

Just as his very arrival had done, the goal scored by Cantona elevated the performance of his team-mates that day. A second goal arrived from a corner, scored by Paul Ince, before the third, which was scored by Denis Irwin. Irwin's, like Cantona's, has a good shout to be the best of his entire career.

Years later, Cantona would describe his perfect goal as the most simple one, where the ball is touched by each member of the team and finished by the last one who hadn't yet touched it. This was as close to that as he would get in a Manchester United shirt, although Pallister, Bruce and Schmeichel didn't get a touch. In all, eight players made 14 passes, and the move was ended with an exquisite one-two between Ince and Irwin before the full-back rounded a defender and rolled the ball into the corner with his left foot. For purists, Irwin's goal was a perfect representation of football at its very best.

"This was not even a contest," said *The Sun*. "It was an embarrassing, one-sided exhibition match. Ferguson's side were so good it was frightening. Frighteningly good, frighteningly unbeaten and frightening for the rest of football."

Ferguson later said it was one of maybe "half a dozen matches every season when the whole team are 100 per cent on song and on top of the game". This was also one of those rare occasions where the team lined up just as everyone remembers it – Schmeichel, Parker, Bruce, Pallister, Irwin, Kanchelskis, Keane, Ince, Giggs, Cantona, Hughes.

It was footballing perfection, almost, and a standard United would reach twice again in the coming weeks. That would not be the case for their next game, though, which was again in London, against West Ham. United scored early and then seemed to become complacent. The Hammers scored twice in three minutes to take the lead, and United needed a very late equaliser from Paul Ince to preserve their unbeaten record.

It had been a physical battle. Hughes, United's first goalscorer, admitted he revelled in it. "I love pleasing United fans but I also get a kick out of being on the pitch and having the power to aggravate thousands of opposing fans," he said. But there was only so long this level of aggression could last without consequences. The casualties from Upton Park were Denis Irwin with bruised ribs and Cantona with a bruised shin. Ferguson rested his talisman for the second leg of the League Cup semi final against Sheffield Wednesday. The game ended with a 4-1 win on the night. One Wembley final booked.

Cantona still wasn't ready for action in the weekend game against Chelsea. Gavin Peacock – who'd scored the winner at Stamford Bridge – was again the scourge of United, striking in the 65th minute to end to that unbeaten run. Ferguson complained about the lack of pace and penetration.

"Without the inspirational touch of Eric Cantona, United looked surprisingly vulnerable," agreed *The Independent*.

United remained on top, but their post-Christmas form had seen Blackburn reduce that lead to just four points. There was a mixed cocktail being brewed with a number of combustible elements. United were still capable of their supreme brilliance but opponents were beginning to believe they could get a result against them, either by being as aggressive as possible, or inciting some aggression from these fiery United stars.

Against Charlton in the FA Cup quarter-final there was a mixture of all these elements. Roy Keane and Paul Ince went into the game one yellow card away from being ruled out of the League Cup final. Telling those two to play within themselves was a non-starter, but thankfully neither were booked. Right on half-time, Peter Schmeichel charged out to close down forward Kim Grant, blocking the ball with his arm. He was sent off, the Old Trafford crowd chanting "Sealey, Sealey!" as veteran favourite goalkeeper Les Sealey replaced Parker.

Hopes of an unlikely upset were soon dashed. Cantona, now with three men on him, won a corner, from which Hughes stabbed home. In the 71st minute, Cantona helped his team seal the win, in typical fashion. The Frenchman had his back to goal but saw Kanchelskis and Giggs running either side of him. Eric chose the right-winger, and played the ball perfectly in his path. Kanchelskis smashed home to make it two.

The Russian got a third before the visitors grabbed a

consolation. *The Sunday Times* reflected: "The problem for Charlton was that United had Eric Cantona back to provide those angles and improvisations that transform the champions from a good side into one of predictable brilliance."

A second Wembley trip was booked, with United facing Oldham in a repeat of the 1990 FA Cup semi-final.

Two weeks after their Hillsborough beating, Sheffield Wednesday travelled to Old Trafford for the fourth meeting between the sides that season. The home fans were treated to one of those supreme performances from Cantona.

"The gods surely hailed Manchester United as champions last night after a display that brought new meaning to the phrase 'fantasy football'," reported the *Today* newspaper. "In an almost ritual humiliation of Sheffield Wednesday, Eric Cantona-inspired United reached new heights on an evening of Arctic weather conditions."

First, in the 14th minute, Cantona's lofted pass sent Ryan Giggs clear to finish. One minute later, the Frenchman nodded down for Mark Hughes to race through and thump in. After Paul Ince got a third, it was Eric's turn to get on the scoresheet. Ince played him through, and Cantona threatened to finish twice before he slid the ball past Kevin Pressman.

Ten minutes into the second half, Eric made it five. Off balance, he got a powerful enough connection with his left foot to finish with style from the edge of the box.

It was a fine answer to re-emerging critics who had found their voices in the wake of the publication of Cantona's *My Story* book that month. The war of words with Howard Wilkinson had been reignited and the doubters who questioned Cantona's ability to remain in the same place without blowing up were about to have their prayers answered.

Swindon Town welcomed United to the County Ground on Saturday 19th March. The leaky Robins defence conceded after just 13 minutes when Hughes crossed for Keane. The game took a bad-tempered turn soon after. Hughes was nudged off the pitch and found himself trying to hold the advertising board to remain upright while the home fans berated him. One appeared to swing at Hughes. Things were turning ugly. Where United had done so well to resist the temptation at Wimbledon, now they got involved a little more.

"I welcomed the intensity of every United road game," Roy Keane wrote in his first autobiography. "But the extra effort by players from clubs like Norwich, Swindon, Crystal Palace, Oldham and Wimbledon led to trouble. Confronted by tackles that were high, late and crazy, our only option was to meet fire with fire. Eric, Incey, Hughes and myself led the resistance."

At the County Ground, one such rash challenge enabled Luc Nijholt to equalise. Cantona, facing intense physical attention, swiped out angrily at challenges from Brian Kilcline and Lawrie Sanchez. Paul Ince got a second for United after battling play from McClair and Keane.

The home side had won a corner minutes after the second goal and Schmeichel collected it calmly, throwing the ball to Cantona. The Frenchman had the company of John Moncur but shrugged him off, finding space in his own inimitable way. Moncur came back with a hard but fair challenge. Cantona was dispossessed, but Moncur was on the floor and the ball was loose. The Swindon midfielder jumped up to reclaim the ball, but he and Cantona got involved in a scuffle. Moncur fell and had one hand on Cantona's shirt; as Eric tried to fight his way free, his right foot stamped down on his opponent's chest. Referee Brian Hill was just a few feet away. Red card.

In an interview for this book in 2019, John Moncur insisted Swindon boss John Gorman had not instructed his team to wind up the United players. "John Gorman wasn't that type of fella," Moncur insists. "Eric wasn't targeted, but he might have been getting frustrated. We were bottom of the league and they were top, we were having a decent day and they were underperforming. I don't think Eric was having a great game...

"I'd had a couple of duels where I'd come out on top. I would always throw a bit of banter about and I think I'd said something to him that might have upset him. Nothing too bad. I think I'd dropped the shoulder on him earlier on as well and he'd given me a funny look. In the second half I tackled him, went to the floor and I was as surprised as anyone when he stamped on me. I wasn't in too much pain, maybe it was the adrenalin and thinking he'd get sent off."

Steve Bruce felt there was no hiding place. "It was a stupid thing to do and we could not dispute the decision," he said.

"Taking Cantona down a peg or two seemed to be objective number one for the opposition hard men," recalled Roy Keane. "Perhaps part-time hard men would be a better description."

The build-up to the game had included references to the presence of referee Hill, who had been the victim of complaints from Ferguson in the 1992/93 season when the United boss asked the FA not to appoint him to referee any more United games. "He stamped on John Moncur and caught him in the chest," Hill said. "I saw it, the linesman saw it. Alex Ferguson did not say anything to me after the game."

"Whatever I say to the players or action I'll take, I'll keep to myself," Ferguson told the press. Cantona was fined but Ferguson wouldn't reveal how much. His 'special treatment' was relaxed. "The gaffer really lost his rag with Eric over the

Swindon thing, and told him to sort himself out, or else," remembered Ryan Giggs.

After the game, Moncur gave a surprising take to reporters: "I've admired Eric so much this season and tried to learn from him. I'll still be voting him as my PFA Player of the Year, despite what happened today."

Moncur confirmed he did just that when being interviewed for this book. "I had a lot of respect for him as a player and that didn't change," he says. "He was a fantastic footballer and I never bore a grudge, those things are part of the game, there was no lasting damage. He had a great year so I voted for him."

After a few near-misses and a couple of 'should have beens', Eric Cantona had finally been given his first official red card playing for Manchester United (let us dismiss the technicality of the Galatasaray incident). Here was a flashpoint the press could get their teeth into.

"The pressure of treble-chasing is clearly getting to United," reported *The Sun*. "They spent this afternoon moaning, groaning and whingeing as Swindon fought for their lives… Cantona was a disgrace to himself and the great name of Manchester United. He was a disgrace to English football."

The next game against Arsenal was bad-tempered to the extreme. Roy Keane was booked for lashing out at Paul Davis, ruling him out of the semi-final. Ince was lucky to escape a booking. A football match was played between the confrontations, with a Lee Sharpe double earning a 2-2 scoreline. In the

86th minute, Cantona found himself in the book again for a foul on Ian Selley.

Instead of seeing out the game, Cantona couldn't resist getting into another tussle with Tony Adams and Nigel Winterburn. And referee Vic Callow couldn't resist pulling out another yellow for the Frenchman, despite it seeming a little of an over-reaction.

This time, Ferguson was more sympathetic. "We've not been doing anything any different," he insisted. "Maybe the referees are reading the paper."

The papers didn't need much of an excuse to pile in on Eric once more. "Eric Cantona's four days of misery will have a devastating effect on United," said *The Sun*. "His second red card in successive games could have cost them the treble." The *Mail* concurred: "The serene stroll towards the game's first Triple Crown has become littered with cautions, rows, players chasing referees, and in the middle of it Eric Cantona is lashing out at the opposition in some kind of wild mist."

The second red card left Cantona with a five-game ban. He would miss away games at Blackburn, Leeds and Wimbledon, as well as the semi-final against Oldham Athletic and the Manchester derby. There may have been hysteria about Cantona's misdemeanours, but it was not an over-reaction to suggest United now had a huge struggle on their hands.

United captain Steve Bruce made a vain plea for the FA to look at video evidence of the Arsenal game to rescind that red. "I felt that Eric did not do anything wrong," Bruce told the press. "He was trying to jump out of the way. To be sent off for that was a mistake. Let's just hope that justice can be done."

In his autobiography later that year, Bruce added: "He was becoming a marked man who could not afford to step out of line in any way. If it was justified at Swindon, it was an error for him to be sent off at Highbury… the knives were out, so as soon as he was involved in anything untoward at Highbury, the odds were stacked against him…"

After giving him the benefit of the doubt over the Galatasaray incident, United chairman Martin Edwards was not ready to agree with the national opinion that Cantona had brought disgrace on his club just yet, but did confess to being worried. "There was a little bit of concern when he was sent off twice in a week," he admits. "That's natural, you're challenging for trophies, you don't want your key players missing games. He was getting a lot of bad publicity. It was a bit of a concern."

There was only one way to respond to the controversy, and Cantona insisted he was going to provide the tonic. "After four days of trouble I have only one answer to give now, and that will be out on the pitch at Wembley," he declared.

"I will not allow two-and-a-half years in this country to be damaged by four days of turbulence. In France it would have been different. Here, with Manchester United, I feel I am in the hearts of the supporters, the players and Alex Ferguson. I am not in a bad mood. I have a bonus, something to spur me on. I have tried to understand the red card at Arsenal and very quickly realised not everyone feels I deserved it. This shows me my love affair with English football can continue."

# Dizzy Heights

**O**nce more, it was cometh the hour, cometh Cantona. In the cup final, he proved to be the man for the occasion. But that occasion was not Aston Villa and not the League Cup. Even in what was to be a record-breaking season for Manchester United, some relative lows must first be endured.

Save for Les Sealey, it was Alex Ferguson's strongest eleven which was sent out to do battle with Ron Atkinson's team. The United boss hadn't counted on his opposite number replicating the tactic which brought him success on the same occasion with Sheffield Wednesday.

Atkinson flooded the midfield, hoping to use speedy wide players to assist his full-backs against Kanchelskis and Giggs. It would be a war of attrition with a territorial surrender from the ex-United boss. Ferguson's team fell into the trap. They started well before Villa suddenly caught them on the break.

Steve Bruce was tempted into a challenge and Dalian

Atkinson finished past Sealey. From then, United were chasing, and with the game reaching a conclusion, became a little more rash and frustrated. Dean Saunders made it 2-0. Mark Hughes pulled one back in the 83rd minute and Ferguson went for broke, taking off Bruce for McClair, but the gamble backfired when United were left outnumbered in injury time. Kanchelskis handled on the line and was sent off, with Saunders scoring the penalty.

The domestic treble hopes were over. Eric Cantona had been ineffectual, Paul McGrath having one of the finest games of his career as he kept a close watch on the Frenchman.

The last game before Cantona's suspension kicked in was another battle – three days later, United played Liverpool at Old Trafford, hardly the thing you need after playing on the energy-sapping Wembley pitch. Cantona was a little quiet but still the most artistic in the United team. After a run of difficult games, United fans were just happy to see their side win 1-0, restoring their six-point advantage at the top.

That was it for Eric for three-and-a-half weeks, which threatened to derail his team's season. In the meantime, United's current stock market value of £82m was reported. When the club were floated on the stock market in 1991, their value was £47m. The club were now worth approximately double what they had been worth when Cantona signed.

On 10th April, Cantona was named the PFA Player of the Year, the first overseas winner of the award. Picking up the trophy, Cantona said: "I hope I will stay a long time. I know I have often changed my mind but as long as I am happy I will stay here." Cantona thanked Alex Ferguson, Brian Kidd, and "all the players – even the ones who did not vote for me – for giving me the pleasure to play in English football."

If this momentous achievement helped to make him feel more at home, then Cantona still found himself in the headlines for the wrong reasons. He had been asked about his suspension and described referee Vic Callow, who had dismissed him at Arsenal, as "just like a little boy". The FA asked him to provide a written explanation for his comments.

United's form during Cantona's absence had been desperately close to disastrous. A 2-0 loss at Blackburn had reduced the gap to three points. United overcame Oldham in a tight league match but laboured against the same opponents at Wembley. The game went to extra-time and with no Keane, Kanchelskis or Cantona, the Latics concentrated on nullifying Giggs. Oldham scored through Neil Pointon and it looked as if United would head to Leeds very tired, and very deflated.

In the last minute of extra-time, United threw everything forward, and following one hopeful lob into the box, Mark Hughes stretched out his powerful right leg to volley into the far corner. It was a reprieve in more ways than one. The replay was scheduled for three days later at Maine Road, and United would still be leggy, but at least they would be facing the same opponent. Furthermore, it meant the Leeds game would be postponed – and Cantona would be back for that.

Galvanised by the Hughes wonder goal, United took Oldham apart in the replay. A returning Kanchelskis was inspired, scoring a sensational solo effort and ripping the defence to pieces. Goals from Irwin, Giggs and Robson sealed a return to Wembley. United would face off against bogey team Chelsea on 14th May in the FA Cup final.

In their last game before Cantona's suspension expired, United travelled to Wimbledon. The game was a late Saturday kick-off, so Ferguson's side already knew Blackburn had lost to Southampton. The teams were now level on points, though United had two games in hand.

But Ferguson's side had a fairly big semi-final hangover and the midfield physical tussle was one too many for Ince and veteran Robson, playing his second match in four days at the age of 37. A mistake from Schmeichel gifted John Fashanu the winning goal. United were unable to punish Blackburn.

In the build-up to the Manchester derby and Eric's return, the City camp were keen to ignite another explosion. Full-back Terry Phelan declared: "The first thing we're going to do is wind Eric up… Steve McMahon will wind Eric up left, right and centre. I don't think Eric will get an inch against us."

City boss Brian Horton felt compelled to take Phelan out of the team, while McMahon was booked inside five minutes for fouling Cantona. The Frenchman didn't react. In fact, he was magnificent in an all-action display. "A move started by Cantona and culminating in two penalty-area dummies by the Frenchman, might have produced their goal of the season had Kanchelskis not found himself crowded out," wrote Joe Lovejoy for *The Independent*. "Cantona was all over the place – dispossessing Rosler in the United area, popping up at left-back with a long pass to put Keane clear, and hurdling Curle's uncompromising tackle with a d'Artagnan leap, followed by an exquisite pass which tested Andy Dibble's speed."

United won 2-0, and both goals came from Cantona before half-time. First, Hughes and Kanchelskis linked up with a devastating show of strength and speed to provide a simple tap-in for Eric. The second was a little more taxing, with Cantona drawing Dibble out of the goal before finishing, after being put through by Hughes.

Alex Ferguson was full of praise for Cantona. "It's good to

have him back. Our record when he plays is phenomenal. He provides that bit of style. No matter the tempo of the game, he's got that ability to compose himself on the ball. In the maelstrom of our league, that in itself is a miracle," he said.

Cantona himself was keen to give gratitude to the display of his colleagues: "I was happy to come back and score but it was more important that the team won… the goals were made easier by the skill and passing of Kanchelskis and Hughes."

It was a huge result – Blackburn drew at home to QPR, and United now had a two-point lead with a game in hand. Victory at Leeds could prove pivotal. Inevitably talk focussed on Cantona's first return to Elland Road since he had won the league at Old Trafford. Considering how controversial that first visit was, Cantona had a minder with him.

"Anyone would think we were playing Cantona United, not Manchester United," Leeds boss Howard Wilkinson said, with a not-so-subtle undertone. This time though it was the wingers, who had spent all season providing the ammunition for Cantona and Hughes, to take centre stage. Kanchelskis and Giggs scored second-half goals to earn a 2-0 win.

United's next game was at Ipswich Town. If they won, Blackburn could not afford another slip. The topic of Cantona's future was never far away, though this time Ferguson was asked about reported interest from Real Madrid. The United boss confessed there had been "lots of interest" but insisted "selling Cantona is not on the agenda".

Eric gave an on-pitch demonstration of his contribution once more at Portman Road. United were struggling, having conceded early and then losing Peter Schmeichel to injury in the 27th minute. Nine minutes later, Cantona met a cross from Kanchelskis with a downward header. Less than two minutes after the restart, Ryan Giggs stabbed in the winner.

It was all on Blackburn to win at Highfield Road, but with United only needing one victory from their last two games at home to Southampton and Coventry, it seemed that unlike the previous year, Ferguson's side would win it on the pitch. That wasn't to be, of course, as Coventry's Julian Darby scored twice to put Blackburn to the sword.

The celebrations this time around were much more muted. The Southampton game at Old Trafford saw United canter to a 2-0 win whilst missing a bucketload of chances; Cantona atoned for his profligacy with a late assist for Hughes.

And Cantona kept his place for the last game of the season, one player Ferguson daren't leave out even if Parker, Keane, Ince, Kanchelskis, Hughes and Giggs all had the afternoon off. Bryan Robson was also playing his last game at Old Trafford. 'Stuck' on 99 goals for the club, the game seemed to be a desperate procession to get him his century. It wasn't to be, but the closest United came to breaking the deadlock was from a Robson cross.

Now he didn't have to try and lay one on a plate for his team-mate, Cantona could chance his own arm. What followed was one of those near misses that would be remembered forever; following a defensive header up in the air, Eric theatrically spun his body and performed the most perfect overhead kick from 15 yards out. Perfect aside from the fact it didn't go in; Steve Ogrizovic palmed it away. Frustration for Cantona and for those in attendance at Old Trafford, who were denied seeing one of the greatest goals of all time.

A couple of days after the celebrations to close the league campaign, Bryan Robson announced he would be going to Middlesbrough as player-manager. Captain Marvel's departure was the first step towards a reframing of the personality of the United dressing room.

Looking ahead to the Chelsea cup final, United had never won a league and cup double before. The squad of players who had made history with their league title win in 1993, and with their club-record league-winning tally of 92 points just the previous week, could enter the record books again.

Superstition could only carry Cantona so far and while the upturned collar had seemingly had a magic effect on his form, the placebo effect on his back pain seemed to have worn off.

On the Friday before the game, Cantona and skipper Steve Bruce had a conversation which foreshadowed events to come. "We went to Bisham Abbey for a spot of light training and I mentioned to Eric that we would be awarded a penalty in the final," Bruce said. "We had been awarded only two during the entire season until that point.

"He shrugged his shoulders, threw his arms out wide and said, 'Penalty? No problem; I'll score'. Eric was going to have a bit of penalty practice, but decided against it as there were cameras about and he did not want Dmitri Kharine to see which way he intended putting a spot kick. He assured me he would score. He was not boastful; he just had total belief."

As part of their all-day coverage of the FA Cup final, the BBC ran a feature interview with Cantona and selected others. Michel Platini spoke warmly of his protege. "He's a very interesting man, one of those rare people who are sensitive and intelligent," he said. "He doesn't come over as he really is. Let's say he has a funny way of getting his message across. But the man himself is very interesting. I'd be perfectly happy to go off on holiday with Eric Cantona."

Howard Wilkinson was asked for his thoughts. "My view of Eric Cantona – for public consumption – is that he was a very good player with a potential for greatness in a great side," said the Leeds boss. "At Leeds, he occasionally showed that. The fact that he left was a situation almost as inevitable as adding two and two and making four."

Cantona, meanwhile, gave a compelling interview about his views on the sport and the path which led him to Old Trafford. "Everything in life can be found in football – like learning how to lose… how to win. So everything you find in life does exist in football," he explained. "And just like football, to enjoy success in life you've got to keep your feet on the ground. You've got to find the right level.

"Football is an art. And I reckon it's the finest art form because it demands spontaneity and the most thought too. My idea of art is that it's all about obeying natural impulse. If you try to make it too elaborate you lose sight of what it's all about. That is why I believe soccer is the finest art. Nowadays in football there are little nobodies… in France, there are players who as soon as the going gets tough, suddenly get injured. And yet they'll still stay at the same club for ten years. They take their wages and don't give a damn about anything else.

"If you have respect for yourself but find that others don't respect you, then you must go. Or you can stay and strike out against the wall. If it cracks, there is a chance you can change things. So then you stay and fight. But if the wall doesn't crack, there's no point in hanging around, being a masochist. It's time to go. The world is big enough; people are waiting with open arms… You are what you are. I am who I am and I'm proud of it. Sometimes you have to go through painful experiences to be able to move on in life."

The forward had certainly done that. His immense potential was finally being fulfilled and while some might say he was being indulged at Old Trafford, the man himself felt he was simply understood. "Manchester United has been like a family," he said. "We've enjoyed great moments together. There have been some rough patches but I realise I've joined a real family. We tend to think of football as one big happy family, but I've come across too many unfaithful families.

"Like any young sportsman I used to think sport would be utopia, but at United I really do find this sense of belonging. We respect each other and we protect each other. That's why I'm really happy to be playing for Manchester United."

And the dark mist which still reared its head? "Let me go back to what I said before, that football is the finest art form because of its spontaneity. Without that, football would be nothing. But because it's so impulsive there are always going to be problems. And just as I can bring happiness to people through my footballing instincts, so there are also going to be dark shadows, black stains. You've just got to live with that. To make people happy as often as possible – that is the only thing that counts."

After a poor night's sleep before the game, Eric was given aspirin for his back pain. It goes some way to explaining the somewhat subdued first-half performance at Wembley, but that could be said for the entire United side. The unrelenting rain was threatening to ruin the game as a spectacle and Ferguson's side were still learning how to adapt to the big pitch. But Chelsea certainly played up to their billing as bogey side, working hard and coming closest to scoring in the first half when Gavin Peacock hit the crossbar.

Ferguson even contemplated the unthinkable – substituting Cantona – but decided against it, ultimately only because of the occasion. United started the second half better and Chelsea were pinned back. On the hour, Ryan Giggs evaded a tackle and played the ball inside the box to the advancing Irwin. The full-back was poleaxed by Eddie Newton, and referee David Elleray awarded the penalty. Bruce's prediction had come true.

The last two penalty kicks in FA Cup finals had been saved. On this most English of showpiece occasions, it was the first time a Frenchman would come up against a Russian in such a situation. One Englishman did attempt to have an influence on proceedings, as Gary Pallister remembered: "As Eric strode forward calmly to take the kick, he was approached by Dennis Wise, who offered him a £100 bet that he wouldn't score. There was barely a flicker of emotion on the Frenchman's face as he accepted the wager, then sent goalkeeper Dmitri Kharine the wrong way. It was an outrageous piece of gamesmanship by Wise, who at least had the good grace to pay up promptly after the match."

Bruce, who had felt strongly enough that United would get a penalty, now couldn't watch. "I must admit that I turned away as Eric took that vital kick," he said. "It was incredible how Eric maintained his self-belief right up to the moment he stroked the ball in. He looked as if he was taking the practice kick he had decided against the day before. When you are the penalty taker in a cup final nerves of steel are required, because the eyes of the whole world are focused on you."

Cantona had sent Kharine the wrong way, placing the ball

with ease to his right and the goalkeeper's left. Five minutes later, Andrei Kanchelskis raced clear and was adjudged to have been pushed by Frank Sinclair just inside the box. Chelsea protestations would not change Elleray's mind. Despite the pressure, Cantona repeated the trick, placing the ball in exactly the same spot as before. You could have replayed the first and not noticed the difference.

The brilliance was in the composure and simplicity. In 2008, some 14 years afterwards, former Liverpool goalkeeper David James claimed to know Cantona's technique. "You can't save from a brilliant penalty taker and Eric Cantona was the best. His technique was so good it was a joke," James said. "You would stand on the goal-line waiting and waiting – his run-up was so slow. He didn't need to sprint and blast the ball: he had control. After he retired I found out his secret – he was watching the keeper. As soon as the keeper's knee went, Cantona took the ball the other way and left him stranded. For any keeper, a bent knee is the point of no return."

Chelsea as a team were also at the point of no return. Two minutes after Cantona's second penalty, Mark Hughes had made it three, and the Blues' misery was complete in the last minute when Brian McClair made it four. Manchester United made history.

"He's the ideal man for that situation," Alex Ferguson said after the game. "He has a sciatica problem and I was thinking of keeping him off at half-time, but I'm glad I left him. Many players would have felt the pressure, but Eric's so confident. It's a temperament thing and he's just got it."

Cantona himself laughed off the very idea of pressure: "People keep asking if I was nervous taking the penalties – but why should I be? It's only a game. If I am nervous on such a big occasion then it's time to stop playing football." He told BBC reporters that his ambition now was to be "kings in Europe", adding: "This United team is the best side I've ever played in and it can get better – if you can't get better as an individual or a team, then it's time to stop playing," he said. "When you begin your career, playing in a big match like this is what you pray for – it's what you play for and it's what you live for."

The player's return from suspension had been emphatic. Those two red cards in four days might well have been the beginning of the end for him, but United's faith had been vindicated. "His importance to the team was shown when he scored a number of important goals after his return, in the Manchester derby and cup final," says Martin Edwards. "He was there when it mattered and that was the important thing."

Cantona was at his own peak, while United were at the highest point in their history aside from the 1968 European Cup final. They had won two trophies and suffered only six defeats in all competitions. Eric's 25 goals and 15 assists made it clear to see who was the most influential performer at the club; Ferguson had described his contribution as a provider as "'incalculable".

The success made it easy for Ferguson and Edwards to think the disciplinary issues were behind them. Little did they know that the most controversial episode in the club's history was just a few months away.

# A Special Case

**A**s recently as the week with the red cards in March 1994, doubters would have felt vindicated in their belief that Eric Cantona was destined to end his career in disgrace rather than glory. There were strong arguments to suggest that might be the case, because for all the brilliance, it could be said Eric's big achievements in winning league championships owed as much to the teams around him.

Marseille had been a great team – they proved that by winning the European Cup without Cantona. Okay, Leeds' disappointing run after becoming champions of England perhaps gave further strength to the argument in Cantona's favour, though those who were a part of the Elland Road set-up still insisted he'd made a marginal contribution. The Frenchman's influence at Old Trafford seemed obvious but he was not part of their earlier successes in the decade and it was possible that upturn, too, was a coincidence.

However, the last few weeks of 1993/94 surely dispelled any

concerns; this was the time when Cantona truly made the difference. First of all, consider the impact of his absence. It is on record from all who were there that Cantona improved his team-mates. Mark Hughes and Andrei Kanchelskis now had different dimensions. It was the imagination, the spatial awareness, the speed of thought, the speed of movement; all these qualities which Cantona possessed which required faith in instinctive ability rather than the extra touch.

United were not ordinary without Cantona but, particularly at 'the business end' of a season, if you don't have the players capable of making the difference, it can lead to some flat performances. Manchester United were far from one-dimensional, but Cantona had become so important to the way his team played that his absence was crucial. His arrival had coincided with a vacancy in the team that suited him to a tee.

"If you play 4-4-2 with two flank men who work hard, then you can afford a luxury player with a roaming role, someone with carte blanche to do what he wants, top open up surprise avenues of attack, to score goals out of nothing; namely, Eric Cantona," said Gary Pallister. "There wasn't much that Eric couldn't do. He had a remarkably delicate touch and the vision to go with it, almost a freakish combination for such a big, strong athlete… At Elland Road they played with long balls, and I think Eric felt he was being bypassed. I can't imagine him conforming to rigid formations and tactics."

The Frenchman's end to the season saw his return to the first team coincide with four consecutive wins which sealed the title, and then he scored twice in the FA Cup final when the game was finely balanced. Cantona was king and kingmaker.

This much was accepted on the continent. Real Madrid's flirtations never amounted to much, but Inter Milan made their first enquiry in 1994. On 10th June, it was reported they were prepared to offer Dennis Bergkamp in exchange for Cantona. "We are not interested in breaking up a winning side. We are looking to add to it," responded Martin Edwards.

Perhaps Inter had gambled on the controversy being enough to tempt United into parting with Cantona on good terms and perhaps if the player had been as isolated as he was at Leeds, they may have been successful. But that wasn't the case.

The first thing to note was that Cantona was not the only naughty boy in the United dressing room. Alex Ferguson famously said the likes of Cantona, Paul Ince, Roy Keane, Mark Hughes and Peter Schmeichel could "start an argument in an empty room", and most of them had come into some other disciplinary problem over the previous season. This unified squad morale. Nobody would back down and each member of the team would be there for another.

So the connection with the fans was forged and cemented. Cantona was always seen out with the players, at a time where the drinking culture was slowly disappearing but still present. The Frenchman would drink champagne while the British players had their beer. "He came as an enigma, but straight away he mucked in with the rest of the boys, fitting in socially and clearly relishing our 'team meetings'," Pallister said.

It wasn't just the players – Cantona would often go to the Bridgewater pub in Worsley near his hotel. He'd buy a round of Guinness for the wide-eyed patrons, then he'd go over to play dominoes with whoever was in the corner, never keeping the winnings should he come out victorious. It was a touch of class and added to that feeling that Cantona was a one-off, yet one of Manchester's own. The working class city that gave Lowry and Morrissey to the world, forging this attachment to the art in a way that was accessible and yet somewhat incomprehensible to the man on the street. You didn't always have to know what it was, but you could enjoy it.

Cantona's individual nature meant he was given what the United players would describe as preferential treatment. There is a famous story of the player turning up to a civic reception at Manchester Town Hall in different clothes to the other players. The event in question was said to be following the 1993 title victory, though details in specific accounts vary.

"A typical example of the extra tolerance towards Eric arose at a civic reception in Manchester after we had won a trophy," Gary Pallister said. "Lee Sharpe turned up in an outrageously trendy suit and the manager berated him for not showing respect for the formal occasion. But five minutes later Eric rolled in wearing a pair of trainers and not a word was said. We accepted it as the extremely canny man-management it was, a matter of dealing with contrasting personalities. The lads would laugh about it, but I'm certain nobody resented Eric's privileged position. We thought he was unique."

Pallister's defensive partner Steve Bruce has a different version of the event, which he says was attended by all of the players dressed in the official club suit; all except for Eric Cantona. He turned up wearing flip-flops, ripped jeans, and a long, multi-coloured coat. That night, the team believed Cantona should be heavily fined and it fell to Bruce to inform him of their opinion: "So I sidled over. 'Boss, the lads aren't happy with Eric's appearance.' Fergie's on the red wine. He puts down his glass, looks over at Eric. 'Tell them from me, Steve,' he says, 'that if they can play like him next year, they can all come as fucking Joseph'."

And Gary Neville's story is different again: "Eric did things his way and no one interfered. When we turned up at a civic event at Manchester Town Hall to celebrate the Double, Eric wandered in wearing a denim jacket instead of a blazer. We looked him up and down and wondered how the boss would react when he arrived. Surely he'd go berserk. The press were there and all sorts of VIPs. But the manager just shook his head and smiled. 'Eh, lads,' he said. 'Some man, that Cantona.'"

The details may vary but the message remained the same. Cantona's individuality was embraced and accommodated, rather than tolerated, or even resented, as it had been elsewhere. Perhaps Old Trafford was the only natural place where that could be the case. With the spotlight shining so brightly on each and every player anyway – Peter Schmeichel, the best goalkeeper in the world, Gary Pallister for a period the most expensive defender in Britain, Roy Keane the most expensive player, Ryan Giggs drawing comparisons with George Best – Cantona's uniqueness was replicated by the others in their own way. This was the biggest stage in British football. Cantona, it could be said, needed those quirks to fit in as well as he had.

Of course, a different dress sense and a taste for the arts is a different matter from being in trouble with the authorities, inside or outside of football. This line would become very blurry over the following months for Manchester United and Eric Cantona and the journey began in Pasadena, California.

The Frenchman was doing TV punditry work for the World Cup semi-final between Sweden and Brazil on 13th

July. Cantona was pushed by a security man and allegedly retaliated, causing police to handcuff him. The situation was resolved within 10 minutes but Eric chose to go back to his hotel rather than cover the game for French TV. Reports in Britain predictably declared Cantona had been "arrested".

Alex Ferguson had already been informed and was not unduly concerned. His priority was making sure his squad were in the best shape for the coming season. He was interested in adding some vibrancy to his front line with the aim of replacing the veteran Hughes but described Blackburn's British record £5m move for Norwich's Chris Sutton as "madness".

There was a premium on English players for Ferguson and his only incoming of the summer was Blackburn's David May for a little over £1m. There were plenty of outgoings – Bryan Robson was in charge at Middlesbrough and took Clayton Blackmore with him, while Mike Phelan moved to West Brom and Darren Ferguson was sold to Wolves. Their places would be filled by young talent coming through at Old Trafford.

Not many changes on the surface. Ferguson would place his faith in consistency. The external changes around United did not only include Blackburn's big-spending, but also a big rule implementation at that summer's World Cup, where tackles from behind were now punishable by red cards. That should have helped a fast, attacking team like Manchester United and yet they found themselves punished initially.

United's pre-season schedule began on 30th July, in Dundalk, two weeks before their Charity Shield game against Blackburn. United won 4-2 at Oriel Park, where those present witnessed a rarity: an Eric Cantona missed penalty. Technically speaking, it was saved by goalkeeper Eddie Van Boxtel.

That hiccup had nothing on the controversy which was to

come in a pre-season tournament at Rangers' Ibrox stadium. Cantona scored against Newcastle in a 1-1 draw but missed in the shoot-out to decide who would play Sampdoria in the 'final' or Rangers in the dead-rubber game. So United played Rangers the following day; with a half-time deficit, Ferguson brought on Cantona and Giggs. Eric was treated to the close attention of defender Steven Pressley and the hostile reception from Rangers and Newcastle supporters filling the ground.

Pressley made a number of poor tackles which Ferguson felt ought to have been punished. Ten minutes from time, the hosts got the reaction they wanted. Cantona had already been warned for retaliating at Pressley and lunging at Trevor Steven. When he did the same at Pressley again, despite making no contact, the crowd were incensed, and Cantona was dismissed.

Ferguson felt the crowd had contributed to the red card and criticised the "loutish hatred". "If he feels there has been an injustice, he has to prove to the world that he's going to correct it," Ferguson complained. "We are told there will be no tackling from behind but it happened several times with Pressley. In these situations Eric can lose his temper. We have to live with his faults and we are delighted to have him."

In his 1995 book *A Year in the Life*, Ferguson wrote: "Eric spent last night in Glasgow. It seemed a good idea to keep him away from the hassle he would get from the press if he came back to Manchester."

He was surprised to learn that Eric did not keep a low profile. He went out with Rangers striker Ally McCoist to a nightclub. "Ally is noted for enjoying himself," Ferguson said. "But it is okay in Glasgow. They are real football people and although there would be a bit of banter, they would be pleased to see him and he wouldn't get the hostile treatment that supporters in London or Liverpool would dish out."

Cantona told *L'Equipe*, referring to the red card: "It's my nature to play like I do and react like I react. It's an instinct and to hell with anybody who is not happy about it."

He had elaborated on that philosophy on the VHS release *Eric The King* earlier that year. "I play with passion and fire," he said. "I have to correct my faults but I must remain true to myself. In the past I have tried to correct myself and I have lost my game. What I have to do now is find a solution that works. I think I've found one now. Nobody knows about it and I can't explain it. People will have to notice it for themselves. You have to do everything to ensure your body and your mind work in harmony. In my case the wires often get crossed. So I have to find a way to achieve harmony."

Clearly that was a work in progress. Cantona would be present for the Charity Shield but would miss the first three league games. Ferguson was looking at the positives, saying: "At least Eric's ban gives me time to get the attack sorted out for the European Cup, when he misses the first four matches."

Those attempts at rejigging the front-line saw Ferguson try Giggs and McClair with mixed success. McClair scored in a 2-0 win over QPR on the opening day and United followed that with a 1-1 draw at Nottingham Forest and a 1-0 win at Spurs; yet the invention of Cantona was missed. In the Charity Shield, Cantona had underlined his importance, not only scoring a penalty in a 2-0 win but showing a gulf in class between United and their closest challengers Blackburn.

Captain Steve Bruce had told Paddy Barclay on the eve of the season: "Eric Cantona was the turning point. The players appreciate it. It's just that he's got this flash of temperament."

A flash of brilliance, too; after 40 minutes of his return, Eric had scored a magnificent header from a sweeping Ryan Giggs cross to give United the lead against Wimbledon in a 3-0 win. "Cantona was incredible," Ferguson said afterwards. "He gave an unbelievable performance and scored a goal, but his all-round play was just exceptional."

Cantona was in good form too against his former team Leeds; unfortunately, his team-mates weren't, and Ferguson's side were 2-0 down early on. He scored a penalty in the second half to reduce the arrears and created a fantastic chance for Hughes, who was denied by Lukic. Cantona also almost replicated his incredible goal for Leeds against Chelsea, where he flicked the ball over the head of the 6ft 3in Carlton Palmer twice, but shot wide of the target.

The 2-1 defeat was United's first setback of the campaign but they responded in style, first overcoming Gothenburg in the Champions League without Cantona, and then taking down Liverpool 2-0 at Old Trafford.

Cantona was provider for the second goal in that game but found himself embroiled in a bizarre controversy. It had seemed Liverpool were intent on provoking some reaction from the Frenchman. Phil Babb, who had just arrived at Anfield for a record £3.6m fee, would make a controversial reappearance in the press later that season. But this was his first appearance at Old Trafford since May, when he had been playing for Coventry in that effectively meaningless match. He had claimed Cantona had tried to stamp on him and that he could have "had his career ended". The game had passed without that alleged incident getting much, if any, mention aside from Babb and a later recollection from then-Coventry boss Phil Neal who said it was "fortunate" Babb hadn't been hurt. Alex Ferguson said the referee hadn't seen it and didn't know what the fuss was about. "I heard that and I just thought, 'Fuck off'," declared Babb.

There was clearly some resentment, but Babb was only a substitute in September 1994. It was left to Neil Ruddock to wind up Cantona, repeatedly pulling down his collar. Cantona went in hard on Ruddock and was booked.

"Cantona was a really good footballer and used to make me look stupid," Ruddock later admitted, in good humour, in a television interview, before saying the Frenchman told him, "Me and you, we fight, in the tunnel." Ruddock asked David James to walk off the pitch with him and managed to avoid bumping into Cantona in the tunnel. He did not escape in the players' bar afterwards – he claimed Eric tapped him on the shoulder, and just as he feared getting a punch, Eric winked, passed him a pint and then walked away.

If the Londoner's approach was more light-hearted than Babb's, then there was a much more vitriolic attitude waiting for Eric in the press that week.

John Fashanu – at the time seemingly implicated in accusations of bribery levelled at Liverpool's Bruce Grobbelaar, just one season after he had broken Spurs defender Gary Mabbutt's cheekbone with an elbow – launched an astonishing attack on Cantona in his newspaper column. "The talk among your fellow professionals is that you are steadily becoming a dirty, nasty bastard," Fashanu wrote in an address to Cantona. "Running up from behind and raking your studs down the back of an opponents's calf is both cowardly and unpleasant."

Manchester United complained to the FA about Fashanu's comments and the then-Aston Villa striker was charged with misconduct and fined £6,000.

There was no suspension for Cantona, then, but he was in and out of the side for various reasons – the European ban, for one, and international duty, in the case of the game at Sheffield Wednesday. It was proving disruptive to United's chances. They lost at Hillsborough to a David Hirst goal. "That's why United offered £3.5million for him 18 months ago," Owls boss Trevor Francis said of Hirst, though he did admit: "The difference was Eric Cantona."

It was their third league defeat from the opening nine games. Ferguson was frustrated by the lack of opportunity to play a settled team and injuries to the likes of Schmeichel, Parker, Keane and Giggs on top of Cantona's infrequent availability meant that inconsistency reflected in performances, too.

Disappointment followed in the League Cup, with United suffering an early exit to Newcastle. Ferguson had contemplated selecting Cantona, but the Frenchman ruled himself out. "I wasn't sure about Eric. Yesterday I asked him if he wanted to play, but he said, 'I think Scholes deserves to play, they won the game at Port Vale, you should stay by them'," Ferguson said.

The United boss had tried to stress there was not a disparity in his squad earlier in the season when questioned about his minimal transfer business. "I decided they had done fairly well financially and there came a point when I said, 'Right, that's it.' Otherwise we could be engulfed by the tidal wave that's happening everywhere else," Ferguson said. "You hear of huge salaries at other clubs, but that's maybe only for one or two players. One on £500,000 and the rest on £100,000. I can't differentiate between Irwin's contribution to that of Mark Hughes or Eric Cantona or Ryan Giggs. I don't have maybe one big star to deal with, I have nine or 10."

Those nine or ten would have been interested to read the

September headlines of United's reported 155 per cent increase in annual profits of £10.78m. Ferguson may have abstained from the transfer market but would not be free of the consequence of these reports. The value of some players at Old Trafford was not reflected by the fees and wages most had been acquired for. Cantona had been a bargain at £1m, while Ryan Giggs cost nothing as a youth player.

There was no price put on the rumours linking Cantona with a move to Inter Milan but it was said AC Milan were willing to top a world record £13m to bring Giggs to the San Siro. Chris Sutton's move may have been "madness" but United would be forced to pay their stars what they wanted. Negotiations for a new contract for Eric Cantona were planned.

The United boss may have claimed to not be able to differentiate between contributions, but it was becoming increasingly clear that without Cantona, Ferguson's side lacked their personality. Could it be a confidence thing? The boss had claimed his team had been fearful of Barcelona's reputation ahead of their visit to Old Trafford in the Champions League: "Names! That's something our players have to conquer. Romario, Stoichkov... you can get more frightened of their names than what they actually do."

United drew that game 2-2 but were soundly beaten 4-0 at the Nou Camp and Ferguson insisted Cantona would have made a difference. "Cantona is unquestionably one of the best players in the world, because of the weight and vision of his passing. And that's what you really need – a passer who can open teams up," he said.

That game marked the end of the suspension in Europe, and chairman Martin Edwards admitted: "We cannot demand it but we are hoping for a world-class performance from Eric."

The Jekyll and Hyde form appeared to have settled down in the autumn, at least in the respect that you could now distinguish a pattern. As poor as United had been in Europe, they were still capable of showing just how much better they were than their domestic opposition. A win at Blackburn was followed by a victory over league leaders Newcastle.

A Thursday night Manchester derby was United's last game before the November international break, but no matter what the day, this was an occasion made for Eric Cantona. Due to a fitness concern about Mark Hughes, a historic game could well have gone very differently, with Ferguson considering a new formation. "We did a function today, playing Eric right forward because there is the doubt about Sparky," the United boss said before the game. "I played him and Ryan through the centre and Gillespie wide left."

Hughes ended up being fit; it was the same old United, and same old Cantona. He grabbed the first goal in exquisite fashion, controlling a pass from Kanchelskis with his right heel to bring it across his body, and taking it on the bounce to smash past Simon Tracey with his left foot. The majesty of the goal brought a rapturous response from the home crowd. Cantona then turned provider, helping Andrei Kanchelskis score a historic hat-trick in a 5-0 win. In the second half, United's vintage style of attacking had returned, and so hopes of a strong run of form over winter were raised.

There was not much positivity for Eric while he was away

with France. They were held to a goalless draw against Poland as they struggled to get their qualification campaign for Euro 96 off the ground. As captain, Cantona bore the brunt of the criticism; not helped by the fact that Zinedine Zidane, then of Bordeaux, was beginning to make an impression.

*L'Equipe* said Cantona was "completely out of it" and "always late and making the wrong choices", whilst France boss Aime Jacquet said his skipper was "disappointing". French League president Noel Le Graet told the press: "There are doubts over whether Eric will remain as captain or even retain his place."

Back in Manchester, Cantona found his value appreciated once more; he and Kanchelskis again exchanged goals and assists in a routine 3-0 win over Crystal Palace ahead of the Frenchman's return to the Champions League.

That would come in the away game in Gothenburg on 23rd November, on the same day as it was bizarrely reported that four people had nominated Cantona for the Turner Prize.

Alex Ferguson said Cantona would go straight into the team in Sweden: "When he stays up front and drops into spaces he's brilliant, the best in the business. But when he falls back into midfield his passing is not so effective. We're trying to make him stay upfield. It's up to the rest of the team to give him proper service in the last third. The problem is Eric always wants to be involved, wherever the ball is."

He was – Cantona created United's goal, for Hughes, but the familiar problems which had dogged United's European campaign were still present. Schmeichel was dropped so Kanchelskis could play. Ferguson felt Gary Walsh was blameless for the four goals conceded in the Nou Camp and really the reserve stopper was not at fault for the three he conceded in Sweden but the 3-1 defeat left United hoping for improbable results to qualify for the quarter-finals. David May was at right-back in place of the injured Paul Parker, while Roy Keane and Ryan Giggs were desperately missed. An injury to Lee Sharpe also compounded United's issues. It was an unfamiliar side Cantona was reintroduced into; placing this failure on his shoulders would be extreme, unless you were counting the suspension against him.

That list of absentees remained for the following game at Arsenal; another bad-tempered game at Highbury where Cantona was able to get through the 90 minutes without his name being mentioned for the wrong reasons. Instead it was Mark Hughes who was sent off near the end, while Arsenal were also incensed that Paul Ince wasn't red carded. Ferguson was relieved to get it over and done with, even if the 0-0 draw meant Blackburn would go top of the table.

Cantona seemed to be benefitting from a run of games; he scored the only goal in a 1-0 win over Norwich. He made what would be mundane, notable, according to Ferguson, who said the day after: "I watched yesterday's goal on video. At the time it was a great goal but you should see the video! It was poetry, you could set it to music – or use it as a coaching video. You say, 'Quicken the game up in the last third', and nothing could emphasise that point better than Eric's flick. It's just a wee flick of his foot and he's flying away from his marker. McClair gets on to it, slips past one man and cuts it in and where's Cantona? In the space as usual. I keep saying that to players – you look up and in the last third, he's always free. He's marvellous at that. And he finished it really well."

Cantona was man of the match in a 4-0 win over Galatasaray in the final Champions League group game. This game was notable for goals scored by David Beckham and Simon Davies, two youngsters who had won the FA Youth Cup in 1992 and were seeing more first-team opportunities come their way. It will be a point returned to later; Cantona had already had a profound influence on some of the young players at Old Trafford. The European victory, despite coming against a backdrop of ultimate failure, provided optimism for the future.

Eric retained the national team armband for a 2-0 win in Azerbaijan on 12th December (he had missed United's 3-2 win at QPR due to international duty) but his return to United was an unhappy one. Ferguson's side faced Nottingham Forest at home, where they hadn't even conceded a goal all season in the league. Cantona scored, but Forest scored two, leaving the Frenchman with a new experience – defeat at Old Trafford, which he had never tasted (when playing for United, of course).

Cantona was booked twice over the following Christmas games – United won at Stamford Bridge on Boxing Day (Eric scoring a penalty) and drew with Leicester and Southampton in encounters that were more firework than festive. The atmosphere began to feel as it had in the late winter and early spring of 1994; yes, referees were more liberal with yellow cards after the rule changes but the games against Leicester and Southampton were particularly ill-tempered.

The bookings acquired by Cantona were down to reactions rather than poor tackling technique, but it didn't stop Ferguson hinting that may be the case when he said earlier that month: "Eric is not a tackler. I've told him not to tackle because he can't. I'm fed up saying that to him."

The United boss talked to *The Guardian*'s Geoffrey Beattie about some of Cantona's more positive attributes, more specifically, his vision. "I think all the great players have to have it," he said. "Eric will provide a pass in the last third of the pitch and I'll say, 'God, I never saw that'. Most players at some point can't see a pass because their head will be down on the ball, whereas Cantona seems to have his head up like a cocker spaniel. He's got the vision and the imagination to go with it.

"Confidence can be lost in a minute and won back in a minute. There are moments when Eric loses confidence. He's not infallible. He gets frustrated when he's made a few bad passes. He gets annoyed because he has got great pride. Because of the speed of our game, invariably the ball will come back to the individual who has made a mistake the minute before. They have to have an iron will to say, 'Forget that mistake'.

"We say to players, 'Look, when you are having a bad time, just don't be complicated, just keep it straightforward.' But players like Eric will always try to win the game and that's what makes them so different. He's always on for a pass that wins the game."

Cantona scored in the first game of 1995 against Coventry City. And ahead of United's game at Sheffield United in the FA Cup (the third year in succession Ferguson's side were drawn to play at Bramall Lane), even Dave Bassett, erstwhile critic of the United number seven, admitted: "If Cantona has a wonder night we'll have problems."

The Blades, now in Division One after their 1994 relegation, were hoping for the sort of performance you see in the movies; like that of Jimmy Muir, the protagonist of the film *When Saturday Comes,* played by Sean Bean. The relevance? The match was used for scenes in the film, with Bean and his fellow actors filming action footage on the pitch.

For a while, far from it being an encounter fit for the silver screen, there was cause to consider whether it was fit to even go ahead; the blustery conditions in Sheffield were intensified by the fact that one side of the stadium had been demolished. A change of approach might have felt necessary, though the hosts went with the one frequently adopted by Manchester United opponents; get under Cantona's skin. Charlie Hartfield was sent off in the 13th minute for a punch on the Frenchman. The pair had been involved in an altercation minutes earlier. If that was typical Cantona, he was at least leading by example; in an attempt to help young John O'Kane settle down in the dressing room, Eric told him: "Don't be like everyone else." Of course, Cantona would leave this game with a more indelible reminder of his individual brilliance.

Bassett hoped his team would hold out for a replay; ten minutes from time, Hughes finally broke their resistance. Then, forced to come out and play, the Blades were caught out by a sucker punch, and this time it was a moment that deserved to be captured on camera. Giggs' through ball was perfectly weighted into Cantona's path. The forward took a touch and, as if the wind wasn't even a factor, stabbed his foot into the ground, lifting the ball with perfect precision over the goalkeeper and in via the crossbar.

"It was sheer genius," Alex Ferguson said. "People can talk all day about goals blasted from 35 or 40 yards as 'Goal of the Season', but that's power. This was complete precision, awareness, judgement – absolute genius. You saw all the years of practice in that goal, it was fantastic."

The victory had been achieved with goals from both of United's strikers, but Ferguson felt it was time to move in the transfer market. His first port of call was to Nottingham Forest, to see if they would part with Stan Collymore – boss Frank Clark had previously seemed reluctant. According to Ferguson, Kevin Keegan then called to enquire about Keith

Gillespie. Ferguson said no but responded by asking about Andy Cole. Keegan said no but 'didn't dismiss it' as he had done an earlier enquiry.

The following day, Ferguson attempted to get hold of Clark. He was told the Forest boss was ill; this was actually the truth, but Ferguson felt it was an excuse in the time-honoured tradition of Brian Clough who had refused to entertain any conversation about selling Stuart Pearce to United.

So the United manager identified Cole as his man. It would be ambitious – Newcastle had established themselves as challengers for the title. But Keegan was co-operative and a deal for £6m (and Keith Gillespie) was concluded quickly.

A flu epidemic at Old Trafford and terrible weather conditions led to an unusual first day of training for Cole, as remembered by Alex Ferguson: "I'd told everyone with flu not to come in, so there weren't many players there. We had to train at Old Trafford because The Cliff was frozen hard.

"We did a session with Andy. Eric failed to get the message about the change of venue and turned up about ten minutes late. He came onto the pitch, went across to Andy, shook his hand and then patted him on the head as if to say, 'I'll look after you.' Andy said to Kiddo afterwards, 'Bloody hell, that Cantona, he's some player'."

Eric's warm welcome to his new colleague would not last for too long. The next game was, ironically enough, at St James' Park. The clubs agreed that neither of the recently transferred players should play, but then Mark Hughes was injured during the act of scoring. A knee ligament injury would keep him out for months. Cantona looked like he had won the game with virtually the last kick, but his effort was cleared off the line and the Magpies earned a 1-1 draw.

Cole was the focus of the build-up to United's next game – a potential championship decider against Blackburn at Old Trafford. Inside 90 seconds he almost made an immediate impact, latching on to a through-ball only to fail to get the ball under his control (incidentally, in almost the same position, he would score the goal which sealed the title in 1999). On this occasion Cole would have to settle for being the subplot; as usual, one man stood up to become the main event. In a moment that was almost identical to his first league goal of the season, Cantona rose to head in from a Giggs cross in the 80th minute. United had secured a valuable win.

Ferguson described Cantona's performance as "spellbinding"and described the initial talks about the player's new contract, held the following morning, as positive. He added: "Cantona worked his nuts off yesterday. It has been a bad six months for us in terms of all the controversy. But now he's playing all the time and is totally fit. He seems to have settled down and knows where his destination is now. His last six performances have been magnificent."

A turbulent start to the 1994/95 season had finally begun to settle down. For Manchester United, it was starting to feel like business as usual, and with a three-year contract on the table, Eric Cantona was at the most stable moment in his footballing life.

# KING ERIC 13

# The Eruption

And so we arrive at a pivotal moment in our protagonist's story. The headline incident, the plot twist. If the theme of this book is to portray Eric Cantona as the man who changed Manchester United and British football, then one might consider the events of 25th January 1995 as a turning point. It would be a fair starting place for the theory, although the truth is surely that the change had already taken place.

The growth of Manchester United as a football club and a commercial entity was occurring at a rapid rate. The increase in interest in Premier League football meant Sky Sports found it justifiable to charge a subscription fee to watch games on their network. The public subscribed in their millions.

In any cultural movement it takes one moment to transport the medium from the arena in which it is usually enjoyed to the mainstream. Football, enjoyed by tens of thousands on a weekly basis in stadiums across the country, could hardly be categorised as a niche interest and Eric Cantona was not the first footballer to find his face plastered all over the front pages. In that respect perhaps this transitional period was to do with concentrated saturation.

The sheer, unprecedented, scale of what happened at Selhurst Park on 25th January 1995 meant everyone had an opinion and everyone wanted to voice it.

What was a relatively low-key 1-1 draw in South London has become arguably the most-written about game in Premier League history, with more coverage dedicated to it than even football's most glorious moments.

The match had initially followed the template for Manchester United away games over the previous year or so. When then-Palace manager Alan Smith spoke to the BBC in 2015, he appeared to have been seduced by a theatrical vision, saying with foreboding style: "What distinctly hit me was that they played in all black that night. None of them had shaved and they looked a pretty ferocious team. I was thinking, 'This is going to be a long evening'."

Gary Pallister felt the same. United had been through this experience too many times. "Eric was always the number one target for supporters around the country," he said. "It wasn't just players who tried to wind him up but fans felt as though they could do it as well. Some of the abuse he got was terrible. It took its toll and it all came to a head that night. He was such a hate figure because he was such a good player."

Palace's aggression had helped them have the better of the game up until the break. Smith had given defender Richard Shaw the task of man-marking United's star. "Shawsie had this sort of bubbly, curly hair. He used to put a lot of Vaseline around his face. He was the most charming, gentle guy you could ever meet but he looked pretty ferocious on the field. He was really up for marking Cantona," remembers Smith. "If you want to say 'gave him one', Shawsie certainly went in. I don't have a lot of sympathy with Cantona. He is a big man and he had given a fair amount out. Shawsie just thought, 'It's on the halfway line, it's in front of the dugout – I'll go for it'."

In an interview for this book, Shaw gave his own version of events, telling me: "Manchester United coming to town is always a highlight of the season, and they'd just signed Andy Cole to come into their incredible team. We anticipated a difficult and physical game. But I disagree with this reputation we got for 'kicking them all over the park'. It was not that way at all and I've watched the game back. Did we get tight to them? Yes, to Cantona and to Cole. We got tight to Ryan Giggs and Andrei Kanchelskis. They were wonderful players, you have to do that to try and stop them playing.

"It was a high-speed, high-intensity game. United were going for the league title, we were fighting to stay up. It was as competitive as you would expect it to be. We weren't told to kick him about. I was a very good man-marker, I prided myself on that. I loved playing against the top players and the challenges that came with it. To me it was a normal thing that happened on the football pitch. What happened after was not normal, but that has magnified things and changed the perception of what came before it."

The incident Shaw is referring to happened just after half-time. At the break, Alex Ferguson had stressed to Cantona to "not get involved" with the defender.

Four minutes into the second period, Shaw again dug into Cantona, and the linesman Eddie Walsh flagged for a foul, but referee Alan Wilkie (who Ferguson had implored to take note of the aggressive play) waved play on. Seconds later, the ball was being contested between the pair once again, and Cantona sought to exact his own personal brand of retribution.

This came in the form of a swiped kick at Shaw. It connected. Wilkie had no option but to send off the Frenchman, in spite of the provocation. "There's the morning headline!" said Clive Tyldesley, commentating for *Match of the Day*.

Alex Ferguson felt it was inevitable. "Alan Wilkie's inability to stamp out the disgraceful tackles from Crystal Palace's two central defenders made subsequent trouble unavoidable," he said in his book *My Autobiography*. Ferguson remembered Norman Davies rushing to escort Cantona to the dressing room in front of the baying home fans. The United boss concerned himself with a tactical reorganisation. For a second, Cantona remained on the pitch while his team-mates remonstrated with Wilkie. Cantona then walked towards Davies.

The changing rooms at Selhurst Park were in the corner of the pitch so Cantona and Davies still had to walk a full 60 yards. As they did so, the Frenchman appeared distracted by a comment from a spectator. Palace supporter Matthew Simmons had raced down from his seat higher in the stand to hurl abuse at the United player.

Simmons was stood alongside home fan Cathy Churchman. "All of a sudden [Cantona] turned and looked back; I thought he was looking at me," Churchman told the BBC. "I had no idea where this other guy had suddenly appeared from. There was this look on Cantona's face. His eyes were seething. You just knew at that point he was going to do something silly."

Davies was stood with Cantona and, for a second, looked away. "I've been slaughtered for that," Davies, who passed away in 2010, told the *Manchester Evening News*. "I think most of it blaming me for not keeping hold of Eric was tongue in cheek.

But I could do nothing about it. One minute he was there, then whoosh he was gone! But I have never been the appointed club man to escort players off. It is a voluntary action because I just feel sorry for players. I get them a drink and try and make conversation if they want. Eric was very quiet though!"

On the touchline, Davies spotted the flashpoint but it was too late; Cantona ran towards Simmons and jumped off the ground in that scissors style we had seen in the past. His boot connected with Simmons as his body was obstructed by the advertising hoarding. Eric stood up, untangled himself and unleashed a flurry of punches. Davies then managed to get hold of Cantona, as did United's security guard Ned Kelly.

"All hell broke loose as he jumped over the barrier," Churchman said. "I can remember falling into my 15-year-old son and Eric's boot just brushing past my coat. Everyone looked at each other saying, 'Oh my God, what just happened?!' It was all over in seconds."

Richard Shaw recalled: "I was sitting on the floor; I was concerned about the fact I'd just been kicked. All of a sudden I heard this noise which made me turn around. I didn't see what happened apart from a little scuffle on the side of the pitch and for the rest of the game it wasn't even anything that crossed my mind. We got to the changing rooms and people were talking about it, then I saw the pictures the same as anyone else.

"I was surprised by it, I admit. You play in that environment and the pressure can push you to a point where you lose your tolerance. I remember Jamie Carragher throwing a coin back at supporters in a game at Highbury. These were isolated incidents you didn't really see in England."

Many of the other players were similarly in the dark about what had happened. "Eric's got involved with his marker,"

Roy Keane recalled. "It's niggly stuff, not nasty. Shirt-pulling, obstruction, a bit of chat. The purpose is to break your concentration – and with Eric, it can work. This time Palace get a result. Eric loses it and kicks Shaw. He's off... As Eric walks off towards the dressing room, the game resumes. Ten men. Now it's a battle. No Eric. Suddenly there's commotion on the far touchline. Something's happened, we don't know what."

This was similar to Ryan Giggs' recollection. "I didn't see what happened next, and I know most of the other players didn't because we were either remonstrating with the referee or reorganising to play with ten men," said the winger.

Ferguson, too, didn't see anything of the incident. Martin Edwards, however, was looking straight at it. "The incident happened right in perfect view of the directors box," Edwards says. "As soon as he got involved with the player you knew he was going to be sent off. As he was walking down the touchline there were a few of us looking at the players and wondering what had been said.

"Eric's being led down the touchline and suddenly he breaks off and throws himself into a kung-fu kick at a supporter. I was thinking, 'Bloody hell, he's lost it. He's gone mad.' I went into the dressing room afterwards and it was dead quiet. We were all stunned, really. I don't think Alex said anything to him."

"I took it upon myself just to go straight down there," Ned Kelly said. "I pushed a couple of stewards out of the way and found my way into the dressing room and Eric was in there with Norman. I told Norman that I would take over."

In the resulting scuffle, Paul Ince joined in and was later accused of throwing punches himself.

Peter Schmeichel also had a perfect view: "From my goal I saw the Frenchman turn around and, almost in the same second as he caught sight of the man who was shouting the abuse, launch himself into a run-up which ended with a fully-fledged karate kick to the man's chest. I think he also managed to slap Simmons in the face."

"I was stood in the middle of the pitch and there was a roar from the crowd," David May recalled. "I just thought, 'What the hell are you doing'? You run over to see what is going on. It is kicking off and it is a case of one for all, all for one… Everyone joined in."

"I was one of the only players that didn't run over," Gary Pallister said. "I could only register shock and disbelief. I realised the enormity straight away. He had stepped way beyond the mark of what could be acceptable, even though I could understand his reaction to some extent."

Cantona was taken to the dressing room by Ned Kelly and Davies. "He was sitting on the bench, very quiet, shirt off, thinking about what had gone on," Kelly recalled. "It was dead silent, you could have cut the atmosphere with a knife. Sometimes you step back and realise you don't say anything."

Davies' recollection was that Cantona was still raging and wanted to go back out to confront Simmons. Davies recalled: "He was furious. He wanted to go out again. I locked the door and told him, 'If you want to go back on the pitch, you'll have to go over my body and break the door down'."

With everyone at Selhurst Park still in shock, the absurdity which was now a football game again continued. David May scored his first goal for the club from a corner. "I was going to get a nice little bit of positivity in the papers the next day," May said. "That is all I could think of." Ironically enough, May wouldn't even see through the night with that positivity. In one absent-minded moment, Gareth Southgate escaped his attention to equalise. The game ended 1-1 and United's players trooped back to the dressing room with some apprehension.

"Afterwards I ripped into Cantona with a fury I had vented only once before," Ferguson said in his 1999 book. Of course, that is not the version told in modern recollections by almost everyone who was there. (He did, however, rage at Wilkie in the referee's room, saying: "This is all your fucking fault!")

Nor do his contemporaneous recollections refer to any rage. Ferguson asked Davies, who said he wasn't sure, but he thought a can of beer was thrown at Cantona. "At the time I was mainly concerned about the sending off because I assumed Eric had been protecting himself. That would have been bad enough, but at least it's answerable," Ferguson said.

The players were unsure what to do, but were by now starting to form their own opinions now the adrenalin was dying down.

"Cantona's opponents tried everything to needle him. There would be sly kicks, a pulled shirt, an elbow. They wanted him to react and generally they would get what they wanted. In January 1995 at Crystal Palace they hit the jackpot," remembered Andrei Kanchelskis. "Cantona was treated differently. Ferguson rarely shouted at him. I certainly never saw him get the hairdryer… Looking back, it was probably just as well nobody went over to Cantona in the dressing room and asked why he had done it. If we had got into an argument, everything might have got out of control again."

Ryan Giggs said Cantona was calm by the time the players returned. "When we got back into the dressing room Eric wasn't agitated, and seemed unaffected by what had happened," he said. "It was the same on the plane travelling back to Manchester. Nothing was said because none of us, the gaffer included, realised the seriousness of what had gone on. Word just hadn't got through and Eric was giving nothing away. It wasn't until I got the chance to see it on telly that night that I could see how bad it was."

This correlates with Gary Pallister's memory: "Eric was very subdued. He just sat quietly in the corner. He didn't really say anything. I think he understood the magnitude of what had happened. Everybody was trying to come to terms with how we were going to deal with it."

Schmeichel, Cantona's room-mate, recalled: "He just sat there on the bench with his face buried in his hands, shaking his head, slightly amazed at the violence of his reaction."

Ferguson was furious – just not with Cantona. United defender David May had, apparently, been the villain of the piece. "The manager is ripping heads off everyone... Big Pete, Big Pally, myself, Sharpey, Paul Ince," May recalled. "He had a go at me for their equaliser. 'Who the hell was marking Southgate?'. I said 'Eric!'... He turned round and said, 'Eric, I am disappointed in you. You can't be doing those things'.

"I thought, 'Is that it? Is that it?!' Any other player would have been given the hairdryer. I just got the hairdryer off the gaffer for not marking someone I shouldn't have been marking."

Ferguson composed himself to go and have a few words with Palace boss Smith, who recalled: "We shook hands and he said, 'What the bloody hell was wrong with that then?' I said, 'Alex, that's an everyday occurrence in Putney High Street'... Because of his tunnel vision, he was even trying to put a case that Cantona had been badly treated. I just said, 'No Alex, totally agree, nothing wrong with it. Everyday occurrence'."

There was now just the exit from the stadium to navigate. "We let everyone else go to the coach then me and Eric came out together at the end," Ned Kelly says. "There were fans outside baying for blood but I was quite confident I could deal with it and you've got to remember Eric was 6ft 2in and from a rough area of Marseille – he could look after himself.

"We were getting reports Manchester Airport was packed with press but we made contact with security who told the driver where to go. We got Eric into the car on the tarmac and drove him to the car park, where he got into his own car and drove home."

Ferguson's understated response to the incident could be explained by the simple fact that he hadn't seen it. Even when he returned home at 1am, he refused his son Jason's request to watch the tape, planning to look at everything with a clear head in the morning. That didn't work.

He went to bed at 2am but couldn't sleep, and got up at 5.25am to watch the video. He confessed what he saw was "pretty appalling". Ferguson added: "I have never been able to elicit an explanation from Eric but my own feeling is that anger at himself over the ordering off and resentment at the referee's earlier inaction combined to take him over the brink."

Reflecting on events a quarter of a century later, Richard Shaw told me: "Eric was the catalyst of everything United achieved in the '90s. He was a wonderful talent. He was one of the best signings of the Premier League era, if not the best. He was certainly the most influential. It wasn't just his work ethic. He had a little bit of the maverick about him. He could do things others couldn't do, see things others can't see.

"The biggest compliment I could give him is how good he made the simple things look. I played against him several times and just couldn't get close to him. He was so intelligent with his play and movement. The thing is for a player like Eric, he had a bit of a flashpoint to him as we had seen at Norwich and

Swindon the year before. You wouldn't want to take it away from him because it contributed to the player he was."

However, despite Shaw's glowing words, in January 1995 this flash of temper had now exploded in its most dramatic fashion yet, putting Cantona's very future as a footballer in serious jeopardy...

# The Aftermath

I n the wake of the events at Selhurst Park, United were forced to act immediately. There was no time for allowing the dust to settle. It was no easy call. The manager's response was serious indeed. After meetings were held at The Cliff – where the gates had been locked – with Cantona and the manager and then Cantona, Brendan Batson and lawyers from the PFA, Ferguson then met with the chairman. Martin Edwards remained in London and planned to travel back to Manchester after he had talked to officials.

In Ferguson's book *A Year in the Life*, the story is told thus: "We arranged a meeting at the Edge Hotel at Alderley Edge at 8pm – we couldn't hold it at Old Trafford because we knew we'd be besieged. Sir Roland Smith, chairman of the plc, Maurice Watkins and I were present. When we arrived there was already a table of three journalists in the restaurant. I wonder how the hell they found out where we were going. My initial feeling was for letting Eric go and Sir Roland felt the same because although we appreciated his qualities, we couldn't imagine him being able to play for the club again.

"I have supported Eric through thick and thin, but I felt that this time the good name of Manchester United demanded strong action. The club is bigger than any individual. I related that to the board and they agreed."

Ferguson said on the way to the meeting he was phoned by a friend, Sir Richard Greenbury, who likened Cantona to John McEnroe in that "on court, his temper gets the better of him". Despite this, the manager still arrived at the meeting in the mind to sack his best player.

"The next morning I called David Davies at the FA, who came to the Royal Lancaster Hotel," Martin Edwards says. "I thought we'd had an agreement that we would ban him until the end of the season, and he thought that was a good compromise. He couldn't deliver that personally because the FA then set up a tribunal which extended the ban. That was very disappointing... The night after the game Alex, Maurice Watkins and I met at Alderley Edge Hotel. We rubber-stamped the suggestion we would ban him for the rest of the season and hoped the FA would go along with it. I wasn't there when Alex informed Eric of the suspension. But I knew Eric was okay with our action and he knew that in using Maurice Watkins, we were supporting him. We supported him through thick and thin... As chairman I wasn't happy about it. It doesn't hold the club in good light. But it was an individual incident."

Ferguson remained uncertain. "I am sure Eric is haunted by it all now. But I felt he had to go," he admitted. "Maurice took a legal stand and counselled caution because of the police investigation and the player's contract. The chairman put forward the FA's view. Then we discussed suspending him but again there were legal matters to consider. All this happened during the evening and the phone was hot. The debate see-sawed on what the correct length of suspension should be.

"The FA had given the message that action had to be taken, but we also had to demonstrate United were concerned with upholding standards. I am nervous about the future, but we will cross that bridge when we come to it. Time is a great healer and I hope the suspension does the trick, but I have doubts. When we came to our decision, Eric and the PFA accepted."

The club announced they had imposed a four-month suspension on Cantona, ruling him out of the rest of the season. They also fined him £10,000.

"Today was a nightmare," Ferguson admitted in his diary. "I am gutted, devastated; the players were devastated; everybody connected to the club was devastated. It was just a case of getting through the day."

The United squad not only backed their manager's decision, but they also backed their team-mate. They had witnessed Cantona's treatment and also experienced it themselves.

"Eric received a certain amount of sympathy from the lads because we knew he was targeted in games," said Pallister. "We had seen him being spat at at Leeds, being fouled horribly all over the country, and he rose above all that."

In an interview in 2010, David May told me that even in his short time at the club, he felt something like that had been coming. Far from being upset with Cantona, you almost get the feeling some of the United players felt he had taken one for the team. "I was surprised it'd never happened before," May said. "Eric did that, and rightly so. You have people week in, week out, on the stands personally slagging you off... I know you should refrain from doing that, but it was the combination of it all… He'd just been sent off by a referee who wasn't really in the right position to do it, then the lad comes out of the back of the stands, streaming down and calling him all the names under the sun… fair play to him. Honest to God, you'd be amazed at the stick everybody gets."

It's a tone shared by Roy Keane. "My immediate reaction was: so what? Fair fucking play to Eric," he said in his first autobiography. "I might have done the same myself. When I saw the pictures I could see it was a nasty incident. Out of order, of course. But my attitude didn't change. My heart went out to him. All the lads basically felt the same. We didn't pat him on the back and say 'well done', but Eric was a good lad and we weren't going to turn our backs on him now…

"Alex Ferguson resisted the pressure to sell Eric. The media were baying for blood. If the gaffer wouldn't do Eric, the media would do the gaffer. He demanded character from his players, now he demonstrated what character really was. He stuck to his beliefs, which the dressing room shared, that while Eric had been seriously out of order he'd done nothing to warrant his career being ended."

The FA had issued their own statement on the night of the game, which concluded: "It is our responsibility to ensure actions that damage the game are punished severely. The FA will live up to that responsibility."

The newspapers on Thursday 26th were dominated by pictures of Cantona's yellow number seven and his outstretched right leg. Attempts to contact Matthew Simmons had failed but some reporters did manage to get hold of his friends. One, by the name Matthew Pickett, admitted Palace fans were baiting Cantona. "He should be disbarred from football and deported," he said. "We were giving him verbals. It was just the usual stuff about him being French. That is why you pay £20."

Mark Coote, a Crystal Palace fan who was yards away, told *The Guardian*: "Cantona was sent off. He was walking along the line. This guy came down from behind me and started hurling abuse at him, calling him every name under the sun."

The authorities at Palace had been called into question but Chief Supt Terry Collins insisted: "I've never seen anything like it in my life. There could have been a riot."

FA chief executive Graham Kelly added: "What happened was a stain on our game. If any offence is proved, the player concerned is bound to face a severe punishment. We especially deplore the appalling example set to young supporters."

Gordon Taylor, the PFA chairman, simply said: "We will do all we can to help, but we cannot condone what he has done."

Cantona was told to attend a meeting with Ferguson at Old Trafford, where he was informed of the club's position. He did so, and while he was there, took his son Raphael to the club store to get a replica shirt with 'Cantona 7' on the back. "It was just the normal Eric," said a member of staff. "He was cool as a cucumber. You would have thought nothing had happened. He walked around as if he did not have a care in the world."

Close to home, Cantona could feel the support of those who had his back. Paddy Crerand – always good for a pro-United view – did not disappoint. "What happened to Eric was a disgrace," said the Scot. "He has suffered the non-protection of referees ever since he came here. Eric has not created the trouble: Eric is the one that has been abused. We know he is a volatile character but they play on that."

Not all agreed. Alex Stepney, the European Cup-winning goalkeeper, said he was "disgusted" and that Cantona shouldn't play for the club again. (In his 2010 autobiography, Stepney did however describe the Frenchman as a "maestro" with no reference to Selhurst whatsoever.)

Shay Brennan gave a reporter the golden line: "Sir Matt Busby would have hated anything like this." Busby, a gentleman, was indeed a man who detested his club being brought into disrepute. He once told Stepney he had disgraced the club after a violent European game where the goalkeeper threw a punch at an opposing player in the tunnel.

Curiously, Busby had indeed dealt with a similar incident, in almost identical circumstances, as Brennan well knew. After a game at Luton Town in April 1960, goalkeeper Harry Gregg (who sadly passed away just as this book was being published) found his path to the dressing room obstructed by a fan. Anticipating that the supporter was about to punch him, Gregg got the first jab in, and floored his assailant.

Busby didn't see the incident, but on the Monday he called Gregg into his office. "He gave me the biggest roasting of my life!" the keeper later said. Despite speculation that there would be criminal charges against Gregg, none were forthcoming. On the first day of the following season, Harry was approached by the same fan who wanted to 'forgive and forget'.

Gregg's own take on the Cantona/Simmons event: "I kept thinking to myself, what was different about this guy, they were all shouting things at him? Just what was it that this lad said to provoke such a reaction? I thought to myself, 'Bloody hell it must have been bad'. And as is my way, I mouthed at the screen, 'Go on, Eric, hit him again'."

So, despite statements about how Cantona had ruined the good name of Manchester United, there were related precedents. As far back as the 1930s, Everton striker Dixie Dean had punched a Spurs fan. In 1978, Alberto Tarantini of

Birmingham had just beaten Man Utd in a famous 5-1 win when he was involved in a scuffle with his own fans. As recently as March 1994, in the Beazer Homes Southern Division game between Fisher and Wealdstone, Fisher player David Ward ran the width of the pitch, waded into the crowd and punched a fan who barracked him. The FA banned him for two weeks.

Gregg had been admonished by Busby but not sacked. United could be content they had taken a firm line with their star man that was not out of keeping with their heritage.

It would take a month for Ferguson to do an about-turn and become defensive over his player, as he was in his diary entry of 21st February: "I'm sure Sir Matt was faced with the same things I'm faced with. We are proud of the credibility of the club and we tried to uphold it, and the Cantona thing really hit us badly. You can't leave your character in the dressing room, it goes out onto the field with you."

The fallout on 26th January was so plentiful there was barely any opportunity to pause and take any of it in. In a more casual conversation with reporters, Graham Kelly said: "The FA does not have the power to impose an immediate suspension... but we're confident United will meet their responsibilities."

FA spokesman Mike Parry was more direct, saying: "We're going to throw the full weight of the FA rulebook at him."

News had reached the player's homeland and Claude Simonet, president of the FFF, said: "Unfortunately I think Eric Cantona will have to be taken off the French team. I say unfortunately because he is a man of great talent."

It was revealed that almost £3m had been wiped off the club's value overnight (down from £79.6m to £77.2m). It would be a short term hit. BSkyB reported a record number of subscriptions in the week after the Cantona incident; the game hadn't even been shown live, but as Manchester United were their most featured team due to their presence as the most popular, the implication was clear.

Perspective was used by Cantona's sponsors, Nike, presumably overjoyed their product was getting round-the-clock coverage. Cantona's Nike swoosh was becoming as embedded in the British public consciousness as it allegedly had in Simmons' chest. "Nike does not condone violence, what Eric did was wrong and he should be punished," said Mike Perry, managing director of the sports manufacturer. "But Nike will not run away from Eric Cantona."

On Friday 27th January, it was announced that United had banned their forward for the rest of the season, though it was suggested they still wanted him to play reserve games. Graham Kelly told press: "I'm pleased they recognised they have to consider the widest interests of the game. I don't think there is any prospect that he will be playing for reserves between now and the date of commission hearing (on 24th February)."

Martin Edwards responded to Kelly's suggestion. "If he doesn't play at all for the rest of this season it will mean he doesn't play until August and that's a long time," the United chairman said. "Clearly he needs to keep himself fit." The club did however agree to adhere to Kelly's wishes until the hearing.

Meanwhile, Matthew Simmons sold his story to a national newspaper. *The Sun* pulled no punches and on Friday 27th January their front page declared they had the full story of

"The Shame of Cantona" on pages 2, 3, 4, 5, 6, 22, 43, 44, 45, 46, 47 & 48. The headline to Simmons' interview screamed: "Cantona's Studs Slammed Into My Heart".

Jimmy Greaves was almost serving as the sane, lone voice in a baying crowd, writing in the same newspaper: "We've heard a lot about Cantona's responsibilities. What about the responsibility of Simmons and every foul-mouthed yob who thinks his £10 admission gives him the right to say what he likes to a man... to abuse, taunt, spit and behave in a way that would get you locked up if you repeated it in the high street?"

Simmons had been told by Palace that due to the police caution he received for the incident, he would not be welcome at Selhurst Park again that season. Simmons, for his part, lodged an official complaint and intended to sue Cantona.

The story became a gold mine for newspapers. No sports story had ever generated as much interest. Not Gazza's tears, not Maradona's handball, arguably not even England's World Cup win in 1966. The desire for controversy seemed insatiable.

On the same night as Selhurst, Wimbledon manager Joe Kinnear had physically confronted a referee, whilst Aston Villa goalkeeper Mark Bosnich had knocked Spurs striker Jurgen Klinsmann unconscious with a disgraceful challenge where he threw his knees first. Cantona topped the billing on 'soccer's night of shame'; it was clearly the story with most longevity.

Curiously, neither of those incidents were mentioned by Liverpool defender Phil Babb in his column for *The Irish Times*. Babb said: "If it were up to me, I'd ban him from English football for good" and concluded: "It doesn't look like I'll be seeing him again for quite a while. His skill will be missed, but that's the price football has to pay."

Statements were taken by police the following week as they

looked into the actions of Simmons, Cantona and Paul Ince. Each day brought with it a new lurid story; Simmons had not even cashed his cheque before other journalists revealed a different side to the purportedly innocent victim. One reporter discovered Simmons had been sentenced to two years probation in 1992 after attacking a Sri-Lankan born petrol station attendant in Croydon.

As *Independent* journalist Richard Williams put it: "You didn't have to look very long and hard at Mr Matthew Simmons of Thornton Heath to conclude that Eric Cantona's only mistake was to stop hitting him."

On Tuesday 31st January, Ferguson wrote in his diary: "Eric's lawyer is coming over tomorrow. Last week we discussed a public apology, but Eric was still too upset about it. He thought it might be better to do it this week. One thing we will pursue is that Eric's problems always occur in the second half and there are suggestions that might reflect a diet problem – low blood-sugar, which could be solved by a half-time supplement."

On Friday 3rd February, Ferguson decided that after the game with Aston Villa, he would surprise his players with a break in Spain. As he made arrangements he was informed the police had asked to speak to Paul Ince following an official complaint; Ince was therefore left behind.

With United's blessing, Cantona went on holiday to Guadeloupe to keep a low profile until the 24th February hearing. That was the theory, anyway. In reaction to reports, a police spokeswoman said: "We have expressed our annoyance to Cantona's solicitors as we believe this shows a blatant disregard for enquiries. We have no powers to make him return to the UK but will be questioning him as soon as he returns."

However there was no appointment for Cantona to attend

the police station, and, it transpired, United had informed the police that he was away. United solicitor Maurice Watkins responded: "It is just not true that Eric Cantona has failed to turn up at South Norwood police station today."

Alex Ferguson had given mixed messages to the press about Cantona's future, on one occasion saying: "I don't think we can keep him." Meanwhile on 5th February, Martin Edwards insisted the club's stance on their suspended player meant they intended to keep him. "Had we wanted Eric to go he would have been on the transfer list already. He is not," he said. "But we must want to see how the FA view the affair. We also don't yet know how Eric is going to feel about the situation."

Of course, talk of the new contract had been put on hold. Who knows how these negotiations are played out, but it is interesting to note that representatives of Inter Milan had been at Selhurst Park and at half-time had tried to talk Edwards into selling them Cantona and Ince. Little were they to know what would happen within 20 minutes; though it hardly seemed to dampen their enthusiasm to acquire the pair.

If Edwards had hoped Cantona's absence would keep him out of the limelight for a while, he was mistaken. Where the Frenchman went, so did the press. Or, more relevantly perhaps, where the trawler went, so did the seagulls. On the day United defeated City 3-0 at Maine Road, Cantona was enjoying a relaxing stroll on the beach with his heavily pregnant wife.

He was confronted by ITN reporter Terry Lloyd and a two-man camera crew. Lloyd claimed he wanted to know when Cantona intended to return to England, following the (incorrect) report of his missed police appointment. Cantona ignored them initially, but when Lloyd persisted, he snapped.

"He then grabbed me in a headlock and said 'Come with me, I'd like a chat with you'," Lloyd told *The Independent*. "He came running at me, launched into the air and kicked me in the chest." He said Cantona had shouted, "I'm going to kill you!"

Cameraman Mike Inglis told the *News Of The World* that "we couldn't believe it", while the third reporter, ITN foreign news editor Robin Staniforth, said: "We were filming on a public beach. We were about 40 feet away with a camera crew. He spotted us and came off the private beach on to the public beach. He threatened him. Subsequently, he kicked him in the chest and bruised him at the very least."

Police were called but took no action. Maurice Watkins said on the Sunday evening: "I saw the report on ITN and two important factors came out of that. First that the report was perpetuating the misinformation that Eric failed to report for a police interview. The second thing is that the ITV cameraman's film was confiscated by the police, which seems to indicate how the authorities viewed this."

Ferguson was less diplomatic, describing ITN's approach as "deplorable", saying "any husband worth his salt would react". In his diary, Ferguson wrote: "The press are having a field day. There are photos of Eric's wife, who is six months pregnant, all over the papers. It's disgusting. What man would not be protective if guys came up trying to take photographs of his pregnant wife in a swimsuit? I'm not surprised Eric reacted. What kind of country do we live in?"

Martin Edwards, who had previously said: "If Eric repeated the action he took at Selhurst Park we would have to dispense with his services," said, after further deliberation: "No facts have been substantiated to me so I can't say anything. It will be a civil matter." (In being interviewed for this book, Edwards said the matter did not cause him undue concern, and in fact, did not remember it until I jogged his memory.)

Inevitably, though, figures of authority back in the UK were quick to assert their own stance. "It's going to be an even bigger problem now," complained Gordon Taylor of the PFA. "It puts a lot of pressure on the FA to take stronger action."

Cantona did indeed threaten to sue ITN for defamation and invasion of privacy. His lawyer, Jean-Jacques Bertrand, said: "Cantona and his family are the object of unacceptable abuse."

FA chairman Bert Millichip expressed "great sympathy" for Cantona, saying: "People were chasing him all over the world. They have followed him around to take pictures of him. I have sympathy for people who are looking for a bit of peace."

Upon his return to the UK, Cantona and his wife attended a meeting with Ferguson, Maurice Watkins and Ned Kelly. The day before, Ferguson had called the police to Cantona's house because press were bothering them. Eric had moved from the Novotel into a two-up, two-down house in Boothstown. Easily accessible for fans, which was no issue for the amiable Cantona; too accessible, though, for the press.

"The first thing we did was get him out of where he was living," Ned Kelly remembered. "Mark Hughes had a spare house over in the Prestbury area. I was there to look after him. The abuse he was getting from was quite horrific."

At the meeting, Ferguson showed his personal support. He explained his theory on a "possibility of hypoglycemia" due to his blood sugar levels and his intention to run tests. Cantona was receptive to the idea.

Two days before the FA hearing, Cantona was charged with common assault and told to appear before Croydon magistrates on 23rd March. He faced a potential six months in prison and a reported £5,000 fine. On the day of the FA hearing, in front of a three-man disciplinary commission in St Albans, Bertrand told *L'Equipe*: "He could be banned for life. My number one objective is to find a solution Eric will not resent as an injustice. He accepted the club's sanctions, but if the FA's are too heavy he won't be able to stand it. We won't try to justify Eric's acts but to explain them. We talk about Eric only when he cracks up but we forget the TV cameras constantly peeping at his windows, we forget about the British press paying people to film him on holiday."

Behind closed doors, the commission – chairman Geoff Thompson, Oldham chairman Ian Stott and Football League president Gordon McKeag – came to a conclusion.

"The members of the FA Commission are satisfied that the actions of Eric Cantona brought the game into disrepute," their statement read. "After taking into consideration the previous misconduct of Cantona, the provocation he suffered, the prompt action taken by Manchester United, Cantona's expression of regret, the apologies he conveyed and the assurances he gave to his future conduct, the Commission decided Eric Cantona should be suspended from all football activities up to 30th September 1995 and fined £10,000."

Cantona could train and be paid a salary but not any bonuses. This was a blow to United, who felt they had already given their player an unprecedented punishment.

"The controversy went with the territory of being at Manchester United, but I had never seen anything like Selhurst before and I don't think anybody else had. It was deeply unusual. It was new," insisted Martin Edwards in an interview for this book. "We did have to react seriously. But we thought we had acted accordingly with the severity of the punishment. We were hurting ourselves, which showed how seriously we took it. I understand why the FA had to send a message, and there was a threat of a life ban at one point. You have to accept the judgement that is made."

Ferguson reacted: "We feel devastated... It's a savage sentence. His next game may be the beginning of November by the time he gets match fit... There were rumours afterwards that one of them was not satisfied, and had wanted a ban to the end of the year and a £100,000 fine...

"After the verdict was read out, Graham Kelly, David Davies, Maurice Watkins and I went into a room to discuss the FA's statement. We were horrified with what was proposed. Maurice was seething. It was so prejudicial. 'You give that out and you'll be in the High Court by Monday, I can assure you,' he said. So they changed it all round, because it was horrendous stuff."

The club knew the FA would probably deny the request for reserve team appearances but felt the ban would not go any further than the summer. United, and Cantona, were lucky to get away with that short an extension if FA executive David Davies' recollection is to be believed. In his 2008 autobiography, he claimed Cantona's statement included apologies to "the chairman of the commission", "Manchester United", "Maurice Watkins and Alex Ferguson", "my team-mates", "the FA" and "the prostitute who shared my bed last night".

United decided not to appeal. Considering Cantona's alleged statement, the tone of the alleged original statement of the FA, and the likelihood that he would have felt even more persecuted after the extra ban, the club probably acted wisely.

Henry Winter for *The Telegraph* said the FA's response was to be "lauded", whilst Graham Kelly said he did not feel Cantona had got off lightly. Weeks later, Ferguson said the only way he expected another player to receive a similar ban was if they "ran over Bert Millichip's dog", saying: "I think the commission went too far. You can't have people in charge of an organisation like the FA being dictated to by the media."

Interestingly, old adversary Richard Shaw agreed, telling me in 2019 that he thought Cantona's ban was "pretty harsh". He added: "It was a loss for football. We were denied watching a wonderful talent play week in, week out. I enjoyed playing against players like that but I also enjoyed watching them."

Meanwhile, Ferguson looked forward to having Cantona back. "I intend to keep working on him and with him," he said. "There will be players who set out to wind him up. He has to be prepared. I still believe he could have an important role at Manchester United... in the early days, I was told I was taking a risk. But you gamble on every player. You may as well gamble on one who lifts people out of their seats. Sometimes he boils over, but that kind of temperament makes him a great player. Eric is so honest, and sees injustice as the biggest crime of all."

The news of the ban encouraged Inter Milan to make another enquiry, causing Ferguson to go public. "Eric is not for sale," said the United boss. "His future is with Manchester United. How he is going to handle his situation, I honestly don't know. It is difficult to imagine the volcano lurking within. The severity of his sentence should placate his hardest critic."

Having dealt with the sporting authorities, there were now the legal procedures to go through. On 27th February, Matthew

Simmons was bailed to appear before magistrates on 24th March, the day after Cantona and Ince were due in court.

Having attempted to keep a low profile, with varying levels of success, Cantona and Ince went out in London until the early hours on the day of their hearing. They went to Browns in Covent Garden, leaving at around 2.30am to go to the Emporium club in Soho to see Prince give a private concert in the company of actor Mel Gibson. They left at almost 5am.

Ince was first in court and pleaded not guilty. He left on bail until May. Cantona had already entered a guilty plea. The severity of the punishment appeared to depend on the strength of the provocation he endured. The court had to decide which of the three main versions of events to believe. There was Cantona's – that he was on his way to the dressing room, "angry and frustrated" when he heard a man shouting racist abuse. There was that of a Palace fan who claimed Simmons had said: "You fucking cheating French cunt. Fuck off back to France you motherfucker. French bastard wanker." And then there was Simmons, who said: "I joined in the general chanting, going 'Off! Off! Cantona! Have an early shower.'"

David Poole QC, defending, appealed for conditional discharge and asked for Cantona to be treated as an ordinary man. The chair of the bench, Mrs Jean Perch, a music teacher, replied: "You are a high-profile public figure with undoubted gifts, and you are looked up to by many young people. The only sentence that is appropriate is two weeks' imprisonment."

That prison was to be High Down, a category B establishment in Sutton. "You could have heard a pin drop when the sentence was imposed," Maurice Watkins said. "Then it was mayhem. Everybody was stunned. Even the prosecuting lawyer was very surprised as it ran counter to all the sentencing guidelines. One minute Eric was a free man, the next minute he was taken down to the cells for three-and-a-half hours."

Ned Kelly went with Cantona: "I think Eric was in a bit of shock. We all were. I followed him with the prison wardens and we sat down together in the cell. One of the old police officers said, 'Don't have the food in here; I'll get you something'. So I gave him some money and he went down to McDonald's and got some Big Macs and French fries so we ate that and had a good laugh. I gave Eric my phone and he called his wife, and Marseille to tell his family. Then he said, 'I can't be bothered with this, I might be better if I just serve this 14 days and get it over with'. I said, 'No way, wait until Maurice gets back'."

Judge Ian Davies granted £500 bail pending an appeal the following Friday, while Martin Edwards complained Cantona had been punished three times for the same offence.

On French radio, Cantona's adviser Jean-Jacques Amorfini said: "He won't stay in that country a lot longer... We are absolutely shocked because Manchester United's lawyers advised a guilty plea so English justice would show clemency."

United weren't the only people frustrated with the idea that Cantona was an exceptional case. Ten police officers had been assigned to the footballer's case; in contrast to the fact only six detectives had been used in a recent local murder hunt.

Mike Bennett, chairman of the Metropolitan Police Federation, felt sportsmen were victims of double jeopardy: "It should be us or the FA who punishes them, and I would say the FA are capable of dealing with everything that occurs inside a football ground without wasting public resources on another trial. It's a nonsense that in this time of scarce resources they can allow so many officers working on one case."

Sensing an opportunity, Inter Milan didn't even wait for the appeal to be heard before making another formal enquiry about Cantona. Inter president Massimo Moratti told reporters on 27th March: "I have sent a fax to Manchester United to sound out whether they are prepared to sell the player."

Having already responded on more than one occasion, Ferguson left this one to Edwards, who stated: "I still have to discuss the Italian interest with the manager and the player. If Eric is desperate to stay then that is the end of the matter."

Having felt so aggrieved at the original sentencing, Cantona and his representatives were much more satisfied with the outcome of the appeal at the end of March. Judge Ian Davies said: "Whatever the defendant's status, he is entitled to be dealt with for the gravity of his offence and not to make an example of a public figure" after reducing the sentence to 120 hours of community service. "Such conduct would provoke the most stoic, and we believe Mr Cantona reacted in a way that was out of character," Davies added.

The media circus reconvened to the local Croydon Park Hotel where they were told there would be a short press conference. Cantona was reluctant, but agreed, and told Maurice Watkins he would like to say a few words.

"Then we started drafting what he was going to say," Watkins recalled. "He was scribbling on a bit of paper and he asked, 'What is the name of that big ship that catches fish?' I said, 'That's a trawler Eric'. 'And the big bird that flies over the sea?' 'A seagull'. Then he wrote it out and we had the famous saying."

(Incidentally, Ned Kelly also claims that the same conversation was had with him – we must presume that both were talking to the Frenchman.)

So, that famous saying. Cantona, Watkins et al took their seats in front of reporters against the backdrop of flashing lightbulbs, clicking cameras and scribbling pens. Cantona surveyed the room, picked up a glass of water, and began to speak. "When the seagulls…" he said, pausing, to take a small drink, "follow the trawler, it's because they think sardines will be thrown into the sea. Thank you very much."

He stood, to more clicking, more flashes and sound of general bemusement from the assembled press. It was left to others to try and make sense of it. "He's just been under some strain lately," said Watkins, attempting to brush it off.

Bertrand, Cantona's lawyer, was asked about talk of Inter Milan. "Any possibility can happen," he admitted. "Today he is still thinking. He has still this intention to stay at United, but when the pressure mounts, he thinks about it."

Watkins, however, echoed the hopes of the club. "I hope he will stay," he said. "There's no reason why he shouldn't stay and now we can have a greater belief in English justice."

That belief would be tested severely over the coming months. But with even Alex Ferguson wondering if the hostility which awaited Cantona on his return would be too much to deal with, it appeared less than likely that his long-term future would be at Old Trafford.

# Different Class

The reporters at the impromptu press conference at Croydon Park Hotel were given yet more ammunition to portray Eric Cantona as a maverick speaking gibberish.

It added to the caricature that had developed during his time in England. Eric liked poetry, he likened football to art, and oh my God, have you seen what he did at the weekend? Because football belonged to the working classes, and artists (or, let's say, poets) were seen to be from the middle class, there was seemingly an irreconcilable difference in the way Cantona ought to be perceived compared to how he was.

The press thought he had given them another line to mock. Look at him, saying something he thinks is meaningful when it's just a load of codswallop. Eric, meanwhile, delighted in their reaction as the seagulls he had just described them as.

There was, seemingly, an underlying contempt as the Frenchman had realised his friends in British football did not include the press. He had complained before about his words being misconstrued but Selhurst Park and its aftermath strengthened his resolve to make a new stand. He would speak to media only when he had to.

Manchester United could now rely on a direct line to their player without any sagas being played out in the press. They couldn't stop the speculation, but had always counted on the player's honesty. (Alex Ferguson once reckoned that to be Cantona's shining quality above all others.)

In the context of Manchester United's 1994/95 season, Cantona is often seen as taking a different direction to the rest of the United squad. But he was training with them, always present aside from that Guadeloupe break. The daily speculation about his future would have an effect at The Cliff.

"He wasn't happy; he wasn't playing, which left a big hole in his life, and he hated the constant press intrusions," Ryan Giggs explained. "They were swarming over him. He'd moved out of the hotel and lived five houses away from my best mate on a normal estate in Boothstown – nothing flash. The people who lived around there were brilliant with him, but it was the sort of house where you step out of the front door straight on to the road. There was no privacy. Most days photographers were waiting for him. He really hated that. There was a time when we thought he'd pack his bags because of it, but looking back now, I don't think he ever really intended to leave."

Some of the United players wondered if Eric would ever be the same again. Those closest to him concerned themselves with his mentality. "I've always wondered what kind of forces he has inside him that occasionally set off this wild outbursts," Peter Schmeichel explained. "Normally he is a well-informed, quiet man who is interested in art and literature. He is level-headed and witty, easy-going and his behaviour is immaculate…

From what I saw he was completely uninterested in football – apart from when he was playing. He could take part in an intellectual discussion about tactics and strategy, but you never saw him hanging around in front of a TV to watch a game."

Roy Keane had long seen Cantona as an ally. One of the warriors. He was witnessing his friend in purgatory: "Football at the level Manchester United play it is a savage business… yes, the rewards are great. You can earn a lot of money and be a hero. But you can also be a failure, humiliated, blasted in the media, jeered by the crowd. Ask Eric about the price he paid for his moment of madness. Jack the Ripper got better press."

The Frenchman had to find a balance to remain motivated. "We all get a little sad sometimes, we feel a little melancholy," he later said. "But being melancholic can be a pleasure too. The body needs to feel alive and sometimes people can't feel the joy of great pleasure. So they find pleasure in sadness. I strive to be at ease with myself, to find harmony between my mind and my body, and to feel in control of my body and my emotions."

Despite all of the outside events, Cantona was as keen as anyone to ensure his future was settled. None of his concerns about remaining at Manchester United related to the club itself. Now the dust had settled, he just needed to feel reassured.

Martin Edwards and Alex Ferguson had quickly decided they would do what they could to keep Cantona at the club unless the player himself expressed an honest desire to leave.

"There was never a real temptation to sell," Edwards says. "The only reason it was entertained was because he said he wanted to go, and Inter Milan were making offers. It was clear that they had already tried to convince Eric to join them and we felt if he was going to go, it was better that he went abroad."

Instead, the negotiations turned to talk of an extended

contract. Edwards said: "I always found him very nice. He didn't say a lot, I suppose he didn't speak a lot with the directors but he was a quiet man anyway. They used to say that he didn't speak English very well. I think he understood it perfectly well. Whether he spoke it better than he let on, I don't know, but I think he understood it well enough. There was the suggestion he didn't, and I think he enjoyed playing up to that.

"He was honest with me. When I had to negotiate the contract after he kicked the supporter, I said to the board that we couldn't be giving him an improved contract in case he did something like that again. We gave him a different contract. We reduced his basic wage but gave him an incentive to win things. I'm generally not in favour of that, as I think it's better to give the team the same bonus scheme. In this case, we had to protect the club. In Eric's contract we put a clause in that said if we won the league, he would get £100,000.

"I was discussing it with Jean-Jacques Bertrand, who said there was no way Eric would accept it. We went back and forth – Jean-Jacques felt there should be a higher basic wage, whilst I maintained it was too risky an investment. Eric arrived after training and Jean-Jacques went over everything with him. I said, 'Eric, it's a three-year contract, how many times do you think we will win the league?' Eric replied, 'Three times.' Jean-Jacques tried to say that couldn't be guaranteed at all.

"Eric was almost personally offended by that and when I asked again I said, 'What about it then, one time, two times?' Eric held up three fingers and insisted we'd win it every year. So even though it was technically against him, he couldn't bring himself to say United couldn't win the league. He wasn't having it."

But Eric knew not all would be the same when he

returned. This was not solely down to him. Dealing with the consequences of Selhurst Park was not the only headache Alex Ferguson had in the latter stages of 1994/95. The beginnings of the squad transition that had taken place to little fanfare in the summer of 1994 were about to take prominent headline space in the pre-season of 1995. The dressing room Cantona would be returning to would look very different.

This idea did not seem to faze the player. "I'm motivated by a challenge," he once said. "It's the same in football as in life. What excites me is never to stay still, but to do something new, to do something that interests me. I want to be like a gambler in a casino who can feel that rush of adrenalin."

It was not a straightforward process that led Cantona to initially commit his future to Old Trafford. On 2nd April, widespread reports said Cantona had done so, though on the 12th, *The Guardian* ran an article which included the statement: "Eric Cantona was last night reported to have made up his mind to leave Manchester United and join Inter Milan."

Author and United fan Richard Kurt made a public plea in *The Independent* to Eric to stay, saying: "Yours has replaced the Pope's photograph in my house. I used to pray to the Pope, I now pray to you." (Alex Ferguson described it as "fabulous… a great article".)

United assistant secretary Ken Ramsden was the latest to be put on fire-fighting duty: "People seem to forget he is under contract to us until the end of next season. The talks are still continuing and there is no real urgency about the situation."

So, what could be happening to intensify the speculation now that Cantona's case had already been heard? Well, over the preceding week, United had played Crystal Palace in the FA Cup semi-final. Tensions were still high and there were reports of incidents between supporters at Villa Park. At one pub eight miles from the ground, Palace fan Paul Nixon fell under a moving coach following an altercation and was killed. Eighty-nine people were arrested. A row between rival fans apparently started when United fans chanted Cantona's name.

To widespread frustration, the game went to a replay, scheduled a few days later as police felt there was nothing to be gained by delaying. The game was played as arranged, with thousands of Palace supporters boycotting it. It didn't pass without controversy. Roy Keane was sent off for a stamp on Gareth Southgate. It didn't help matters that it was almost identical to the Cantona stamp on Moncur.

Selhurst Park was now almost exclusively portrayed in the press as Cantona's misdemeanour rather than an altercation between player and fan. It was Cantona's name and not Simmons' which was given the most coverage when reporting the shocking events surrounding the semi-final. Without even being in the vicinity, Eric was public enemy number one again.

The day after the game, Jean-Jacques Bertrand said of his client: "He is thinking everything over in view of all the latest developments. There seems to be a wave of opinion which wants him to leave. I formally deny the reports of a move. I don't deny we have been talking with Manchester United and Inter officials but, for the moment, our sole priority is to establish Eric's future in England from October."

Meanwhile, Inter Milan released a statement saying they were yet to receive a formal response to their offer.

Despite best efforts of all to try and make things as smooth as possible for Cantona's eventual reintroduction into the game, it seemed unlikely that it would pass without further trouble. Tony Kershaw, chairman of the National Federation of Supporters Clubs, said: "There is a good chance there will be near anarchy at every ground in the country when he appears. He will be baited by fans and goaded by rival players."

Whatever the future held, there is no underestimating the importance of Eric beginning his community service on 18th April, six days after the semi-final replay. He was to run a special coaching programme for youngsters, teaching more than 700 kids aged nine to eleven at The Cliff. Probation officers in Manchester were flooded with requests from schools and youth clubs to have Cantona attend after judge Ian Davies said he hoped the Frenchman might help young boys and girls develop their football skills.

Even on such an occasion, reporters tried to prise information from the children and their parents to see if Cantona had given any indication about his future. There were 12 boys from Ellesmere Park Junior Football Club amongst others. Cantona "told young Manchester United fans he had no plans to switch clubs" according to *The Guardian*.

Cantona seemed very much a 'do as I say' and not 'do as I do' mentor. He told 13-year-old Simon Croft: "If you think you're going to get a yellow card, don't argue with the referee. Walk away." Ellesmere Park coach Les Harris said: "I'd rather see these boys kick a ball than each other. He has taught them the tricks of the trade."

It was a timely reminder for Eric. Needing to take stock, working with these children was more of an opportunity than a punishment. In a peculiar turn of events, Manchester United would benefit from this period more than anyone probably realised at the time. Cantona was able to undergo something of a personal reinvention.

"Above all, I need to be free," he later said. "I don't like to feel constrained by rules or conventions. Everyone has to live according to their own principles, but there's a limit to how far this idea can go. There's a fine line between freedom and chaos. To some extent I espouse the idea of anarchy. What I'm really after is an anarchy of thought, a liberation of the mind from all convention. Perhaps it ends up being more like surrealism than anarchy. It's like the way children think. It would be wonderful if we could communicate in that way too.

"There's something magical about children. When children are free, there's an incredible honesty about them. An honesty you can feel every time you come into contact with them. Honesty sets you free, and we should recover the freedom of childhood."

The experience seemed to be a turning point in settling Cantona's future. On Monday 24th April he spent all day locked in talks. "We spent the whole day negotiating with Eric – a really good day because it looks as if he's going to stay," Ferguson said. "The initial meeting went on for 80 minutes, but then Eric had to go off for community service. Jean-Jacques Bertrand, Maurice Watkins, the chairman and I carried on talking until about 3pm… Eric came back around 5.15pm and we agreed a deal at 8.40pm.

"The most important thing was that he wanted to stay. He turned down a lot of money from Inter Milan. We agreed we would take a couple of days to decide that this is definitely what we want, and Jean-Jacques will return on Thursday so that we can announce it on Friday. The contract reflects the situation, the need for Eric to play and, in fairness, Eric suggested that the pay should be tied to him playing."

On 28th April 1995, it was reported Eric had signed a new deal to stay until 1998 on £15,000 a week. Confirmation came a day later at a press conference. "It's a love story," Cantona said. "It is something very strong for me. The love of the club is the most important weapon in the world. I just couldn't leave."

And how would he deal with inevitable further provocations? "Easy," he smiled.

Ferguson admitted he had been concerned. "I thought he was almost certain to leave," he confessed. "There was so much pressure on him, and you have to think if you are doing right by the player. When you think what has happened to him since January, you wonder who else could have coped with it.

"The easier route would have been to go, but he has put himself in the firing line. You worry what sort of effect all this has had on him inside, but outwardly he has reacted to everything very well. It's that which persuaded me he can handle it. He knows this that this is the last chance."

Cantona ended the press conference telling reporters "you fear me more than I fear you" and then prepared to leave, saying: "I'm sorry, I must leave for training. I need to be fit for my next match." United skipper Steve Bruce reacted positively. "Eric is a superstar and people have been forgetting what a fantastic footballer he is. We have missed him a great deal and he's very popular in the dressing room."

Ryan Giggs confirmed as much in his autobiography, saying the squad had given him plenty of good-natured banter about the 'seagulls' quote. "The players loved that," he said. "The older lads gave him some stick, which he found very funny. He was taking the piss, which he liked to do with the press. He used to pretend he couldn't speak English to get out of doing interviews. He knew it would stop him being pestered…

"While the post-Palace soap opera was going on, the rest of us played football. He trained with us every day, then minibuses full of kids would arrive at The Cliff and Eric would stay on to do his community service, coaching them for two or three hours. The United coaches helped him, but it was definitely hard work for him."

One party, of course, was not happy with the new contract. Inter Milan. Moratti's aide Paolo Taveggia said United had "agreed to have him play for Inter next year. I am disappointed with Cantona's representatives, his manager and his lawyer."

Manchester United's end to 1994/95 was disappointing, by their high standards. On the last day of the season, they travelled to West Ham United knowing they needed to win to claim the title; they also needed Blackburn Rovers, managed by Kenny Dalglish, to drop points at Anfield.

Ferguson's side were missing five names from their FA Cup final team from 1994. Parker, Kanchelskis, Cantona and Giggs were absent while Mark Hughes was deemed only fit enough for a place on the bench.

There was a hot atmosphere in the air. United might not have their Frenchman but they had Paul Ince, the former Upton Park midfielder who received just as hostile a welcome as ever, with banners emblazoned 'JUDAS' held high in the home end.

Ian Darke, commentating for Sky Sports, expressed a hope that "that kind of thing won't sour the occasion."

Of course, if it did, Sky would not necessarily be too disappointed, although the sporting complexities of the day made for compelling enough drama. Upton Park had also been the venue for a damaging defeat for United in their 1992 run-in. When Michael Hughes gave the Hammers the lead and news came through that Alan Shearer had scored for Rovers, then all seemed done and dusted. But early in the second half, Brian McClair equalised for United. Then John Barnes levelled things up at Anfield. There would be more twists to come.

United brought on Hughes, who had a chance to give United the lead. But most opportunities fell to Andy Cole, who was frustrated time and again by Ludek Miklosko in the West Ham goal. In the last 20 minutes, under siege, the frenetic scenes barely resembled a football match so much as simply eleven men trying to force a football to go between two posts.

As the final whistle went at West Ham, Liverpool provided a desperate sting in the tale when Jamie Redknapp scored with the last kick of the game at Anfield. Blackburn thought they'd blown it, but heard almost immediately that United's game was over. They were champions.

United's Mersey misery wasn't over just yet. A week later, Everton defeated them at Wembley to win the FA Cup. Ferguson's side put in a flat performance, unable to lift themselves and shorn of players to make a real difference. While Ferguson's United were far from a one-man team, many pinpointed Cantona's absence as a reason for the trophyless end to the season.

"I'm sure the fact he wasn't allowed to play again cost us

the title," said Ryan Giggs. "In one mad moment we lost our inspiration, our talisman. In passing judgment on what Eric did, I think it's important to remember that the spectator he had a go at wasn't exactly whiter than white. He had provoked the attack with a stream of abuse, and it later emerged that he had a conviction for assault with attempt to rob."

Andrei Kanchelskis later reflected: "Had Eric, under extreme provocation, not launched himself at a fan, Manchester United would have beaten Blackburn to the league title."

And, finally, Roy Keane: "If only Eric had kept his head at Selhurst Park. There's no doubt in my mind that with Eric we would have claimed our second double."

Gary Pallister saw it a little differently. "His absence was a heavy blow because he was a great player, but we were by no means a one-man outfit and, if the breaks had gone our way, we could easily have repeated the League and FA Cup double."

Ferguson felt United had surrendered the title by imposing the ban they had. "The decision we took at the time was, in effect, giving up the league and the cup," the boss later admitted. "If Cantona had remained in the team, he would have at least made and scored a dozen more goals. We lost the final to Everton and I think Eric would have made or scored a goal in that game."

Martin Edwards agreed. "The difference Eric made is easy to see by how successful we became," he said. "Okay, we should have won the league in 1992. With Cantona we win the league in 1993, the Double in 1994 and again in 1996, and we miss out on another in 1995 by one point and one goal in the cup final. I think with Cantona we would have won three doubles in a row. He was that influential."

Not so influential that his mere return was a guarantee of

success, however. Ferguson might have planned for further transition within his squad in 1995 but was almost certainly forced to do some business that he hadn't anticipated.

One obvious matter to resolve was Paul Ince, whose influence in the dressing room was becoming a negative. Peter Schmeichel said: "It doesn't take much psychological discord to begin to make a good team less effective, and to prevent this from happening Paul Ince just had to be weeded out. Ince was a good player... but I felt he was, to put it mildly, self-centred and arrogant, and his potentially adverse influence on young players was something I know worried Alex Ferguson."

Ince and Ferguson's relationship had become increasingly abrasive. The manager had tolerated the Londoner's cocky attitude, and insistence that others called him by his self-appointed nickname of "Guv'nor", but far less palatable was the apparent refusal to adhere to instruction. Ferguson felt Ince had ignored the plan in the defeat in the Nou Camp and tore into him at half-time.

Similar problems followed. Ince ignored instructions to remain tight to Steve McManaman in a game at Anfield in March; leading to Liverpool scoring and winning 2-0. Ferguson later described United's loss here as the one that cost his team the league. Ince's performance in the FA Cup final was the final straw and the United boss welcomed the advances of Inter Milan. Supporters were not happy – Ince was popular. Losing him for £6m seemed like a bad move, and fans were outraged further when they learned the Italians had apparently only paid £3m up front.

The previous season, Martin Edwards had revealed plans for Old Trafford's North Stand to be redeveloped at a cost of £28m. "It means we will be restricted in the transfer market for the next two seasons," he said. "That is why we invested £6m in Andy Cole."

United fans were furious at the idea they would have to sell without replacing in order to build the stand. Meanwhile Ferguson was trying to bring in players but couldn't. In fact, the manager was on holiday when Edwards called him to say Mark Hughes had signed for Chelsea. The fee would be decided by tribunal; a contract agreed earlier in the year had never been signed due to a disagreement over one clause. Hughes had been a vital part of the team in which Cantona played; so too was Andrei Kanchelskis, who eventually moved to Everton in a protracted saga.

None of this influenced Cantona ahead of the new season. Ferguson said he was "training like a beast" in the summer and said "Eric has suffered too, I cannot believe he would want to endure anything like the last six months again."

United were keen to not take any chances. They decided that Eric would stay in Manchester while the first team went to Kuala Lumpur on their pre-season tour. Ferguson arranged for teams from Bury, Oldham, Preston and Rochdale to play in training sessions against a United team with Eric in it at The Cliff. As these were not organised friendlies, it was deemed acceptable for Eric to participate.

The first of these, which Ferguson was present for, was against Rochdale on the 25th July. The junior United players were told to give the ball to Eric at every opportunity. At half-time in this most laidback of sessions, Ferguson berated the youngsters for occasions they did not pass to the Frenchman.

The press had reported on this session and it provoked a response from the FA, reminding the Reds that Cantona was banned from football-related activities until October. United cancelled the other sessions. Preston manager Gary Peters was confused. "From what I gather the friendly with Rochdale was just a glorified training exercise for several players, not just Eric," he said. "And that's what we were going for."

It transpired years later that the Preston session did actually go ahead. Speaking to *Off The Ball* in 2019, Kevin Kilbane, the former Deepdale winger, admitted Peters took the young team over, and remembers that Cantona was on the pitch.

"I was a young YTS player, about 17, so we went over and played against Cantona. It was great for us," Kilbane recalled. "We couldn't have an official referee, it had to be someone from Man Utd, a physio or one of the coaches, it couldn't be classed as an official game… Cantona didn't really run around much, but he just sort of had a few touches, everyone was just watching him in awe. It was just great to play against him."

The FA, however, felt the sessions could be considered friendlies that fell under their jurisdiction; going against the ban. Cantona, frustrated, told the club he wanted to move back to France and submitted an official transfer request.

"Eric Cantona was very upset at the recent inquiry by the FA concerning his involvement in a training session held on 25th July. He told Martin Edwards he felt he had little future in the English game," said Ken Ramsden.

"Even after all of our support, Eric decided he wanted to leave," Edwards confirmed. "We tried to organise friendly games but he couldn't play in them and then we were told he couldn't even train. It was frustrating as we obviously wanted to keep him fit so he would be ready to play in matches."

On 8th August, Ferguson told reporters: "Eric feels persecuted by the FA inquiry and it seems like the final straw to him. Obviously we don't want to lose him, we just have to

**Going rogue:** Cantona emerges from his Boothstown house after the Palace incident, ahead of some memorable meetings with the press and a community service assignment with local youngsters.

**The resurrection:** The Frenchman in training (below) ahead of his comeback against Liverpool – a match which sees him stroke home the equaliser from the spot before celebrating in style...

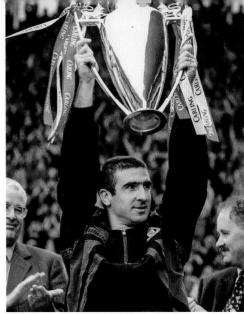

**Driving force:** Eric is in magisterial form as the 1995/96 campaign approaches its climax, with a succession of winning goals helping the Reds overhaul Newcastle in the title race after trailing Kevin Keegan's side by 12 points.

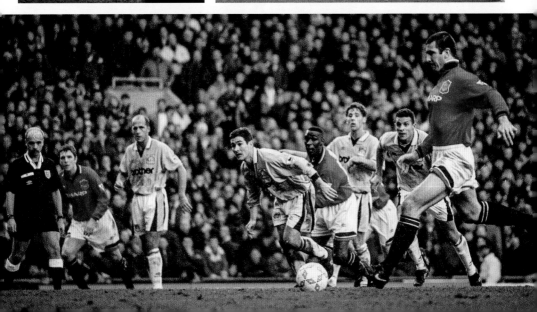

**Crowning glory:** Cantona completes his rehabilitation in English football with a dramatic winning goal late on in the FA Cup final clash with Liverpool in 1996. He leads the Double winners up to collect the trophy wearing the captain's armband – a fitting tribute to his newfound sense of serenity.

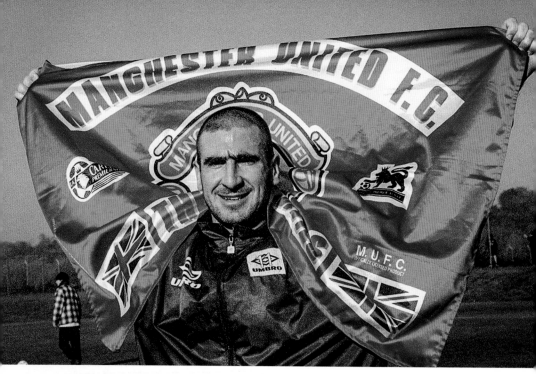

**The last stand:** The 1996/97 season sees Eric come under fire for some below-par performances, but he silences the critics with arguably the finest goal of his career – a mazy run and chip against Sunderland at Old Trafford.

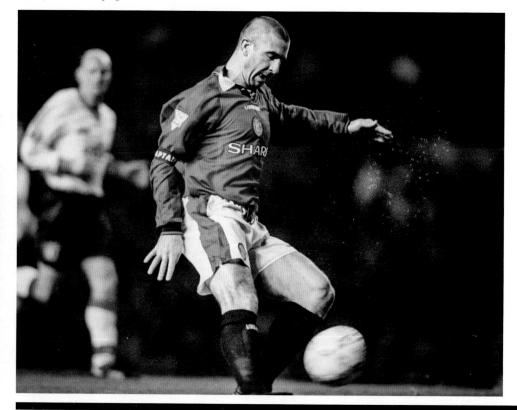

**Continental kings:** Cantona inspires United to a stunning 4-0 victory over Porto in the Champions League quarter-finals, raising hopes that the Reds are ready to take the next step in European competition...

**Down and out:** Eric rues a missed chance in the Champions League semi-final defeat against Borussia Dortmund – a match which seemingly solidifies his desire to retire from the game.

**The end:** Sombre scenes around Old Trafford as fans, manager and chairman try to come to terms with the Frenchman's decision. Rumours of his departure had swirled after the friendly game against Coventry City (left).

**Life after football:** Post-retirement, Cantona fills his time with beach soccer and acting amongst other things, as well as making the occasional trip back to Old Trafford, where he's always guaranteed a rapturous reception...

hope that things settle down." The United manager's concerns were far deeper than he was letting on. That same day, he went to see Cantona back in the Novotel in Worsley, where Eric insisted he wanted to go to France.

Ferguson feared Cantona was slipping away from United. "Eric had been sent into exile and forbidden from training or travelling on our pre-season tour, so it was natural for him to feel isolated and forgotten," Ferguson said in his autobiography.

That evening, Ferguson talked to his wife Cathy, who persuaded him to try and talk Eric into staying. The following morning, he contacted Bertrand and asked if he could meet with Eric the next day in Paris. Bertrand agreed. Earlier that day, United had played a friendly at Bradford City.

News had filtered through that Cantona wanted to leave; the United supporters unveiled a flag that read: '1966 was a great year for English football, Eric was born.' Their stance was clear.

After the game, Ferguson left for Paris via a book launch in London. In his autobiography, Ferguson recalls a speedy dash though the Paris side-streets on the back of a Harley-Davidson, driven by Eric's lawyer Jean-Jacques Amorfini. When they arrived at an empty restaurant, closed by the owner as a favour to Cantona, Ferguson and his star player enjoyed "a wonderful time". Ferguson had deduced that Cantona needed reassurance, and explained how the club would do everything possible to ease his troubles. He would also have to move out of the hotel he was living in. Ferguson recalled: "Eric agreed and the rest of the evening was spent reminiscing about great football matches of the past…Those hours spent in that largely deserted restaurant added up to one of the more worthwhile acts I have performed in this stupid job of mine."

Cantona agreed to return. At Manchester Airport, Ferguson

told reporters: "Eric trained very hard and was looking forward to playing in the private games but suddenly that was all taken away. With his wife and kids in France, he was left sitting alone in his hotel room in Manchester. He started dwelling on things. I told him any action was aimed not at him but at us. I don't think it had been fully explained that the FA were not going to punish him. That troubled him a great deal. There is no doubt about his future at United. He will be back on Monday and here when his suspension ends in October."

Inter Milan claimed to have been approached by a United intermediary after the transfer request and on the morning of Cantona's return to training, they had a spokesman tell newspapers: "It's not simple to work out what the player or Manchester want. If it's possible, we'll sign him." For once in this saga, there was finally an answer – it wasn't, and they wouldn't.

Alex Ferguson had achieved a more remarkable coup than he had when originally signing Cantona, in convincing him to stay. He had also taken another big gamble. He hadn't signed a single player and was now putting his faith in the temperament of the most volatile footballer in Britain. This at a time where he was also renegotiating his own contract with the club. The risk was enormous. So was the pay-off.

# Young Pretenders

I t was all change back at The Cliff once Eric Cantona had joined back up with his colleagues on Monday 14th August 1995. He was familiar with the young men who were now occupying the seats of his former senior colleagues. He had made it his duty to familiarise himself with them much earlier in his career at Old Trafford, though at the time, nobody had realised how mutually beneficial that approach would be.

There had been a changing of the guard, as Roy Keane explained: "I socialised with the lads in the 1994/95 team more. I was into the drinking sessions, the banter with Robbo, Brucey, Incey and Eric. A different team."

Keane remained, of course. But he was right to highlight the transition and the impact it would have. Cantona, having been in a position where he was an example to young children, was not in too different a scenario now. He would have to lead by example. He would also have to adapt his own style. Ryan Giggs was the only member remaining of that potent quadrant of attacking players which had brought such incredible success and had Cantona in the most imperious form of his career.

The dynamics were shifting all the time. The balance on the right-hand side was yet to be decided. It was not clear how Eric and Andy Cole would combine, though the relationship would be very different to that with Mark Hughes.

Any future success depended largely on Cantona's ability to deal with this transition. One thing was clear – the youngsters certainly looked up to the Frenchman. The distance between them and Cantona helped cultivate the sense of mystery.

"None of us got to know Eric well, although there was a vast, unspoken respect for him," Gary Neville remembered. "In training, if the ball didn't get played to him as he wanted he would look at you like he was going to knock you out. He had massively high standards; he was a perfectionist. But you didn't feel belittled, it just made you strive to do better.

"We were desperate to impress him. Respect for him contained a little dash of fear because we had all seen how he could erupt, even though we knew he'd never take it out on us. We found incidents like that amusing – after the event, anyway – because Eric was so mild-mannered, quiet even, the rest of the time. He wasn't arrogant but polite and considered."

For a better sense of perspective, it is worth getting the full picture from those around The Cliff at this time. Those who can remember the likes of David Beckham as a hopeful adolescent rather than as decorated global superstar.

Eric Cantona became a totemic, influential presence for the younger generation, but he'd been doing his bit to raise standards from almost the moment he joined the club. In his first few days Cantona had set the example with his extra training sessions. "There are a lot of people who stay on a bit longer," remembered Steve Bruce. "The last one off the training ground is always Eric Cantona. People might be amazed by that as the game appears to come so easily to him, yet he is always wanting to practise his technique that little bit longer. It is not physical work, but he likes to practise his finishing. If he has to do that, it shows what the rest of us need."

Peter Schmeichel recalled that Eric would often have company: "The secret behind his ability was an enormous amount of dedication to training, where he incessantly practised his game's little details and tricks, often after the rest of us had finished for the day. But he was never entirely alone. The young players – Paul Scholes, Nicky Butt, Gary Neville – used to stand there and watch the big Frenchman's ball juggling – out of admiration, naturally, but also as a means of enhancing their own footballing development."

Cantona would ask some of the young players to practise with him. Pretty soon, he didn't need to ask, as those youngsters witnessed what a difference he made.

"There were huge reactions from Eric arriving," Class of '92 member Chris Casper says. "One was his influence on the first team in a side who were struggling. The first team took a real influence from him, observing his quality and technique. We had some great characters but he really turbo-charged things. We were putting in the training but not to the intensity that he was. He'd got the ultimate respect of everyone.

"He was the catalyst, he put a bomb under the place. The manager took the decision because he had to win the league. If there was one thing about the signing, it was that he'd just won the league and had experienced it. Pressure didn't affect Eric, it was just like he arrived and said, 'I'll win you the league.' In the game against Norwich away in 1993, he just ran the show, and calmed the entire team down. The team were outstanding but they needed that extra something which Eric brought."

Pat McGibbon, a young defender in the reserve team, confessed to a bit of a man-crush. "Eric was an enigma," he says. "He drove a small Renault Clio and lived in a two-up, two-down in Boothstown. Myself and my wife lived a mile further up the road in Walkden. We used to go to The Moorings pub just to see if we could spot him. I was more like a stalker than a team-mate but he just had that aura about him.

"One morning at training I watched him line ten balls up, 30 yards out for a crossbar challenge. He ended up hitting the crossbar eight out of ten, and they all rolled back to him."

The kids would try and imitate him. "We all had a go at what he was doing, he used to kick the ball as high as he could and keep it up," John O'Kane remembers. "That's why his touch was so good. He was a unique player and person... when he said hello in the morning you felt ten feet tall."

Those small moments of validation or interaction became just as exciting for the United young players as they would any regular supporter. "He wasn't a massive conversationalist. In the dressing room, he would always be on the periphery, but you knew for sure he understood exactly what was going on," Ben Thornley recalls. "On the odd occasions during the season, we would train at Littleton Road instead of the The Cliff.

"One time Eric was getting into his car as I was leaving and he gestured to me if I wanted a lift back to The Cliff. I was only a young lad and this was an idol of mine. He started a conversation; I said that my parents and my sister could speak French, and I was taking it at A-level. I mentioned writing in French was difficult. He turned to me and said, 'Even for French people, writing is difficult!' I thought it was a strange but poignant thing to say. It was only a short journey to The Cliff but it left an impression. He was polite, he would always greet you and say goodbye when he was leaving."

Those FA Youth Cup winners had already enjoyed their success prior to Cantona's arrival. There is then the consequential conversation about how influential Cantona was on this group of already gifted stars but as Casper stated above, his impact on the first-team success had spoken for itself.

"He was always the last one to leave," says Thornley. "He would always do things in his own time, taking his time to wind down and to have a shower and get changed. But he would always take his time with the fans who were at The Cliff. Every autograph that needed signing, he'd do it. Everyone would scream for him. He'd do it every time. On school holidays it was packed with hundreds and he would go through it all.

"There are only two players I've felt genuinely in awe of when I was on the same pitch of them, Eric was one and Zinedine Zidane was the other. They just had a presence, such an aura, about them. They always seemed to have just as much time as they needed on the ball, one because of that aura and two because they were such gifted footballers.

"The manager indicated the procedure that Eric would go through, his routine in preparation for matches. He would do it alone, in silence, away from people. He would focus. It was like *Stars In Their Eyes* where they disappear behind the screen and become the singer, that's what Eric would be like from his persona on a daily basis to getting ready for a match.

"It wasn't just the young lads who looked up to him, it was the senior players as well, we all knew he had something that could unlock an opposition defence. He was brilliant at that."

Just as the mood at the club changed with the success, so did attitudes at those training sessions. United's fledglings were now not only happy to be picked by Cantona to help him train, they would be desperate for their own sessions to end so they could go and play with the Frenchman. It did not have to be the holidays for the first-team sessions to end with young hopefuls praying for some attention from United's star player.

"We'd come back from Littleton Road and we'd see Eric was still out, wanting to practise his free-kicks or his shooting," Thornley recalls. "He didn't have to ask, we'd be queuing up almost, hanging about sheepishly hoping to get invited or that the ball might roll to you so you could get involved.

"There were times when he specifically wanted certain players for certain things, so if he wanted someone to cross for him, for someone like myself or Becks, it was perfect. You would instantly go from, 'Oh great, he chose me!' to, 'Oh no, I hope I don't mess this up!' You had the manager watching out of the window, and we knew he was full of admiration for those of us who had already done a full training session and wanted to come back and better themselves by practising with Eric. We wanted to put on a good show for him and for Eric."

Asked about Bruce's theory that Cantona would try to engineer situations he might find on a matchday, Thornley says: "It could well have been an attempt to replicate the unpredictability of a game scenario. But how many times did he do something in a match and you would think never in a million attempts would anyone be able to do what he just did? He could do things others just couldn't."

Over time, this attitude became more serious. Extra sessions with Cantona evolved into extra sessions by themselves, with Beckham endlessly working on his shooting.

"During my time at Manchester United I was lucky enough

to have a lot of people who put in countless extra hours to get better," Sir Alex Ferguson said in 2016. "Gary Neville turned himself from an average footballer into a wonderful one because of his work ethic, as did David Beckham... I remember Eric's first day and after the training session had finished he asked for a goalkeeper, two players from the junior team who were still there, and a few footballs.

"He said he wanted to practise. When word got back to the other players, one or two more turned up the next day for an extra session and so the number grew. That was all because of Cantona's work ethic and influence."

Ben Thornley agrees with the point. "That was something schooled in those sessions with Eric and influenced by his desire to be as good as he could be," the former winger says. "And when you considered how we aspired to be at his level, and then how we witnessed how much he wanted to improve, it was an education in how to conduct ourselves. And we wanted to prove that we were keeping up with him. There was immense potential in the group of lads but the benefit of the time spent with Eric proved to be incalculable."

That view went right the way to the top. As well as Ferguson, Martin Edwards could easily see the impact his signing was having throughout the club. "Eric had a big influence on the young players coming through," Edwards says. "They were breaking into the first team, he was in his prime, and he was a bit of a hero to them. His work ethic and attitude to training rubbed off on them. He was somebody they admired, and it is easy to see that he was instrumental in their careers."

As those players started to realise their potential, that influence from Cantona would become more noticeable. By January 1995, most of the Class of '92 had made their first-team debuts. But the period of education was almost brought to a staggering halt by Selhurst Park. The night before, the reserves drew at Derby County, and most of those young players were back in Manchester when they heard the news.

"We were playing pool in a pub and they had the news on the big screen there," remembers Kevin Pilkington. "We thought 'oh no'… it was one of those moments where you always remember where you were. Everyone looked up to him. He was a joy to watch, some things he would do in training you'd never see anyone able to replicate. But when you saw what he did at Selhurst you realised he would be gone for a while."

Others were in the city centre. "Myself, Becks, Gaz, Mark Rawlinson, Chris Casper, if we weren't with the team, we might get together and go into Manchester and have something to eat," Ben Thornley says. "We heard about it when we were on Deansgate. We heard snippets and weren't too sure what to believe until we saw the footage later on. I can remember thinking, 'Wow!' We knew he had a fuse from what we'd seen in France but it was still shocking. It was unprecedented.

"We didn't know how to react because it was something we'd never seen before in England. You don't expect to see it at the club you're representing and especially not from someone who you've looked up to from the day he arrived. It opened our eyes to the different side of him. He was a gentleman to us but we realised he was human, that he too could be pushed too far."

The young players appeared to adopt that feeling within the senior squad of sympathy to Cantona. However, despite being a group of immense potential, the general mood in the summer of 1995 was one of doubt that they could compensate for the departures of Kanchelskis, Ince and Hughes, as well as for the remaining six weeks of Cantona's suspension. United's first three away games were imposing tasks at Villa Park, Ewood Park against the champions and then Goodison Park against the FA Cup holders. Cantona's suspension would have included the home game with Liverpool on September 30th, but Sky selected it for broadcast and moved it to Sunday, 1st October. The date for the return of the King had been set.

There were still those opening weeks to navigate. In addition to the names already missing, Steve Bruce, Ryan Giggs and Andy Cole were all injured for the opening game. At Villa Park, it was Gary Neville's 20th league appearance, Nicky Butt's 25th, Paul Scholes' 18th, Phil Neville's third, David Beckham's fifth and John O'Kane's debut.

Villa were 3-0 up at half-time. Beckham's long-range consolation goal would eventually be the most prophetic moment from this memorable game but on *Match of the Day* that evening, Liverpool legend Alan Hansen seemed to say what everybody else was thinking. "You can't win anything with kids," Hansen declared.

This was the commonly held opinion: the *Manchester Evening News* held a poll on the eve of the season asking whether Alex Ferguson should be sacked. The majority said yes, though Ferguson later said this was probably mischief from City fans.

As Cantona continued to train with the new-look senior squad, Ben Thornley doesn't recall the Frenchman showing any loss of faith. "There was no change in his demeanour," Thornley says. "He trusted the manager. Eric just seemed to shrug his shoulders and take on the mantle like, 'These are the guys I'm playing with now, if the manager thinks they're good enough, then they obviously are.' With Eric at the helm everyone came on quicker than if he hadn't been."

United responded well, defeating West Ham and Wimbledon

at home to bounce back after that Villa disappointment. A big task awaited Ferguson's side as they travelled to take on Blackburn. Bruce and Cole were back while Giggs was fit enough for the bench but the United team still included Gary Neville, David Beckham, Nicky Butt and Paul Scholes.

It was a brave call but the right one. On this big occasion, the young midfield trio in particular impressed with heir confidence, tenacity and fluency. United scored twice in the second half by pressing Rovers into their own box. The winning goal from David Beckham was a jewel carved from the rough, a scrappy passage of play finished by a beautiful angled shot.

The confidence gained from this win had a massive impact on United's young squad. It helped them defeat Everton away in a fantastic 3-2 win, before one of the most thrilling performances in the past year when Bolton were demolished 3-0 at Old Trafford. In that game Ferguson's choice was a 4-4-2 shape, with Terry Cooke and Lee Sharpe providing the width and Beckham and Butt in the middle, and Paul Scholes and Ryan Giggs the front two players. The vibrancy, speed and positional interchanging of these players proved impossible for the newly-promoted Trotters to handle.

There were immediate consequences to this run of form. The surprise element had well and truly gone. If Blackburn and Everton had been unsure how to approach this young United team, nobody else would be making that same mistake. Teams would face United and treat these young players as if they were the double winners of the previous year. They would eventually stand up to the task but there would be hiccups along the way.

The first of those came in spectacular fashion in the Coca-Cola Cup against York City at Old Trafford. York won 3-0 in one of the great shock results. Six days later, United were eliminated from the UEFA Cup in similarly surprising fashion, when they drew 2-2 with Rotor Volgograd at home. They exited on away goals.

Cantona's return, then, couldn't have come at a better time. "He'll definitely play on Sunday," Alex Ferguson told the press on Friday 29th September. "His rightful place is playing in big games. His fitness is very good, and the adrenalin will help him through the game… Liverpool at home? I don't think I'd be able to stop Eric playing."

But Liverpool at home also meant there would be a certain level of hostility waiting for him. In the Scouse defence would be Neil Ruddock and Phil Babb. If Cantona had thought absence would make the heart grow fonder he was given a timely reminder about how deep rivalries continued to burn.

On 6th September, a death threat was made by someone claiming to be a Leeds fan, who said they would be carrying weapons when United played at Elland Road on Christmas Eve. They called *Football Monthly Magazine* editor Tony Flood and said: "If me and my mates can get to Cantona or Ferguson we'll kill the bastards. We will give them hell when they come here. This is a serious threat. We're all carrying weapons and know how to use them."

Cantona, meanwhile, took the time to insist he was a lover, not a fighter. On 19th September, he sat alongside Diego Maradona in Paris to launch a 'world players' union' which aimed to encourage communication between players and administrators. "Soccer is beautiful – it's not war," Cantona said. "They need us and we need them. We hope that whenever there is an important decision affecting the sport, affecting spectators, affecting us, that it goes through us."

Had Cantona, without kicking a ball for nine months,

become a spokesperson for better relations between players and the sport's governing bodies? Certainly, the world's eyes were trained on the Frenchman ahead of one of England's biggest games. Would the Frenchman be a reformed character?

Meanwhile, on 29th September, the FA launched a new anti-racism campaign. Liverpool player John Barnes stated: "A lot of good may come out of what Eric did because it's brought home the issue to a lot of people. If Eric hadn't reacted like that, no-one would have realised the abuse he was getting. You can't condone what Eric did but I'm sure there are players who have felt like doing the same thing. I bite my tongue and I don't react. But then people laugh it off and say, 'Well, it can't be that serious because you don't react to it'."

With Cantona mainly maintaining his silence with the press, it was left to Ferguson to discuss the game. He told reporters he would take more time talking about controlling tempers: "A bit of dialogue, one to one… I did that when he first came to the club, and I'm going to be doing more now."

On the day of the game, inevitably there were dozens of features across the mainstream media, with Ferguson's interview with Paddy Barclay in *The Guardian* perhaps the most insightful when it came to what people could expect.

"The impact Eric has had on this club concerns something we need to address in our game – the practice aspect, the technical aspect," he said. "Even when he's not been playing, he's still been training. There's a real professional attitude to it all. It's as if he's saying, 'This is what I've been brought up on and this is what I'm going to do.' And it doesn't change from day to day, no matter that he's been out all this time. And now, fortunately, we have eight or nine followers because of it.

"He started off with three or four – Paul Ince, Ryan Giggs, Lee Sharpe and then Roy Keane – and gradually it grew until pretty well all of them stayed back for extra practice. Apart from Steve Bruce – he needs his rest! Sometimes on the day before a match I'll shout over, 'Come on in, it's Friday'. And they'll shout back, 'Just give us another minute.' It's terrific to see that work ethic, and it all comes from Eric. People from outside won't notice that.

"I think the effect Eric has on our youngsters is perhaps best illustrated by something that happened after the Galatasaray game here last season. I'd been doing a radio interview and came back to find him at the tactics board with David Beckham and Gary Neville, talking the game through. You could see how much it meant to them."

Barclay asked Ferguson what Cantona had to do to ensure he remained a positive role model. "I don't see why he should change," Ferguson insisted. "If you look back over the best teams, you tend to find that it's the captain who is the leader in that sense. Bryan Robson did it for us. He was a fantastic leader. But players like Cantona are not that type. George Best wasn't. So I don't accept Eric should take that sort of responsibility. I mean, if he's playing well, his vision and ability will improve others, maybe even inspire their imaginations.

"Because of the way we play football in this country, we lack players of vision, players who can see out of the corners of their eyes. I remember a goal Cantona made here against Coventry. From where I sit I can see everything and I'm saying things like, 'Put it there, pass it now,' but this pass... I just couldn't see it until it happened. You would hope that kind of thing would help someone like Paul Scholes, who is imaginative by nature."

Having convinced Cantona to remain at the club, Ferguson felt the Frenchman would not have enjoyed the move to Italy as much as some expected he might. "There are too many things that weigh heavily against that," he said.

"He is never going to get the same adulation as here. He is never going to be looked after as he is here. I have already intervened. I went to Paris because I was determined not to accept what Eric was saying. He maybe felt that he couldn't win. Once I had convinced him otherwise, it was all right."

To repeat the point, Ferguson's fateful Paris dash was probably an even greater gamble than the one he had taken to sign Cantona in the first place. If the relationship between Manchester United and Eric Cantona had ended at Selhurst Park, the perception of the success of the relationship would be hotly debated.

It was Ferguson's, as well as Cantona's, reputation which now lay on the line, as the Scot admitted: "I hope my reputation doesn't have to be judged on Eric Cantona's life with Manchester United. If that is to be the only blip in my career, I'll accept it and go to the big penalty box in the sky quite happy... in fact, very happy."

# Returning Royalty

I f it was fair to describe Manchester United's decision to invest in Eric Cantona as the leader of their next generation as something of a gamble, then it is worth noting the club had recovered from their short-term financial hit inflicted by events at Selhurst Park in January. Their shares were now at a record high, with Cantona remaining as popular as ever – the Frenchman alone was responsible for more than 20 per cent of the club's merchandising revenue.

From that point of view, Cantona had never been missing, but he had of course been absent from where it mattered most. "Naturally I am delighted to have him back," Alex Ferguson wrote of Eric in his programme notes for the game against Liverpool on 1st October 1995.

"Nine months without playing football is a long time for a professional and Eric has been very quiet this week, no doubt making his own personal preparations. There is no point opening up all the rights and wrongs of why he did what he did and the severe punishment he received. All I really want to say is that he has trained hard during his ban and he did well in his community service. He has served his punishment and all he needs now is some football."

His return was universally welcomed by his team-mates. Peter Schmeichel explained Cantona as having survived an "eight-month nightmare" and said: "He has changed... I'm sure you'll see a different and better Eric. I rate Eric as one of the five most gifted players there have ever been in the world. To have him back will be a huge bonus; his reappearance will add to the young players' confidence."

Schmeichel had been beaten by a late winner scored by Cantona in a rare practice match that had been arranged at Old Trafford the Thursday before the game, presumably for the benefit of the hundred reporters in attendance.

United skipper Steve Bruce hoped opponents would treat Cantona fairly. "We all hope our fellow pros will give him a break and not try any silly antics," he said. "Let's just enjoy Eric and his football... he is a special talent, and it will be a shame if he can't show that."

In fairness to Liverpool, their captain Ian Rush was as good as his word when he insisted they would not be trying unnecessarily to get Cantona into trouble. In charge of the game was David Elleray. He had claimed the spotlight was on him just as much as it was on Cantona. He had sent off Roy Keane for an alleged dive at Blackburn, incensing the midfielder.

One shining light so far as potential trouble was concerned: restrictions due to the rebuilding of the North Stand meant there were no Liverpool supporters (officially, anyway) among the 34,934 at Old Trafford. Just over a minute had been played as United opened the game attacking the Stretford End. Andy

Cole found Cantona in space on the left; the man who would surely be demanding the closest of attention from Liverpool had already, as was his speciality, found a way to escape it.

His cross was slightly behind Cole, but perfect for the run of Nicky Butt, whose first touch was a little heavy. Perfectly heavy, one might say; it tempted David James to come out of his goal, but Butt continued with his momentum and cleverly fired past him. Just 67 seconds were gone; Cantona had created a goal.

The atmosphere was frenzied, but Liverpool grew into the game as the hosts tried to settle into shape. The Nevilles were playing either side of Bruce and Pallister and that was comfortable enough; Cole in front of Cantona, as unfamiliar as the pair were, was a fairly conventional partnership.

But where the Frenchman had left behind a comfortable pattern where he was flanked by Kanchelskis and Giggs, now there was an altogether different dynamic behind him. The tigerish Butt was playing from the right, with Roy Keane partnered by the left-footed Lee Sharpe in the middle.

Liverpool took the initiative and turned the game around with goals from Robbie Fowler either side of half-time. (Fowler who, in his autobiography was surprisingly supportive of Cantona, saying, "When Cantona went into the crowd to sort that fella out who was giving it to him, I reckon most of the professionals were thinking, 'Good on you Eric'.") Ferguson had already made changes to try and combat the possession mismatch in the middle. David Beckham came on for Butt and United moved to a 3-5-2. United were struggling to find any fluency, but Cantona – despite being the man responsible for most of the maelstrom of the day – managed to maintain his composure in two key moments. First, he timed a perfect pass into the path of Giggs in the 71st minute. Giggs raced into the box and was chopped down by Jamie Redknapp.

Cantona took the penalty himself, sending the ball past David James (who had yet to learn of his opponent's technique from the spot). United's number seven raced to the crowd, twirling around on the post that held the netting up behind the goal.

Late on, Eric clipped in a cross that Andy Cole met with a bicycle kick which went agonisingly close to answering just about every question mark over the Frenchman's head. There was one last moment of minor controversy, though it was more pantomime than confrontation; after being barged by his old friend Ruddock, Cantona gestured that it was the Londoner's large frame that had felled him. The game ended 2-2.

"We got off to a dream start, then we forgot we were playing a game of football," Ferguson told the press before facing numerous questions about Cantona. Eventually he had enough. "I've finished talking about Eric Cantona. I'm happy to talk about the game," he sighed.

If anyone had deserved equal billing with Cantona on the day it had been Robbie Fowler. Even his brace could not, however, take the spotlight away from the returning Frenchman.

It was widely expected that Eric would be rested for the second leg of the tie with York City. But with United's needs fairly urgent, and Ferguson keen to get as many minutes as possible under his player's belt, he decided he would not only play him at York but also in a reserve game against Leeds United.

So Bootham Crescent was the unlikely venue of Cantona's first away game since Selhurst Park. A York official told the press: "It's just a normal game. Whether it was Cantona or Maradona makes no difference – no player needs protection here. Our security is more than sufficient to cater for the game and we're not employing anybody more than usual."

Ferguson's team came close but not close enough. Their 3-1 win at York saw them eliminated by one goal. Cantona had played his part but couldn't inspire his team to ultimate victory.

He also ignored provocation from midfielder Nigel Pepper. "I had a couple of dips at Eric, and he didn't react," Pepper said. "There was no intent, but I still got him. Eric didn't even say a word to me. I can applaud him now for not reacting… he's such a good player, people will always get tight and try to hit him. In any game the knocks are going to come his way."

Ferguson was more frustrated with the close attention paid to Eric by someone else on the pitch: "I always remember the referee Jeff Winter kept following him about the pitch," the United boss said in 2006. "It was amazing, it's the thing that always sticks out about the return leg, he kept following him about as if to say, 'I'm ready for him!' It was pathetic."

Of course, referees did not need to push their own name into the spotlight. That would come naturally as a consequence of handling the first few games of Cantona's comeback. They were being sought out by journalists to provide some extra explanation that might reveal the truth about Eric Cantona and his explosive personality. Those reporters were in luck as the referee for the forthcoming Chelsea away game was Alan Wilkie, he who had dismissed Cantona at Selhurst Park. The excitement to speak to him was almost too much.

Wilkie's comments make interesting reading: "If it is offered,

I will be only too glad to shake Eric's hand. I'm looking forward to the game... I have refereed Eric in three matches, including his first-ever game in England, and I've never had to speak to him before that Palace game. The main reason everyone loves refereeing United is because there's such a cup tie atmosphere."

Those cup upsets had caused a ripple on the club's valuation. But the long-term forecast seemed solid. United were due to renegotiate their kit deal and the 55,000 capacity from 1996 would also increase revenue. The short-term forecast, and whether United could recover from their mixed start to the season even with Cantona back in the fold, seemed less clear.

The decision taken to play Eric in the reserve game was made partly because the French FA had excluded him from their team. So Eric lined up on Saturday 7th October against the second string of his former club. The game was held at Old Trafford rather than Bury's Gigg Lane, where the reserves usually played. 21,502 turned out to witness Eric's participation, where goalkeeper Kevin Pilkington recalled the instruction was to feed the ball to the Frenchman at every opportunity.

But there were few. After just 17 minutes, Eric was hurt by a challenge from Leeds player Jason Blunt. He was immediately taken off nursing a knee injury. It was a precaution, but a sound one, as Cantona was forced to miss the Manchester derby after the international break. Cantona waved apologetically to supporters as he came off and even arranged an apology to go over the public address system at half-time.

Come the derby, City were brushed aside in a poor game decided by an early Paul Scholes goal. *The Observer* described it as the "youngest United team in memory". Meanwhile, Eric's media blackout left press searching for ways to weave him into their narrative. The game at Chelsea was fairly easy – his first league game away since returning, reuniting with the referee who sent him off and coming face-to-face with the man who had been his strike partner back in January.

Ahead of the game, Mark Hughes told reporters: "The hostility from crowds to United players is worse than anything I've ever experienced, even when I was playing for Barcelona … the venom from opposition fans reached a higher level than ever in the wake of the incident at Crystal Palace last season.

"The backlash to Eric made it worse. A lot of people wanted United to fall flat on their faces. That feeling has probably carried on now.… Eric will have to live with that. The one big difference I've noticed from being a Chelsea player is that there isn't anything like the hostility shown towards me now in away games that I felt when I was playing for United."

He said that his old colleague must be protected: "It's talent like Eric's we need to nurture and protect. People are trying to destroy his kind of ability. Hopefully, he won't be sparked into doing anything silly again in the future."

Cantona was back in the team for the game at Chelsea and would play virtually every minute until the end of the season. For *Match of the Day*, Clive Tyldesley observed: "Every mood and every move will be monitored by the camera lens."

What United needed was an early goal to take the sting out of the atmosphere. It came in the fourth minute. The travelling fans had already gone through one rendition of *Ooh Aah Cantona* when Giggs, Keane and Neville combined to find the Frenchman on the edge of the area. Eric dummied, and the ball went to Scholes, who squirmed a shot into the corner.

Cantona had a more present role in the second six minutes later. If Wimbledon in 1994 saw Irwin score as close to the perfect goal in Cantona's vision as any he'd participated in, then this one comes pretty close. In an interview with ESPN in 2011, Cantona was asked about the 'tiki-taka' style played by Barcelona at the time. "This is nothing new," he said. "It goes back to Cruyff and Total Football. It's all about knowing what you're going to do when you receive the ball. Who is free, where is the space, always with one touch."

There was no less craft in this goal. Ryan Giggs and Cantona tried elaborate flicks to find a team-mate in space. But no pass – from over 20 in the move – was wasted, and only Andy Cole in the outfield did not touch the ball. In the penultimate moment, Cantona was played the ball in space. The jeers from the home fans were drowned out by the roar from the United fans as the Frenchman's wonderfully timed, stabbed through-ball found Scholes, who smashed it in.

Mark Hughes did pull a goal back, but that only provoked a late flurry; Ryan Giggs scoring a wonderful solo effort before Cantona and Cole combined to get a goal for Brian McClair. Alex Ferguson later described the first half as the best his team had played all season.

It was another case of meeting familiar faces in the following game as Middlesbrough travelled to Old Trafford, coached by Bryan Robson, who had earned them promotion. He had signed former United stopper Gary Walsh, who pulled off a fabulous early save to deny Cantona a brilliant goal.

In what appeared to be a fairly good-tempered game, Roy Keane suddenly took offence to a tackle from Jan-Aage Fjortoft, and lashed out with a punch. One could only presume he had been missing the aggressive old days. He was sent off with not even 30 minutes on the clock. Ferguson opted for a tighter midfield three and his team scored just before half-time.

With three minutes remaining, Cantona (described by the *Telegraph* as the game's "major creative influence") thrilled Old Trafford with the sort of control from a high ball that John O'Kane had previously drooled about. He then used his frame majestically to create space; adjusting his body so that his through ball to Andy Cole had enough power on it.

Cole's shot nearly didn't; it bounced just in front of the goal, and looked as if it was going wide, but the ball hit a divot which pushed it into the net to seal the victory. It was the slice of luck that the former Newcastle player had needed.

Cole, much like Cantona, had borne much of the responsibility for United's failure to win the league in 1995. For the Englishman it seemed more personal, as the doubts concerned his ability. His status as English football's record signing meant more was expected than 12 goals in 18 games (five of those coming in one match, the 9-0 win against Ipswich Town) and his failure to put one of multiple opportunities past Ludek Miklosko on the final day of the season was tainting his reputation. It hadn't helped that as soon as he'd joined, the team had immediately lost their best player to suspension.

But now Cantona was back and there were question marks about the compatibility of the pair. On one occasion at Stamford Bridge, Cole threw up his arms in frustration after Cantona played him the ball in an area he didn't want it. It was clear, though, that if Cole wanted to succeed it would be he who would have to adapt to Eric.

But it's safe to say that Eric was amongst those critics if Alex

Ferguson's observations are to be believed. In his first auto-biography in 1999, Ferguson wrote of Cole: "He had hardly arrived when Cantona was suspended. Upon Cole's eventual linking with the revered Frenchman, Cantona's body-language was as acid as a Dorothy Parker putdown – but without the subtlety. Shrugs and grimaces erode confidence and Cole, not surprisingly losing his, became a butt of humour."

In his 2013 book, Ferguson said that "displeasure had been apparent" in Cole's relationship with Cantona, which seems a strong enough indication that the dislike was mutual.

Cole disputed that in Andy Mitten's book *Glory Glory*, saying: "He was the only player I saw who the manager never had a go at. We all went to a film premiere and were told to wear black ties. Eric turned up in a cream lemon suit with Nike trainers. The manager told him that he looked fantastic. I liked Eric and considered him friendly."

But the two failed to find any genuine compatibility. The wins and good football enjoyed over Southampton and Coventry City were mostly earned by the craft of Cantona in tandem with the new-look midfield.

After the 4-0 win at Highfield Road, Ferguson said: "They all played well but, again, I find myself picking out Cantona and Giggs. They are both having a massive influence this season. Ryan's contribution has been outstanding and Eric just possesses that composure which spreads throughout the side."

When United needed their forwards to work together, however, it was often their inability to do so which proved costly. A draw at Nottingham Forest was salvaged by a Cantona penalty and the *Mail* concluded: "All the possession in the world grants United nothing if Cole cannot fit more profitably into the passing shapes around him."

The former Newcastle man missed chances against Chelsea; Cantona looked less than impressed. Cole was eventually brought off with Ferguson later saying he thought his record buy had been careless, but reaffirmed his belief that he would become a "great goalscorer" for the club.

Cantona had at least found a rhythm with players like Butt, Beckham and Scholes, whose non-stop engines helped to create space for the Frenchman, even if the dynamic was not quite the same as when he had played as a central ringmaster, sending Kanchelskis away down the right or Giggs down the left. While the partnership up front wasn't working, Cantona was doing enough to prove that his own form wasn't the reason. He scored twice in a home draw with Sheffield Wednesday.

"Cantona was the best player on our team today," admitted Ferguson. "He was marvellous. He inspired everything we did that was good."

Ferguson was having to deal with injuries; Gary Pallister was out, Steve Bruce was playing through pain. Paul Parker was struggling, Roy Keane and Nicky Butt were missing. United went to Anfield depleted and lost by two goals but that did not spare them a dressing down from Ferguson. Unusually, the hairdryer was kept on for the press afterwards.

"I don't think the players showed the passion required," he blasted. "When we play Liverpool I expect the players to fight. Particularly in the first half, it was the most lifeless United performance for years, especially coming to this place."

It wouldn't get any better the following week. United were beaten at Elland Road on Christmas Eve. Newcastle United were league leaders and had a 10-point advantage over Ferguson's side; the two teams would meet on the 27th. It was the third huge game in a row and Cantona was quiet again;

this time, though, his team-mates did put in a shift worthy of the shirt and picked up an impressive 2-0 win.

Pallister and Bruce were now both out. David May picked up an injury and United were already making do with Gary Neville at centre-half. Ferguson needed to make an emergency signing and noted French defender William Prunier had been released by Bordeaux. Knowing Cantona had played with Prunier at Auxerre, Ferguson asked if he should sign him, and Eric gave his positive recommendation. A trial was arranged.

On December 30 1995, Prunier played in a 2-1 win over QPR – and the talk was about him after the game. Writing for *The Independent*, Alan Nixon observed: "Prunier's passing was superior to that of any other defender at United... he would be a perfect asset for the moment."

Prunier spoke about his time in Manchester to *Le Parisien* in 2019, being taken aback by the affection United fans had for Cantona. "When I left Auxerre, Eric was a guy that the whole of France seemed to hate and who was booed on every pitch, and when I met him again, I found a God, because Cantona in Manchester, he really was God," Prunier said.

"I didn't stay there long, but I had the time to live through something special. It was during my first game against QPR. The crowd started singing *Ooh Aah Cantona*, and then *La Marseillaise*. I knew it was for Eric and not for me, but it gave me goosebumps... In Manchester, they saw his charisma as genius. When I say he was a God, I'm not exaggerating.

"One day, we went to the restaurant. People recognised him, but no one bothered us during the meal. A long and silent queue started to form next to our table. In the end, everyone asked him, one by one, for an autograph in the utmost respect."

As for Prunier, rarely have consecutive games yielded such

wildly different perspectives. From possessing passing ability "superior to any other United defender" to looking "like a gendarme asked to do traffic duty at Piccadilly Circus", as the *Mail* described him at Tottenham Hotspur. United lost 4-1.

Ferguson, who had wanted to see how Prunier fared against Teddy Sheringham, now wanted another look. Prunier's representatives refused another trial. Unlike Sheffield Wednesday a few years previously, Manchester United would not live to regret their missed opportunity.

Cantona scored a late equaliser against First Division Sunderland in the FA Cup but it was widely agreed his performance levels had dipped in recent weeks. A 0-0 draw at home to Aston Villa on 13th January left United nine points off the pace. Worse still, Newcastle had a game in hand.

That day must have been a tough one for Cantona. He was visited by France boss Aime Jacquet and coach Henri Emile to discuss Eric's return to the French team. Their issue was that in Cantona's absence, Youri Djorkaeff and Zinedine Zidane were both shining in the sort of areas Cantona loved to occupy.

The role available was one of the lone striker, but a player whose responsibilities, as described in Phillipe Auclair's biography, resembled "a kind of advanced water-carrier who was expected to disrupt the back line." Cantona refused; when Jacquet asked if he would change his mind if Zidane or Djorkaeff were unavailable, Eric said he would discuss it.

Ferguson later conceded that Eric hadn't been at his best. "Yes, we've had the dip. More than one. There've been periods when his form's been off, and then he's come back quite well," he said. "So there's been inconsistency. It's what we expected."

That could have been down to the different shapes played by the manager. He'd tried three in defence again at White

Hart Lane. Then he came up against Sunderland, who fielded a five-man defence to crowd out Cantona, with Ferguson admitting "the way we played in the first half didn't suit him" while insisting he planned to build around Eric's strengths.

"I haven't asked Eric to do anything different," he said. "His game is about movement, floating into spaces where defenders can't find him. He still does that. But we've got to get back to playing with two wide men. We've tried one or two things to give us penetration on the right. We played Eric with Paul Scholes and Andy Cole, which didn't work at home. It all got too congested. But it's been hard to find the right formation."

Ferguson said he had seen changes in Eric: "He's still quiet, but what's happened has been the kind of experience that can't help but have an effect on your life. They say even a bad experience can be good for you, and maybe some good has come out of it. Perhaps his attitude to injustice has been altered.

"Since he came back into the team there have been refereeing decisions that he hasn't agreed with but he's chosen not to argue. I've seen him walk quietly away from incidents that might have drawn a different reaction before.

"Nobody's tried anything. The fans he can handle. But the nice surprise has been the other players. And the referees, who've treated him fairly and generally haven't tried to make a name for themselves. In fact there was one who did something unusual. He made a decision Eric didn't like but, when play stopped again, he quietly took him aside and explained it. That impressed me. He's been magnificent in training, just like he always has. It's been difficult for him. But when he gets his consistency back, his best form will be back, too."

It's impossible to know just how defining that meeting with Jacquet on 13th January 1996 was. Cantona once famously said that he "played against the idea of losing" so of course when he had discussed potentially playing for France in the 1994 World Cup and the European Championship, he would have envisaged his participation as a successful one.

In 2007, Cantona claimed he would have at least continued to the World Cup in 1998 if he had been selected for Euro 96. "And if we'd won the European Cup with Manchester, maybe I'd have carried on too," he said. But an interview in 1996 was perhaps closer to the truth. "When I do quit football it'll be at the very top," he said. "I certainly wouldn't contemplate playing for teams that are less successful than Manchester United. Nor would I contemplate playing for the reserves. Once I feel I'm not at the top any more, I'll quit football."

It's possible Cantona could have continued as he said. He acted on impulse, and if there is one consistent thread in Eric's personality it is that he embraced the emotions of each journey he went on. So just how true was the idea he could have been done with football if France had qualified for the World Cup and United had enjoyed further success? It does not seem unreasonable, at least.

And suddenly, you are left with a conclusion you cannot escape. Eric Cantona did not view football as a career to be endured in the long-term. He would not linger on the pitch until his body gave up. He was on the hunt for the most glorious farewell he could make in the sport.

# A Reformed Character?

**A** game in London, at West Ham United – a team featuring former foe John Moncur – was the perfect setting to test the theory that Eric Cantona had become a reformed character since his suspension.

Neil Harman, writing for the *Daily Mail* (and one of Cantona's harshest critics in January) had said in November 1996: "He's not quite angelic, but such a sense of serenity has descended on Cantona that United can be carried to the Premiership title on the cultured spread of his wings."

Manchester United's form since then probably gave Harman cause to reconsider part of that prediction, but events at Upton Park only served to reinforce some of it. "Has English football ever experienced such a transformation, from the devil incarnate to docile dogooder?" Harman wrote in his report.

Cantona had sported a newly-shaved head in the previous game, the FA Cup replay against Sunderland. He had done this in his early days in France, explaining his reasoning to *France Football* magazine. "I'd do it again," he'd said. "I regret other people's reactions, but they'll never make me regret my actions, or prevent me from fulfilling my whims, my desires, my fantasies. If a great painter shaves his head, they'll say, 'That's normal, he's a creator, he's a bit crazy.' In football, people are too used to seeing healthy boys, with nice haircuts, who weigh everything they say…"

It's probably fair to conclude this was an act of defiance. A reminder of his individuality. It's also fair to connect it with the meeting with Aime Jacquet. Cantona, asked to be something other than what came naturally to him? No, that couldn't be. It was time to remind the world who Eric Cantona was.

The game at West Ham got off to the perfect start. In the eighth minute, Eric met a cross from Giggs to finish at an angle. This was enough to win the game, but the headline story came later. Referee Steve Lodge missed a two-foot lunge by Julian Dicks on Andy Cole in the 75th minute. Cole was furious and got a yellow for dissent; it took Cantona to calm him down and move him away before he got sent off.

Moncur felt he had seen a different Cantona. "My thinking was that maybe the long time he had out of the game helped him mature," he says. "That he couldn't afford to see the red mist so often. The last thing he would have wanted would be to spend more time not playing and that incident made me think that maybe he had changed a little bit. Maybe he felt like he had something to give back to United, they stood by him, Alex Ferguson really did.

"He wasn't much of a communicator in matches. He never gave you verbal, never really acknowledged banter, although perhaps he was storing it up, bottling it up. He held his cards close to his chest. The times I played against him, I never heard him arguing. He let his actions speak for themselves."

If that was the first real test of Cantona's self-control, more were to follow. A trip to Reading in the FA Cup, for example, where one home fan threw a coin at him, only to miss and hit a linesman. It wasn't the only item thrown. "It was the story of the banana skin that wasn't," read the report in the *Daily Mail*. "United's sure-footed progress was conspicuous, not only for Eric Cantona's polite return of the half-eaten banana some ignoramus threw at him in the second half."

Cantona's answer was to score a goal in a 3-0 win. Referee Jeff Winter commended the player, saying: "If this was supposed to be a test for Eric, he passed with flying colours."

In spite of this, Cantona only seemed to fall more deeply in love with English football. His exile from the French national team would make him a champion of the England team, and he was happy to praise the quality in the domestic game. "English football has its detractors," he said in his book *Cantona on Cantona*. "Critics have claimed it is not up to the level of its international counterparts. I disagree. I've always thought it was among the best in the world. English football is the best technically, up there with the German game – and much better than in Italy, France or Spain."

A return to Selhurst Park to face Wimbledon was next on the horizon. Eric would later insist the perception of this dramatic change in his personality was blown out of all proportion.

"I often get asked about the change in my temperament. The truth is there hasn't been such a big change," he said. "People think I've suddenly learnt to feel at ease with myself, but I was never ill at ease in the first place. Everyone has their bad moments. I do, however, have a little more experience now.

"I seem to be able to cope better with situations. I'd hesitate to say that what happened was a mistake, or that it was foolish or silly. It was far too complicated to be characterised in such simplistic terms. There was a time when I would lose my temper regularly, when I felt that I had to stand up and say something about things that made me angry... but not anymore."

Was he protesting too much? There was one thing that remained surely true in his insistence; Eric was led by impulse. He was also motivated by fresh challenges and United's regeneration had certainly presented that. This new role as mentor was one he had embraced but in the coming weeks and months, Eric was to step up his game a level.

Cantona's journey towards redemption had a few more symbolic milestones at Selhurst Park. In the 15th minute, when Steve Bruce had to leave the pitch, Eric took the captain's armband. He scored the game's decisive goal in the 70th minute, putting away a header and swinging on the pole behind the goal.

This time, there was no aggression from the home crowd. He scored a fourth goal to seal United's win. He decided not to tempt fate by celebrating in the same fashion; just as well, as the Dons had been charitable hosts, with owner Sam Hammam having invited Eric's father Albert over as a special guest.

Joe Kinnear was equally gracious afterwards. "People may say that he's a lesser player because of the way he's controlling his temperament," he said. "But I don't see it that way. I just wish he was playing for us."

Writing for *The Guardian*, David Lacey observed some changes: "Cantona is a different player, but United are a different team. The mood has changed. Ince and Hughes have gone. These days the football does more work than the eyeball."

United continued to pick up pace. Four impressive wins against local rivals followed, with Cantona involved in a major way. He was chief creator in home wins against Blackburn and Everton, and also played his part in a 6-0 demolition of Bolton at Burnden Park, but his only goal from the eleven his team managed in those four games was a controversial penalty in the Manchester derby in the FA Cup fifth round.

Five league wins in succession had kept United in the hunt to peg Newcastle back. The gap at the top, heading into a seismic game between first and second at St James' Park, was four points, though the Magpies had a game in hand.

Cantona had been quiet in the first game back in December, but, having helped his colleagues have so much of the glory, it was the Frenchman's time to return to centre stage.

In the 50th minute of a game where the hosts had spurned chance after chance, Cantona's moment came; United built up on the edge of the box, Phil Neville clipped in a cross and Eric was there at the back post to volley back across goal and into the net. Cantona was the match winner but man of the match was Peter Schmeichel; that description of 'spurned' is hard on the Newcastle forwards, who found the 'Great Dane' to be a brick wall. In Schmeichel's autobiography, he said: "Cantona and I had a standing agreement which went more or less as follows: 'Peter, I score one and you keep a clean sheet, okay'?"

That agreement made a huge impact on United's fortunes, on and off the pitch. The result at St James' Park saw the club's shares soar by 13p to 280p each (from their season low of 197p after the League Cup exit) – the value of the club had increased by £7.9m overnight, and by 42 per cent over the season.

A week later, Cantona scored the decider in the FA Cup quarter-final against Southampton. He then set up a goal for Lee Sharpe to seal the win. "The Frenchman with a fuse as notoriously short as his shaven hair would not be everyone's obvious choice for the calm head in a storm," the *Express* reported, "but on a night when United were forced to navigate choppy waters, King Eric proved his side's leader of men."

At Loftus Road, United took on relegation-threatened QPR. The hosts took a shock lead with a deflected goal. Cantona kept up his end of the bargain, netting a dramatic late equaliser. Earlier, the Frenchman had been visibly frustrated with Cole, remonstrating with him after a miscommunication. Cantona could not comprehend Cole's single-mindedness.

"Your colleagues are doing the best they can to improve themselves; it's up to you never to let them down. That's respect," he later said, though he was speaking in general terms and not specifically about Cole. "If someone's on my team I expect respect from them and I give them respect in return."

The issue appeared to be Cole's insistence he ought to be the figurehead of the attack, the finisher, which was in direct conflict with Cantona's feelings of it being a team game. It was more than being aggravated at a technically inferior player.

Against Arsenal in the next league game, Cantona was like a man possessed. "I've said in the past that I could play single-handedly against eleven players and win," he said later. "I believe in myself. Sometimes it's crazy, I know… No matter what the situation, I always think I have a chance of winning."

Eric was the best player, creating numerous opportunities – United had more than 25 shots on goal, and created more half-chances which Cole could not get on the end of. But Cantona, as so often, took responsibility. Seizing a headed clearance, Eric chested the ball down and thrashed it over David Seaman on the half-volley with such ferocity that it smashed down off the crossbar and into the net. It was akin to an adult grabbing the ball in a game between toddlers and showing them how to score. At the other end, Schmeichel made a number of saves late on to preserve this latest 1-0 win.

Gary Pallister was in awe of the performance levels. "Victory at St James' Park signalled the start of an astonishing run of six successive games in which Cantona scored, many of them the only goal," he said. "Equally sensational was a sudden volley which looped over David Seaman to beat Arsenal… Big players rise to big occasions, and Eric was doing that twice a week during that unforgettable spring."

Alex Ferguson was delighted at the performance, describing it as "one of the best of the season" – and the goal, describing Cantona's body shape as "thrilling… like a ballet dancer."

United were second as the whistle went against Arsenal but were top before they played another game; Newcastle's 2-0 defeat at Highbury meant their goal difference was now one inferior to United's.

Tottenham came to Old Trafford and Ferguson was right to predict "another tough game". United were not as brilliant as they had been against Arsenal, and again needed the intervention of their talisman. Just after half-time, the ball landed at the feet of Nicky Butt, who passed it to Gary Neville.

Neville clipped it into Cantona's chest just in front of the centre circle. The Frenchman controlled it imperiously, turning to face goal as if he had all the time in the world. As if the two Spurs players snapping at his heels didn't exist.

"Collar turned up, back straight, chest stuck out, he glided into the arena as if he owned the fucking place," Roy Keane once famously said of his team-mate. "This was his stage. He loved it, the crowd loved him. His finishing was deadly. We'd give him a bollocking for not tracking back. Then, just when exasperation was being felt, Eric would produce a bit of magic to turn the game. He'd seize half a chance, and bang, it was in the back of the net. I'd never seen anyone finish like him."

This was one such moment. Eric advanced, approaching the penalty area. Sol Campbell hesitated then committed with a block; the United player feinted to the left, leaving the young defender unable to react. Cantona took on the shot as if it was his comfortable side, the precision on the effort leaving goalkeeper Ian Walker helpless. United won 1-0.

It was the latest in a series of goals that were as enjoyable to watch as they were crucial. "They were fabulous, and some of them he created all on his own, like the one against Spurs, when he ran from deep," said Gary Pallister.

"Compared with the speed and flair against Arsenal on Wednesday, this was a lean-footed Cantona with his fifth goal in five games," read the report in *The Guardian*, while *The Times* said: "The picture is becoming clearer. When the championship jigsaw is complete, it will surely reveal a central image. Eric Cantona of course, for this brilliant Frenchman seems determined to bring the trophy back on his own."

Ferguson's team were three points clear, and though Newcastle had two games in hand, there was a mental shift they would struggle to recover from. From being rank outsiders 12 weeks ago, United were now favourites with most bookmakers to regain their title. That stunning upward trajectory continued off the pitch. As United prepared for their FA Cup semi-final against Chelsea, there were fresh reports that the club had "increased its market value 65 per cent to £158m since August". Much of that was due to the recent agreement of a new £60m five year deal with Umbro.

Football was enjoying a boom the likes of which nobody had predicted. When BSkyB had first won the television rights to broadcast the Premier League in 1992, they cost £191.5m. Those rights were due to be renegotiated and were tipped to top £500m. When BSkyB again won the rights in 1997 for a continued deal, they had to pay an eye-watering £670m.

There was no denying that the star, the man who defined the storyline, was Eric Cantona. The interest levels were reflected by the skyrocketing financial figures. The Frenchman's own influence had been pivotal. He was as important to the Premier League as he was to Manchester United.

Back to actual sporting matters, the Chelsea-United game at Villa Park was dubbed a battle between the foreign stars. Cantona, of course in the red corner, while Dutch legend Ruud Gullit had enjoyed a fantastic year at Stamford Bridge since arriving on a free transfer. On the comparisons between the pair, Gullit insisted: "That's interesting for you and your readers, but it's not interesting for me because I know that the game isn't going to be resolved by two players."

Technically speaking, he was right. But for once the narrative was proven with Eric and Ruud the most influential players on the pitch. Gullit scored Chelsea's goal, but Cantona came up trumps with a display Ferguson described as "just magnificent". He was unfortunate not to score twice. The first, an inventive volley from distance which rattled against a post, and the second, an effort that seemed as if it might go in via the woodwork before Andy Cole made sure at the far post.

United then got a winner through David Beckham while Eric had the last word, popping up to deny John Spencer an equaliser with a goal-line clearance. United were through to the FA Cup final for the third year in succession.

Cantona, who had signed that renewed deal on reduced terms less than a year ago, had already repaid any debt he had to Manchester United and Alex Ferguson. He could have been forgiven another kung-fu kick, because even if this wiped another few million off the club's value, it barely touched the amount it had multiplied since the player arrived from Leeds in November 1992. He could have walked off into the sunset in April 1996 and we would probably still be discussing the merits of an argument which holds Eric Cantona as the single most influential player in the history of the British game.

Those young team-mates who had shown vibrancy in Eric's absence were now blossoming with a technical style which had bettered the apparently cosmopolitan offerings at Stamford Bridge. Twice against Chelsea, United's young stars had put on a dazzling display of football, with Cantona at the heart of it. They had shown a composure beyond their years and a culture that should have been beyond them. Except it wasn't.

Earlier in this book the term osmosis was used to describe Eric's influence on his team-mates. It was probably even more relevant in 1996 than it was in 1993. Back then, there were senior players raising their own game. Now, these youngsters had absorbed the daily lessons in technique, yes, but also in conduct, patience and composure. The three years of behind-the-scenes education were paying off.

And still, even in this period of maturity, Cantona's exceptional form made him the headline act. "He is performing like a player possessed," Alex Ferguson said ahead of the Manchester derby.

United came into the game with the boost of Newcastle's loss to Liverpool in a 4-3 thriller and once more showed their cool heads thanks to Cantona, who scored an early penalty and then created goals for Andy Cole and Ryan Giggs in a 3-2 win. Two days later, Cantona scored the only goal in a game against Coventry City at Old Trafford (a match remembered mostly for an horrific injury to City defender David Busst).

These weeks saw the fledglings get another important lesson. The Coventry game had been a strange one that United appeared to sleepwalk through; it was a similar scenario at The Dell but the opponents here were fighting for their lives in a relegation scrap and stormed into a 3-0 half-time lead.

When they came out for the second half, United were in their other change strip of blue and white, having started the game in grey. It made little difference, though Ryan Giggs scored a late consolation. It was a reminder for the youngsters that quality enough was not alone. If United did not match the work-rate of their opponent, they could get beaten comfortably.

That said, United's defensive shape hadn't helped. With Gary Pallister injured, Ferguson plumped for Gary Neville in the middle, with Denis Irwin on the right and Lee Sharpe on the left. The unfamiliar combination, led by Steve Bruce, did not work. "When you defend as badly as that, you are going to lose games," said Ferguson, who shut down talk of the kit, saying it was simply because the players didn't like the grey strip.

It was fitting that United faced Leeds at Old Trafford a

few days later. Ferguson had complained about Howard Wilkinson's team apparently putting in more of an effort against his side than other teams following that Christmas Eve defeat at Elland Road (Leeds had just lost 6-2 at Sheffield Wednesday) and was presumably thinking along the same lines after their resolute performance in this game.

The Yorkshire side had, since Christmas, lost 2-0 at Everton, 5-0 at Liverpool, 3-0 at Aston Villa, and four days before playing United, had shipped four goals down at Chelsea. Yet not only were they digging out a draw against Manchester United, they were doing it without their goalkeeper – defender Lucas Radebe had been in goal for most of the game.

Cantona once more appeared frustrated with Cole's inability to convert chances. Ferguson agreed, bringing off his record signing for Paul Scholes. Immediately Cantona played him the ball; Scholes was tackled, but the ball rolled to Keane, who finally found a way past Radebe.

Ferguson was irate afterwards: "I just cannot understand Leeds. Howard does not deserve his players to play like that. If they played like that every week they would be in the top six. It is pathetic, because it seemed like it was only against Manchester United. No wonder managers get the sack. Howard deserves better. Leeds play Newcastle in their next game and I would like to see the video of that. We have watched Leeds in our last three games and I could not identify them."

In a television interview Ferguson then said he felt the players were "cheating" their manager and said: "When it comes to Newcastle, you wait and see the difference."

The difference in Ferguson's favour this season had been Eric Cantona. It was a feeling shared by most; it was revealed on the eve of United's final home game of the season that Eric had been named the Football Writers' Player of the Year. The Sunday newspapers were full of tributes for Cantona, who – regardless of what happened in the title race – had already, in most people's eyes, achieved redemption.

Reporter Neil Harman had been converted in the space of a year. "He changed, so why couldn't we?" he said. "The coronation of Cantona justified both his astonishing meta-morphosis and that of those who were his chief accusers." Not everyone agreed. Sportswriter James Lawton said Cantona was "not, suddenly, a combination of Superman and Mother Teresa" despite being "unquestionably Footballer of the Year."

Emlyn Hughes, he who had been so critical back in 1992, blasted: "There is no way Cantona should have been named Footballer of the Year. The fact he has picked up the award is an indictment to all the past winners."

Alex Ferguson, of course, was more generous. "A lot of players come to me and ask if I can sort out their problems but not Eric," Ferguson told the *Daily Mail*. "He has sorted things out himself. The end result tells you everything about his moral fibre. This is a man who possesses unbelievable determination. The players love him… A lot of players can never experience the pleasure of having such a wonderful player. I was not going to kick him out. I was determined to see it through."

Cantona himself said: "I am proud and privileged to have been voted Footballer of the Year. It is a tremendous honour for me and my country… it is also a great tribute to the players at Manchester United."

One player not buoyed by the mood was Andy Cole, who was finally dropped, with Paul Scholes brought in. It was a tough decision for Ferguson, but turned into a fine tactical move. United played Nottingham Forest knowing if they won their games by big margins they would win the league. So they set out to do just that. Cantona thrived alongside Scholes, inspiring those around him to put on a display that wowed Old Trafford, which boasted a new record attendance of 53,926.

"As United struggled for the breakthrough, Cantona repeatedly made the space which eased the desperate pressure on passing outlets from midfield," reported the *Express*. The *Mirror*'s take: "Cantona showed why he deserved those votes from his biggest critics with another gem of a display."

For a while, the Frenchman let the youngsters take the spotlight, with Beckham (two), Scholes and Giggs making it 4-0. But Cantona saved the best for last – having failed to execute a through ball, he instead intercepted the interception, beating Colin Cooper for pace, chesting the ball down and then half-volleying it past Mark Crossley.

Ferguson celebrated as if it were the match-winner, knowing every goal was reverberating on Tyneside like the punch of a heavyweight. Cantona's might well have been the knockout blow for Newcastle, who now had to win at Leeds and Forest by a combined tally of seven goals just to have parity on the final day. If Ferguson's theory about Leeds was proved correct, then Keegan's men might get all those goals at Elland Road; but Wilkinson's men forced Newcastle to work hard for a 1-0 victory. Keegan then unleashed an outburst live on Sky Sports where he responded angrily to Ferguson's comments and declared he would "love it if we beat them, love it!"

More box office television for Sky, then. No matter what the result at Forest, the league title race would go down to the last day of the season, inviting a new flood of subscribers to the only place they could watch English league football.

Newcastle drew at Forest to change the landscape.

United now only needed to avoid defeat at Bryan Robson's Middlesbrough (sparking conspiracy theories) unless Keegan's side could muster a hatful of goals. The occasion passed with far less drama than the year before, though this time Cantona took a back seat.

David May was in for the injured Bruce, who now faced a race to be fit for the FA Cup final against Liverpool, so Eric had inherited the captain's armband. May scored early on. Nerves were settled, especially when news came through that Spurs had taken the lead at Newcastle.

The Magpies levelled, but Andy Cole came off the bench to score with his first touch at the Riverside to set aside any remaining doubts. The team now played with style and rounded off the win with a fine goal from Ryan Giggs.

Manchester United were champions again.

# A Final Flourish

Eric Cantona made an exception to his self-imposed ban on speaking to the press in FA Cup final week of 1996. This transpired, probably, for a number of reasons. First of all, an obligation part of the tradition of the competition. Secondly, a softening of his stance considering that British journalists had named him their Player of the Year. And thirdly, events in the week building up to the last league game.

Matthew Simmons was in court to face his own charges related to his behaviour that night at Selhurst Park. It was alleged he'd provoked Cantona with racist language. Prosecuting lawyer Jeffrey McCann, on his last day in court before retirement, asked magistrates to ban Simmons from all football grounds. He was then attacked by Simmons, according to *The Guardian*, "grabbing him around the neck, trying to haul him over a table and appearing to kick him in the chest."

Simmons later apologised but was sentenced to a week in prison. In an interview with *Hello!* magazine, it was clear

Cantona felt Simmons' true colours had been revealed. "The hooligan? His behaviour shows he's not all together. I don't want to talk too much about him, that would give him too much importance," Cantona said.

"The hardest thing was having to put up with the endless comments, the swift judgments, the resounding criticism. My family were shocked but they were also there. Every time I go through this kind of experience I react the same way.

"First I feel like going away, escaping. Very quickly pride and maybe a deep sense of honour urges me to take action. Then I can stand tall and face up to it. I'm not easily beaten. The easiest part was the community service. I found myself going beyond the stipulated commitment. I devoted myself to these kids. I hope I did bring some light into their lives. As for United, you know we made up for it this year. I'd set my heart on it. We owed it to them."

In the *Express*, Cantona said: "I wanted to win the Premiership title for Alex Ferguson and it's exactly the same with the FA Cup. I have tried to pay back everyone at Manchester United. As long as I am in England, I hope to win the title every year..."

He also spoke to *L'Equipe*, saying: "I've signed and that means I'll stay, to be honest and faithful to those who surround me. I can't think of any reason that could make me change my mind... My confidence dates from the day United got me to sign up again. I have tried to pay back Alex Ferguson in kind. I tried to pay them back, him and my friends in the team."

He told the publication that he was resigned to missing Euro 96. "I've got good friends in the French team and I do hope that France will go far with or without me," he said. "I stay French in my blood and in my heart."

Finally, Cantona was asked by the BBC to do another

feature interview for their final coverage. He sat down with Des Lynam to discuss the events since January 1995.

On winning the league: "The first one with Manchester was great, this one was very important for the club after last season, and very important for myself, because I had a lot of things to prove after... well, everybody knows, last year."

On some good coming out of Selhurst Park: "I always try to put things in that way. I think we learn from everything, and a bad thing can be turned (into a) good thing. It's very difficult at the moment but in the future, we look to put the future under the sun."

On how persuasive Ferguson had to be to keep him at the club: "He just asked me if I wanted to leave English football because he knew it was a difficult time for me, but I just said no. But he didn't try to persuade me. I wanted to stay. Just... I was close to signing somewhere else because I wasn't sure if Manchester United wanted me to stay, because I receive a lot of critics, and them too. I just wanted to stay...

"When I arrived here I felt 'now I am in a big club, a great club'. I knew I had a lot to prove but I wasn't afraid about it. I'm very confident, always... No, I don't think I have really changed, not really. I just do what I've always done. I just try to live in harmony with myself and perhaps the way I now play."

On whether the cup final would be less pressurised because of the league win: "Yeah, I think so. I think, last season we lost in the final because we didn't win the league the week before..."

"Mind you, you weren't playing," Lynam interrupted.

"Yeah, but... it was my team-mates, it was me. It's like a big family."

On how he felt about the departures of Ince, Kanchelskis and Hughes: "I'm a true optimist," he responded. "I think I can win a game if I play only on my own against eleven players, so I'm worried about nothing. But I respect them, though, because we had a lot of great times together but life is like that. Before us, it was a life, afterwards, it will be another one..."

On winning the Champions League: "It is important for us and for English football, or nobody will remember us."

"And what about after that?" Lynam posed.

"When we win I want to stay in football, when I lose, I want to quit!" Cantona laughed. "But... I don't know. Maybe a manager, or maybe something else."

Lynam asked Eric about his relationship with the United fans. He said: "I respect them very much. I love them. They never stopped singing. I'll never forget it. Ever. I will try to give them the pleasure they need, every time."

"For the next two years?"

"For the next two years. Or maybe longer... or maybe shorter. We never know in life. But I am very, very, very happy."

He was also in the business of making others very happy. After participating more than most in the media duties, Cantona might have felt entitled to keep more than his share of the proceeds of payments for those duties. The squad, as usual, pooled that money together, and gave each individual the chance to either take their share from the communal pot or leave it in a draw.

Most of the young players took their share but Paul Scholes and Nicky Butt stayed in the pot, as did the senior players. The bonus pot had been £15,000, but stood at £12,000 once the shares were removed, remembered Roy Keane.

"When the draw was made, Eric Cantona's name came out of the hat," Keane said. "He got his cheque. And plenty of stick. Next morning Eric arrived with two cheques made out to Paul and Nicky. This was their reward for taking the gamble, Eric explained. This was Eric to a tee. The unexpected, a touch of class, also an appreciation of the plight of two young lads more in need of money than himself."

According to Ferguson, the reason Cantona gave was: "Because they have balls."

Cantona, the leader of this squad without question, had joked about becoming a manager in some of the press coverage. Yet on the eve of the cup final, he provided advice which turned out to be just as crucial as the winning goal itself.

"I spent time with Eric Cantona and Peter Schmeichel figuring out how to deal with Steve McManaman," Ferguson recalled. "Eric suggested we drop Roy Keane in front of our back four to keep tabs on McManaman. It was an astute observation, which we followed; as a result, McManaman was silenced and we won what was a tedious, uneventful game when Eric scored the only goal. Eric's advice was crucial."

The game went almost exactly as planned. Keane was the man-of-the-match and played arguably his second best game ever for the club. United started brightly, but it soon became a stalemate. Andy Cole was taken off, with Ferguson hoping Scholes' introduction would reignite his team. Liverpool took off their own star striker, Stan Collymore, hoping that departing legend Ian Rush might have one last moment of destiny at the club. He did. Sort of.

But this was Cantona's story, and not Rush's.

United were just about the better team in a poor final. Liverpool could be hit with that old cliché of having 'not turned up' if only they hadn't arrived at Wembley in garish cream suits. With extra-time looming, Phil Babb sliced behind the goal. Beckham took the corner. David James got a fist on the ball, which hit Rush's chest and bounced out of the area.

The footage reveals the most remarkable thing. As Beckham swings the ball in, just as James comes for it but before he has connected, Cantona moves back. He stands wide-legged for a moment, watching the play unfold instead of getting amongst it. In the half-second between James' punch, Rush's chest and the first bounce, Cantona has retreated five yards.

The ball bounces again. Cantona's natural momentum carries him back a further yard – now just outside the penalty area, having been stood just above the penalty spot.

His body shape is perfect. He turns slightly and pulls his right foot back. David James remains on the floor. There is a narrow gap between David May and Jamie Redknapp on the edge of the six-yard box for the Frenchman to aim at, but the shot has to be inch-perfect. By the time he has connected, Rob Jones and John Scales have rushed to position their bodies between Redknapp and May; they are stood just one yard off the line and approximately two feet away from each other.

It is perfect. Rob Jones swings a leg, but the ball has already gone into the goal. There are still five minutes left to play, but Manchester United have won the FA Cup.

On the final whistle, broadcaster Clive Tyldesley grabbed an interview with Cantona and asked if it was the best moment of his career. "It was important," admitted the player. "After winning the Double two years ago, it was a great moment… now we can go on holiday. We can have a nice holiday."

Tyldesley said it was a big contrast to how he must have felt a year ago. "That's life," Eric smiled. "Up and down."

That may be so. But it was yet another up for Manchester United, thanks to the number seven. What had already been a quite remarkable comeback had ended with the most glorious conclusion, achieved in cinematic fashion.

Not befitting the script was the Liverpool supporter who spat at Cantona as he led the United team up the Wembley steps to collect the FA Cup. Cantona showed class by refusing to allow the incident to overshadow the day. "We all know the difference between Manchester United and Liverpool fans, but that is life, it does not matter," he said.

"It is not important. What is important is the last game and the last victory and we have won today, we are the first team to win the Double twice, so maybe today was more important than when we won the Double two years ago, but it was also important two years ago."

Cantona revealed he had asked Steve Bruce to lead the team up. "Steve has been injured and I feel very sad for him," Eric said. "I wanted him to pick up the cup but he did not want to. He said, 'I have done it before', but I tried to persuade him to go up. It was a great time for me going to collect it, and it has been a great season. There is more to come. I have got ambition and everybody here has ambition so we are never content.

"We are happy today, but we always look to the future and that is what makes it a great club, and I am very proud to be with a club like that. I always want to win like my friends. We know that it is very important that we try to win the European Cup next season. It is historic to win the double Double and next year we will try to win the European Cup, and the championship, that would be a great double. A treble Double!"

Gary Pallister was full of praise for Eric's contribution: "The sides cancelled each other out for most of the match, then Eric stepped forward to win it in the style we had come to expect from him. After all the crucial goals he had scored on the title run-in, it shouldn't have surprised anybody. What a goal it was! What a story for Eric."

Gary Neville, one of the youngsters who had done so well, also gave Cantona his due credit. "We'd done it with kids, though there is no doubting who made the greatest contribution," Neville said in his autobiography. "Eric was immense. We'd looked to him for leadership and he'd been incredible as a match-winner. Winning titles is all about teamwork, but there are a couple from my time – certainly that year, and also 2006/07 with Cristiano Ronaldo – when you are so indebted to one player that you feel like giving him your medal. That was Eric's championship."

Peter Schmeichel made a bold claim. "In actual fact, he was a better player on his return to the top flight," the goalkeeper said. "When he finally began to play again, he quickly demonstrated that he had learned how to control his temper."

However, Aime Jacquet, who had been at Wembley to witness the moment of majesty, resisted the temptation to select Cantona for Euro 96. The dream of winning a major championship with his country was over for Eric, who would have to make do with another push at the European Cup...

ｉｖｙ

# The
# Protégés

On his second return to Selhurst Park since January 1995, Eric Cantona had once more seemed set to take the headlines after scoring the opening goal in a routine win for Manchester United. The Frenchman showed exceptional control to bring down a pass before lashing a ferocious shot into the roof of the net. He smiled and raised his arms to receive the applause like an actor before the curtain goes down.

"One Manchester United goal of stunning brilliance changed the destiny of their opening game against Wimbledon," wrote Frank McGhee for *The Guardian*. "It seems almost unnecessary to add that it was scored by Eric Cantona."

The game was so comfortable that Alex Ferguson indulged in one of the rare luxuries; bringing Eric Cantona off for a rest, 15 minutes from the end.

The United bench was right in line with the halfway line. In the last minute, they all watched as Brian McClair nudged the ball towards David Beckham just inside his own half.

Beckham swung his left arm back and suddenly all inside the ground knew he was trying what he had attempted just a few minutes earlier; a frankly ridiculous attempt on goal.

That first effort had not troubled Neil Sullivan in the Wimbledon goal. But this one did. Sullivan was on the penalty spot as the ball floated in a perfect arc. He made a half-hearted jump towards it, but it was so fruitless that he didn't even extend his arms.

Beckham had scored one of the most extraordinary goals of all-time. He had been but a young pup desperate for League Cup opportunities when he saw Cantona try a similar shot at Stamford Bridge in September 1994. Players across the world had tried to replicate Pele's effort against Czechosolovakia in the 1970 World Cup, which had narrowly missed the target. Beckham's was the first high-profile success of its kind. A global superstar was launched.

Beckham stretched out his arms just as Cantona had earlier in the game, and smiled with the sort of cheeky arrogance that led you to believe he wasn't surprised by what he'd done. However, he couldn't contain the excitement once back in the United dressing room. Cantona congratulated him on his "beautiful" goal. Beckham had idolised Cantona so much that he had posters of him in his bedroom back at his digs as he dreamed of emulating his heroics. That day had come.

"I say how important it was for me in my career, but I was more happy about the fact Eric Cantona came up to me afterwards and said, 'Good goal'," Beckham said in 2013. "That was better than scoring the goal for me. He was a quiet man, Eric, but he was a man of few words, and when he talked to you it was always something special."

Alex Ferguson remembered the exchange well: "Eric was

a man of few words, but when he offered praise it had a dramatic effect. It was more meaningful to David Beckham, after he scored his miraculous goal against Wimbledon, that Eric considered it the best goal he had ever witnessed, than the fact he had pulled off the impossible."

Cantona later said: "Yes, I would loved to have scored it, but it is very difficult. David is a very good player and he has been picked for the England squad and he deserves it. Every game he becomes better, him and the other players."

It says everything about the respect held for Cantona that validation was actively sought out and when it was provided, it could have more impact than even a moment which genuinely changed Beckham's life forever.

The goal was a seminal event which almost served as a complete introduction for those players who had been doubted less than a year before. A league title and an FA Cup should have been enough to speak for themselves, but now these youngsters were capable of producing moments of magic that you could barely comprehend. Moments of magic that you would really, normally, only associate with one other player.

"The emergence of some of the lads felt as if it wasn't coincidental," remembers Ben Thornley. "Suddenly there were other players who, largely because of how they had learned from Eric, were able to contribute similarly. They took some of the responsibility. They showed it wasn't just Eric who could inspire Manchester United to win titles. This group of lads were young enough to help them do it for almost a decade."

However, United would not be favourites heading into the new season – that would be Newcastle, who had signed Alan Shearer for world record £15m. When it became clear Blackburn were willing to sell, Ferguson (boosted by the new contract he had been awarded days after the cup final) went in big with a £12m offer. Rovers owner Jack Walker had no option but to accept. It seemed that Ferguson finally had his man four years after his first attempt. Shearer agreed to the move to Old Trafford.

But Walker was reluctant to sell to local rivals and, according to Martin Edwards, offered Newcastle the chance to sign him too. The Magpies put in their record bid, and Walker now had all the reason he needed to refuse to sell to United, with Shearer moving to his hometown club instead.

All was not quite as serene as it appeared it might be at United over the summer. In June 1996, a statement issued on Cantona's behalf read: "Eric Cantona will quit football if English companies do not stop associating his name with products he has not given permission for his name to be used on… They have scandalously abused his name and have nothing to do with him. The public must not be fooled."

The Shearer saga rumbled on to the end of July. Meanwhile, Blackburn made their own offer for Eric Cantona. "We have made a bid for him and are awaiting a response from United," said Rovers chairman Robert Coar of their derisory £4m offer.

"There is no way the matter will be considered," said Ken Ramsden. "The offer has been rejected out of hand. Eric will not be going to Blackburn Rovers or anywhere else."

Instead of being sold, or quitting, Eric was named permanent captain as Steve Bruce departed on a free transfer. Bruce's natural replacement was David May, but Norwegian Ronny Johnsen had also been brought in. Johnsen was one of five foreign players signed as Ferguson splashed the cash.

Even on those five, though, he didn't quite spend the £12m he had available to buy Shearer. Johnsen cost £1.2m, while Dutch goalkeeper Raimond van der Gouw and Czech Republic winger Karel Poborsky cost £500,000 and £3.5m respectively. Completing the summer incomings were Jordi Cruyff (son of Johan) for £1.4m, and little-known Norwegian Ole Gunnar Solskjaer for £1.5m. The total spend was £8.1m. With the exception of Poborsky, who had impressed at Euro 96, all of the signings were squad players brought in with the hope they would add experience for European football.

To succeed on that front, they would need Cantona at his very best. "Different people have different needs, and the trick is to know yourself so well that you get the preparation right," he said in the book *Cantona on Cantona*.

"I know my needs. I know my own body. I need to train hard, to eat well, to drink lots of fluids, and to sleep a minimum of ten hours a day. Eating the right food is important. I don't eat red meat more than once a week. I eat pasta once a day, usually in the evening because you need energy through the night…"

There is no suggestion Cantona suddenly abandoned this approach but as the weeks wore on and the pre-season bulk showed little sign of subsiding, the natural question was whether Eric's heart was in it anymore. It seemed an absurd thing to even consider at the time, but looking back, the summer of 1996 appeared to be another pivotal period.

Cantona had his heart set on winning the European Cup. The events in the summer and autumn of 1996 surely made him wonder if that was possible. We will come to the Champions

League later, but the failure to add a world class striker to partner Eric may have disappointed him.

It stands to reason, anyway, especially considering Ferguson's later statement in his autobiography that Cantona felt "United were not ambitious enough in the purchase of players". That was one of two complaints the Frenchman had in this conversation; the other being he felt he like a "pawn" of the club's marketing department.

The mood of the country was almost the exact opposite; the European Championship held in England had created a feelgood factor as Terry Venables' men reached the semi-finals. The same happened to France, although Eric had contrasting thoughts about the performances of those teams, describing England as "beautiful" and being direct in his assessment of France. "They just waited for one of their star players to do something and hung on grimly," Cantona opined.

Some reservations about United's capability to kick on were allayed when the Reds crushed Newcastle, Shearer and all, 4-0 in the Charity Shield. Cantona was instrumental, scoring the opener and creating another for David Beckham. Easy. Too easy, perhaps.

*The Telegraph* swooned over Eric's display: "Maybe for a half-second at least, Shearer might have been caught in two minds about his career ambitions. He must have targeted the majestic Cantona with envious glances."

In the 65th minute, a sign of the old Cantona came to the fore; Belgian defender Philippe Albert was confronting Gary Neville when Eric raced over, grabbed Albert and threw him to the ground. The Frenchman was booked. Asked afterwards, Eric smiled: "I must be very strong. I just pushed somebody and he fell down. It was nothing much."

Strong indeed. But the next time United came up against a team in black and white stripes, the accusations against Cantona would be a lot stronger, and the test for the English champions would also be much more stern.

The responsibility to be a leader was a little more pronounced now he was captain. "I have always felt that I must have a lot of responsibility even when I was not captain. It is important that everybody feels that they have got a lot of responsibility so that we become stronger as a team," Cantona said, whilst insisting he was enjoying the "happiest time" of his career.

United, with their new squad players, struggled to get into a proper rhythm. Ferguson had selected Beckham on the right at Wimbledon but planned to introduce Poborsky into British football at home. But Beckham had created a selection headache with his goal; and the United boss' attempts to give all of his new signings game time resulted in some inconsistent performances. The first two home games were both drawn 2-2, first to Everton and then to Blackburn. In the second, a point was rescued by Ole Gunnar Solskjaer, with his first Reds goal.

After an international break, United drew again, this time away at Derby County. Beckham scored another long-range screamer. Cantona's own form had been as indifferent as that of his team. Those handsome early wins seemed a long time ago, so a trip to Leeds was, for once, just what the doctor ordered. The home side were struggling and the champions took them apart, scoring early and controlling the game. Two minutes before half-time, Ferguson's side were awarded a penalty. Cantona sent Nigel Martyn the wrong way, but for once, hit his shot wide of the post, much to the delight of the Leeds fans. It was his first competitive miss from the spot.

That *schadenfreude* was quickly returned in the second half as United smashed in three more goals to win 4-0. Cantona rubbed salt in the wounds by tapping in the last one and standing with his arms outstretched in front of the Don Revie stand, aggravating those who had been laughing at their former player an hour ago. "The Frenchman had the last word as he converted Ole Gunnar Solskjaer's far-post cross then stood in front of the Kop with arms outstretched," reported the *Mirror*. "It was a provocative gesture that might have sparked a riot – but many of the Leeds fans had already walked out."

The identity of the club and player who had inflicted such embarrassment was enough to force Leeds to dismiss Howard Wilkinson soon after the game. Their decline since winning the league was deemed irreparable by their present management.

Sympathetic as Ferguson would have been to Wilkinson's plight, he now had to concentrate on a competition where he too had come in for criticism. There was no foreigner rule, there were no suspensions – this time Manchester United needed to make an impression on the Champions League.

They faced holders Juventus in their first game. The Turin side, probably the best in the world, had strengthened with the signings of Zinedine Zidane and Alen Boksic. With Roy Keane and Paul Scholes injured, Ferguson adopted a different approach, haunted by the home game against Galatasaray in 1993 and the away game in Barcelona in 1994. He moved away from the 4-4-2 system to a 4-5-1.

Wide in midfield were Poborsky and Cruyff. Alone at the top was Eric Cantona, effectively playing the same role he'd been asked to play for France. It was a thankless task. United's midfield three of Beckham, Butt and Giggs had nowhere near the experience of Antonio Conte, Didier Deschamps and Zidane. Cantona was isolated and couldn't get into the game.

"Eric Cantona spent much of last night with his back to goal gazing down the pitch at what Juventus were doing to Ferguson's tactical plan," reported *The Guardian*. "This was not the Frenchman's ideal role, any more than it was against Galatasaray in Istanbul."

United went 1-0 down and never looked like recovering. There was a lesson to be learned but one neither manager or squad would take on in time as far as Cantona's own arc was concerned. It had been a gamble on the quality of United's precocious young midfield trio and it didn't work (Ferguson ripped into Giggs at half-time, bringing him off for McClair) but Eric, who had 'failed again', bore the brunt of the criticism. Italian broadcaster Bruno Longhi accused Cantona of being unprofessional and being 5kg overweight.

Former United winger Ben Thornley believes the relatively poor contribution from Cantona in Europe was down to the formation changes. "You do have to adapt in Europe, but, without ever wanting to be critical, I didn't ever really understand why Sir Alex moved away from the 4-4-2 with Eric being the deeper lying of the forwards," Thornley says.

"I thought the way we were set up was perfect for that and it felt like that was a big reason why we went on to win the European Cup in 1999. It was back to 4-4-2. I think the manager had so much respect for some of these brilliant European teams and that's why he adapted. Eric in a 4-5-1 was asked to plough a lone furrow and that wasn't his game.

"European teams were fearful of us and they were particularly fearful of Eric and Ryan. Eric had the ability to drop into spaces and do the impossible but he was unable to do that."

Cantona had taken the lion's share of the criticism for Turin, despite effectively being blameless. Back in familiar territory, he produced a fine display against Nottingham Forest, scoring twice and setting up a goal for Solskjaer. The Norwegian was not a Mark Hughes replica but he did remind Eric of another strike partner he was fond of – Jean-Pierre Papin. Cantona likened the quick feet of the 'baby-faced assassin' to those of his legendary compatriot.

"He would say to me, 'You'll score today, don't worry' before every game," Solskjaer recalled. "It made me feel ten feet tall."

The Rapid Vienna assistant coach, who went to see the game as the Austrians were United's next European opponents, felt bemused by the criticism of the Frenchman. "Every attack comes from Eric Cantona, the brains of the team," he said.

The *Independent* shared the view, praising Eric's involvement in the other goal of the game: "Cantona started to retrieve his natural effrontery, back-heeling to Poborsky, whose centre found the too-often subdued Ryan Giggs who headed in."

The report in *The Guardian* suggested not all were convinced: "A nagging problem is their profligacy in giving away chances – Cantona is especially guilty."

Against Vienna at Old Trafford, United played a familiar 4-4-2, with Beckham in the middle and Poborsky on the right. Ferguson's side put on one of their most impressive performances in Europe to date with a 2-0 win that could have been five. The *Daily Mail* deemed "lessons had been learned".

It seemed that United, when faced with inferior teams, generally had enough quality to comfortably win, compensating for the transitional issues caused by the new faces and the positional shifts. Cantona seemed to enjoy playing with the craft of Jordi Cruyff and the guile of Solskjaer. The trio combined to good effect to put Tottenham to the sword, with the Norwegian scoring twice.

These small crumbs of comfort were unlikely to placate Eric's mood. The autumn seemed to bring a cumulation of minor grumbles that weighed on his mind. In mid-September 1996 there was a court case brought against Cantona for an incident in May 1994. The Frenchman had to pay £350 after a judge ruled he had attacked a man from Liverpool during a brawl at a hotel in Chester after a day at the races. Cantona denied the accusation, but did not contest the charge at Liverpool County Court as he wanted to avoid a "media circus".

During the international break, Cantona was training in Manchester while many of his team-mates were away with their national teams. It can be a lonely place for top players; not the ideal way to prepare for a game against Liverpool.

At this time, there was also speculation about a takeover of Manchester United by media group VCI, who valued the club at £300m. The stock market value in the early weeks of the season was £281m, with a share price of 453 1/2p. By 15th October, that had hit another boom. Granada Television and brewery company Whitbread had expressed interest in buying Manchester United for £450m. The share price went up to 558p – it had tripled in 1996 alone.

All of which may well have flustered Cantona, who'd hoped the club would invest more heavily in the dream of European glory. Instead, he had watched helplessly as Alen Boksic – linked to United before his move to Italy – had scored in Turin whilst Eric, the club's most valuable player (or commodity) was cited as the reason his team were toothless.

Certainly Cantona was disillusioned over the coming days. United defeated Liverpool but Eric had an off-day. He was quoted by Steve Millar of the *Mirror* as saying: "There is something wrong with me and I don't know what it is. I can't understand why I am playing so poorly." He was also quoted: "I forgot I could play so bad. I am very unhappy but we have got a game on Wednesday and I will try to play better, much better, because I am very, very disappointed about my performance."

The remark is interesting and illustrates Eric's high standards. Around this time he was quoted as saying: "If I perform very well but my side loses, I can't be happy. Some players seem to feel it's fine to be pleased with a strong individual performance. As far as I'm concerned, if the team wins, then and only then do I allow myself the luxury of feeling pleased with myself for certain small details that may have led to that success. But winning is ultimately more important than my own happiness."

Before United travelled to Turkey to face Fenerbahce, Eric appeared on Canal Plus show *Nulle part ailleurs*. Producer Jean Teule said later: "Cantona turned up looking like a zombie. He seemed to have one foot in reality and the other in dreams and madness. I can see everything ending in tears for him."

Curiously, in Turkey Cantona had one of his best European nights for the club, scoring one and being involved in the other in a 2-0 win. *The Times* described it as "unquestionably the most impressive English performance on foreign soil in the European Cup since the end of the ban, six years ago." Eric was not the isolated figure he had been in Turin, and often dropped deeper into midfield to dictate the play.

A return to England saw a return to the punch-drunk form United had showed and they were finally given a hiding against Newcastle United. The Magpies won 5-0.

On the morning of the game, *The Guardian*'s Paul Wilson ran a piece titled 'Whatever happened to Cantona?', including the following: "Cantona was United's goal saviour last season, but this season he is a mere shadow of his previous influential self... it is a matter for debate whether Cantona exerted a greater presence on United's behalf during his suspension than during the last few games."

Scathing, but accurate on this occasion. Indeed, the Frenchman's only notable inclusion in the match reports was to mention he should have been sent off. He was involved in a late tussle with Peter Beardsley; this after Eric had been booked for shoving old foe Philippe Albert, who said: "I think he will agree that he was really lucky to stay on the field. He seemed to be upset with all the things going on around him."

The problems continued. At Southampton the following week, Cantona missed an early chance. United were battered 6-3 in a crazy game; Eric lashed out at Dutch defender Ulrich van Gobbel and was fortunate to escape a red card once again.

Ahead of the home match against Fenerbahce, Richard Williams of *The Guardian* wrote: "Cantona has come close to being sent off in both United's recent heavy defeats. It seems unlikely that the strategists at Fenerbahce will have let these events go unnoticed. How much easier the Turkish team's task might be were the Frenchman to be persuaded to take an early bath. And how depressing would be the consequences of this decline for those of us who defended Cantona after the Selhurst Park affair and who were delighted by the success of his eventual rehabilitation within the English game."

The previous incidents where Eric had been sent off had not come from runs of bad form, but rather, after moments of frustration. Hopes that he might build on the quiet restoration project that was his reputation in European competition were dealt a blow when Alex Ferguson fielded a conservative shape at home against the Turks to get his team used to it so he could play the same system against Juventus again.

The way the Italians had dictated the game only strengthened the United manager's theory that he had to control the game in the middle. But Cantona was once more by himself and while United suffocated the midfield, they offered no penetration going forward. The visitors scored with a deflected effort 13 minutes from the end to inflict the first ever defeat at Old Trafford in European competition.

The club's official yearbook says Eric, suffering from a "lack of confidence", "fluffed chances he would normally despatch with arrogant ease."

Cantona was understood to have taken the defeat personally, as it had occurred under his captaincy. He didn't speak after the match; he got changed quickly and left the ground.

When United lost at home three days later to Chelsea, their misery was complete. Emphasis was placed on the first game after the international break – Arsenal at home – with United having lost three out of their last four matches. And though Ferguson's side were better against the Gunners, they still lacked a cutting edge, winning 1-0 thanks to an own goal.

That cutting edge deserted them in the home game against Juventus, though United were a little unfortunate. Ferguson had gone bold this time, conceding that the conservative shape hadn't worked. A midfield of Beckham, Keane, Butt and Giggs started behind Cantona and Solskjaer. But 13 minutes in, Phil Neville pulled a hamstring; Keane moved into defence, and Zinedine Zidane and Didier Deschamps were able to run things in the middle. Juventus scored a penalty in the 35th minute.

In the second half, United were sent out to play at the frenetic pace their home fans were used to seeing, and Old Trafford responded in kind. Ryan Giggs terrorised the Juve defence but couldn't provide a goal. United were now creating chances but Cantona found Angelo Peruzzi equal to his efforts.

The 1-0 defeat was unfortunate but at this level, the finest of margins was bringing the hardest of evaluations. "Cantona given a French lesson" was the headline of the match report by *The Guardian*'s David Lacey who asserted that Zidane was the most influential player and that Deschamps' midfield display "did enough to close the case for Cantona being restored to the French national team". Lacey wrote: "As a footballer in England, Cantona is like Kipling's man who would be king, a senior NCO accepted as a God by natives who have never seen anything quite like him."

Lacey predicted that the final group game against Rapid Vienna could well be Cantona's last match for the club in Europe: "Despite Cantona's consistent failure to come to terms with the demands of a higher level of competition, Ferguson continues to defend the enigmatic Eric with the old ferocity. It is, he argues, simply a matter of confidence."

United's league recovery continued with a win over Leicester City. The Foxes were hard to break down – usually a scenario the Frenchman excelled in. Here, he was merely the final act, setting up Nicky Butt for the third goal. Journalist Michael Walker wrote: "Eric Cantona has been described in many ways. But for the past six weeks only two words convey his standard of performance. One is 'poor', the other 'unaccountably'."

It seems a little harsh. The way United and Cantona had been written about, you might have been forgiven for thinking they were relegation candidates. But the win over Leicester meant they were only five points off the top. Still, predictions of an ultimate demise were being prepared as United travelled to Vienna. Ferguson played a 4-4-2. When it came to the crunch, there was no experiment. A midfield of Beckham, Butt, Keane and Giggs, with Cantona and Solskjaer in his attack. United performed admirably.

"Giggs settled United's nerves after 23 minutes with a goal of calculated accuracy after a fine through pass by the rejuvenated Cantona," reported the *Express*. "The Frenchman finished things off in style with a simple goal from Beckham's cross."

David Lacey of *The Guardian* showed he was prepared to praise Eric when he impressed: "Giggs, like Keane, Beckham and, crucially, Cantona, found the sort of form this level of competition consistently demands."

Four days later, United drew 2-2 at West Ham; Eric setting up Solskjaer with a great through ball. Yet the headlines from this game, and United's draw at Sheffield Wednesday, were two fantastic goals from David Beckham and Paul Scholes respectively. Beckham in particular was a player demonstrating confidence that could be directly traced to his professional relationship with Eric Cantona.

The education had now reached a stage where examinations had been passed, certificates had been awarded and these young men had not only served apprenticeships but were out in the big bad world carving a name for themselves. There was something distinctive in their individual and collective style. Manchester United had one real Eric Cantona and, suddenly, three or four mini-Cantonas.

"Eric's close control was brilliant, something that Scholesy was exemplary at," says Ben Thornley. "The ability to strike a ball with ferocious power from distance as Cantona did became one of Becks' trademarks. Giggsy had already been in the team but you could see the benefit of playing with Eric in the way he was now able to switch the ball; Giggs was brilliant anyway and if it was possible that he could have improved, then that improvement was thanks to Eric. Every single one of those lads picked up something from Eric, even Nicky Butt, who observed the way that Eric used his physical prowess to seem bigger than he was.

"It was almost as if they each picked an attribute of Eric's and distributed them amongst themselves, working on it until they became masters... I still think the lads were incredibly talented. What Eric gave them was the belief to express themselves on the field. Belief to not be intimidated, that they had a lot to offer. The way he conducted himself gave them a pathway to succeed. Our group had already won the FA Youth Cup before he even arrived so there was obviously a lot of talent, but it was more about education and enhancement."

# Signing Off In Style

Just when many were starting to believe that Cantona's magical powers had gone for good, the Frenchman rolled back the years to provide Old Trafford with yet another glorious moment.

In the last game before Christmas 1996, United were 4-0 up against Sunderland. Cantona had already exorcised one ghost, scoring his first league goal for 97 days with a penalty. But the game's iconic moment occurred eleven minutes from the end.

David May fizzed a pass to Eric who was just in front of the halfway line. Two Sunderland players paid close attention. One, Richard Ord, swung at him, but Eric evaded the challenge; the other, Kevin Ball, snapped at his heels, but with three touches, he moved the ball away from the tackle, away from another challenge from Ord, and away again from another challenge from Ball.

Ord followed as Cantona advanced, but the Frenchman used his body well, and the Sunderland player collided with team-mate Andy Melville. With just defender Gareth Hall to beat, Eric played a one-two with Brian McClair to create space. Hall was unable to close down Cantona in time as he let the ball run across him and pushed his instep into the ground, lifting the ball over the Sunderland goalkeeper.

Ben Thornley, on the left wing, remembers what happened. "I could see the play developing through the centre," he said. "Eric picked the ball up, played a one-two with Brian McClair, and when you thought he was going to try and pick out another pass, I was haring up the left, thinking this would be my chance.

"He took the shot on and I thought I'd follow it in, thinking it's going to come back off the woodwork. But it dropped straight in. I was still running. I just thought, 'Wow, that was immense'. Immense but not surprising."

Cantona's effort clipped the inside of the post before going in. Old Trafford could scarcely believe what they had witnessed. Eric – back straight, collar up – turned to face his team-mates, and then effectively did a 360 to all sides of the stadium, slowly raising his arms in acceptance of the adoration, and allowing himself a smile of self-satisfaction.

"It was a privilege to play in that game," Thornley admits. "I remember how he just stood on one spot and turned around, absorbing the adulation, for what was a brilliant piece of skill. It's what he did at Wimbledon and Sheffield United; that precision, when you are playing at that sort of a level, you just need that extra dimension."

Alex Ferguson was thrilled: "Cantona inspired the performance today and his goal… absolutely marvellous."

With his confidence returning, Eric had a renewed belief in glory that season. Before Christmas, he joined some of his team mates for a festive drink, as per Gary Neville's autobiography: "'Together, we will win the European Cup.' It was quite a promise to make, but this wasn't coming from just anyone. The man saying it across the pub table was Eric Cantona. We were in the Bull's Head in Hale. It was December 1996, and our Frenchman had pulled up a seat with me and Becks.

"The young lads had always been in awe of him and Eric was a quiet man. But this time we got chatting. Over a drink, Eric told us we were going to become kings of Europe… Eric had staked everything on winning the Champions League."

Eric was in fine form again on Boxing Day. Beckham had already notched another stunning effort of his own, but the skipper was beginning to show he was still the one most capable of the most outrageous things. In the 67th minute Beckham played a fine pass in Cantona's direction. The Frenchman showed exquisite control to take the ball on his upper thigh to stop the momentum. He flicked the ball up before it bounced and flicked it again over Crossley's head. The bemused Forest keeper was helpless, but the magnificent effort hit the crossbar. Solskjaer followed in to convert the rebound.

Next up, Eric scored from the penalty spot against Leeds in the last game of 1996 to earn his team a 1-0 win. Ian Ross of *The Guardian* described Cantona as "half the player he can be but twice the player he was three weeks ago."

Some were more willing to get on board with the idea of Eric's return to form. Take *The Mail on Sunday*, who reported: "Either George Graham was caught in the Old Trafford traffic or he has taken on board the age-old Leeds grudge against Eric Cantona. 'Radebe more or less eliminated Cantona from the game,' declared the Elland Road boss. Oh yeah? Then how come the Frenchman's sublime touches sent Leeds to their second defeat inside three days and nudged the Champions even closer to the Premiership summit?"

They closed the year two points behind leaders Liverpool. The Anfield club had 39 points, three teams were on 37, and Aston Villa in sixth were on 34 points. Had United not dropped so many careless points, they would have had a huge advantage.

Hopes of a mercurial return to form for Cantona and United were dashed. There were some good wins but scarcely anything outstanding, aside from Beckham's breathtaking winner at White Hart Lane in January. In a win at Coventry, there was another indication of a changing of the guard in the *Manchester Evening News* report: "Paul Scholes was the man grasping the nettle and Cantona let his heir apparent have free rein."

On the first day of February, there was a neat reminder of Cantona's contribution when he struck a late winner against Southampton, with *The Observer* saying Eric "played a captain's part", but three days later the skipper was unable to prevent United from being eliminated in the FA Cup to Wimbledon.

It was the first time he had ever tasted defeat in the competition. He was also booked, which ruled him out of the next two games – trips to Arsenal and Chelsea. These were games that would surely test the mettle of this United side but they didn't appear to miss their French star. Particularly at Highbury, where new strike duo Andy Cole and Ole Gunnar Solskjaer each got a goal in a 2-1 win.

*The Independent's* report was predictable: "Who needs Cantona? The absence of United's French captain merely gave the armband, the aura and the leadership to the man who, in spirit, has dominated the team throughout the season: Roy Keane… United rippled with skills, the quality of which took some believing given the demanding conditions."

At Stamford Bridge, Beckham scored yet another marvellous goal in a 1-1 draw. Eric was back to face Coventry ahead of the Champions League quarter-final first-leg against Porto at Old Trafford. After three minutes, he played in Andy Cole, resulting in an own goal. Sixty seconds later Cole had scored himself. After the 3-1 win, it was difficult to ascertain what difference Eric made.

"We're in transition," Ferguson said. "There was a time when we desperately needed Eric, and people said that without him we couldn't win anything. Before Eric, people used to say the same about Bryan Robson. Now we have Giggs, Beckham and Keane all maturing to the extent where they have their own impact on matches. We are less reliant on Eric, and there is no question he has helped greatly in the players' development. He's done a terrific job, but Eric doesn't feel his job is over. He tends to look on the end of the season, the part of the year when there are prizes to be won, as his best period."

Having seen mixed results with his tactics in Europe, Ferguson once more gambled on a 4-3-3 at home to Porto, only with a slight variation. Cantona would play in his normal role, with Cole and Solskjaer in front of him.

The positive variation paid dividends, with the Frenchman at the heart of everything. It wasn't so much his goal in the 34th minute which made the game 2-0, as his second-half display alongside Giggs which terrorised the Portuguese champions.

In the 61st minute, Eric played a wonderful pass down the left touchline for Cole to race on. Cole held the ball up and timed his own pass to Giggs perfectly; the Welshman made it 3-0. Cantona then turned provider for Cole; a famous 4-0 win was secured. United's value soared another £10m to £430m the following day.

The British press fawned over what they felt was finally the magic formula. *The Telegraph*: "United they attacked, Ryan Giggs and Eric Cantona conjuring pass after precision pass to embarrass the pride of Portugal."

The *Mirror*: "This was breathtaking. The renaissance of English football led by a French captain and Scottish manager."

The *Guardian*: "Ferguson's decision to play Cole and Solskjaer up front, allowing Cantona to drift in his old manner, gave United's movement both pace and stealth."

The second leg finished 0-0; Ferguson this time choosing a 4-1-3-2 shape which did its intended job of protecting the advantage. A 2-0 win at Everton (with a goal from Eric) at the end of March gave United a six-point lead over Liverpool, though Roy Evans' team had a game in hand and still had to welcome their rivals to Anfield on 19th April.

The day before the win at Goodison Park, the *Evening Standard* published a story that Cantona was joining Israeli side Beitar Jerusalem for £4m. The story had been run in *The Jewish Chronicle* for the festival of Purim, a traditional time for practical jokes.

But events at Manchester United were being taken very seriously indeed. The upcoming Champions League semi-final against Borussia Dortmund was so vital, in fact, that United took their eyes off the ball against struggling Derby in the league; the Rams won 3-2 at Old Trafford. Cantona was his team's star performer. With his side 2-0 down at the break, Eric responded with inspiring purpose, taking down a ball from Solskjaer, shrugging off three defenders and rifling a bullet of a shot home in front of the Stretford End. Those in attendance weren't to know it, but it would be the last time he would score at Old Trafford.

And so to Germany. Despite a pre-match injury to Peter Schmeichel, United were the more impressive team for the majority. Ferguson played a 4-4-2 formation and it was the right blend of bold and conservative. Cantona created chances for Butt and Beckham. Neither went in. The former hit the post and the latter saw his effort cleared off the line.

"Fourteen minutes from the end, Eric jumps out of tackle in midfield," Roy Keane said in his first autobiography. "His challenger Tretschok breaks forward, shoots, the ball takes a deflection off Gary Pallister. Back of the net. Perhaps the moment Eric's future was decided."

Watching the footage again, the accusation seems a little unfair. There is a bouncing ball and Eric attempts to flick it past his marker. The Dortmund player wins it, though, and because of the momentum of his own run, Cantona is caught out ten yards away. The ball is then played to Tretschok, whose deflected effort goes in. It was no more Cantona's fault than Pallister's, though, more fairly, it was a bit of a freak. The 1-0 defeat left United's European hopes on a knife-edge. Before the second leg, there were league games at Blackburn and

Liverpool – no time, then, for a lapse like against Derby County. None came, either.

Midway through the first half at Ewood Park, Nicky Butt was taken down in the box. Cantona stepped up as usual. The kick was not struck with conviction; Tim Flowers saved. The ball squirmed out of his grasp, but as Cantona tried to convert the rebound, the ball was cleared.

Ten minutes later, Eric atoned, controlling a Scholes pass, allowing the bounce and timing his own ball perfectly to Cole, who finished in style. Blackburn levelled and Scholes regained his side's lead before Cole created a late goal for Cantona. The 80th minute strike turned out to be the winner.

Cantona played well at Anfield but this was Gary Pallister's day. Or, should we say, morning – Sky Sports arranged the game to kick off at a ridiculous 11.15am. The defender scored two fantastic headers before noon, in a 3-1 win to all but seal the title. United were five points ahead of Arsenal and Liverpool with a game in hand.

Tentative talks had been taking place on a new contract with Martin Edwards and Cantona's advisors. The player himself had not yet entered into serious discussion with anyone. The Frenchman was concentrating on facing Borussia Dortmund. Schmeichel was back, but Denis Irwin and Ryan Giggs were only fit enough for the bench, while Roy Keane was suspended.

After eight minutes, Lars Ricken hit a tame shot that crept into the far corner. United now had to score three. Cole was played in on the angle by Solskjaer and went for an early shot. Goalkeeper Stefan Klos parried it in to the path of Cantona, though it was slightly behind him. It seemed a player of the class of Cantona had only to tap the ball for it to go in; but his imbalance and the spin on the ball made him delay. Defender

Jurgen Kohler was able to clear. Might the Cantona of three years previous put it away? Most would probably say yes. Eric missed another chance when he fired past Klos only to see his effort cleared off the line. Those were his best chances but the team weren't found wanting for them – 21 in all.

According to the *Daily Star*, Manchester United had "outplayed their Bundesliga opponents twice... and have nothing to show for it but broken hearts and disappointment."

Inside the United dressing room, as the home players tried to pick up their morale in order to win the league and have another crack at the competition next year, there was one person harbouring more hurt than the rest.

"We'd soon discover that losing to Dortmund must have had a massive effect on Eric," Gary Neville said. "We hadn't been beaten by a great team, we'd just not taken our chances. Tiny margins. There were several factors, and no one inside the dressing room blamed Eric, except perhaps himself."

Roy Keane, who later criticised him for his lack of European impact, also cut him some slack. "Eric struggled in Europe – to be fair, we all did," Keane said. "He was superb in the domestic game, where his poise and technical brilliance meant he was always one step ahead of the chaos. And because we were so strong around the park we could spare him the chasing back, the graft, the tackling we happily did on his behalf."

Andrei Kanchelskis strongly disagrees with the Irishman about the European issue. "Keane once said that Cantona was not a player he could ever remember changing the course of a game in Europe," the Russian said. "If Roy was implying that Eric was part of the reason why Manchester United fared so badly in the Champions League, I cannot agree. The biggest reason Manchester United did not do well in Europe in those years was nothing to do with Cantona but the UEFA rule that then stated you could only play three foreigners in your team."

But Gary Pallister does conform to that generally accepted view that Cantona struggled with European football. "Although he played some tremendous games for us in the Champions League, I don't think he thrived as he did in the Premiership because the continentals marked him more tightly," he said. "European coaches routinely detailed some very competent man-markers to spend the whole match slowing him down."

To this writer, however, it feels like too much of a coincidence that Cantona's best games came with a familiar team around him and an attacking line-up. Play him in Turin as a lone striker, with Poborsky and Cruyff to supply him, when they had never played as a trio before? Play the same system at home? As we saw at Leeds, Cantona had to be more involved. Eric had shown himself to easily be competent enough to deal with men marking him.

His strength was to make them work to find him, which created space for others. And, of course, there is the fact that he was never able to play alongside both Kanchelskis and Giggs in Europe. His form in Europe will remain a 'what if' and a 'why?', but surely the one thing we can say for certain is that it had nothing to do with ability.

Not that this would have been any consolation for Eric Cantona that evening. When talks resumed about his future, they were about to take a very different direction.

# The Final Curtain

In the early February of 1997, Eric Cantona was given permission to go to Barcelona to play a charity game, due to his domestic suspension which ruled him out of matches at Arsenal and Chelsea. On Eric's return, Alex Ferguson was sufficiently concerned about his player's mood that he called him into his office for a chat.

"For some time I had been worried by changes I discerned in Cantona," he said. "He was subdued and did not seem to be enjoying his football… It was almost as if part of him was already somewhere else. My concern about his mood, and about form that was moderate by his standards, deepened as I observed subtle differences in his body shape.

"He was a big man with the kind of physique that demanded rigorous training, and now there were hints that, at the age of 30, the thickening process had begun. The worries were serious enough for me to call Eric in for a chat. In the past our meetings had invariably been positive and fruitful… this time there was not the same liveliness in his responses." Ferguson said Cantona had "voiced no specific problems", but the manager was not at ease with how the conversation had gone. He kept an eye on his player.

It was obvious after the Dortmund game that his captain was detached. "Conspiracy theorists were telling us that the loss of his edge was related to feelings of mutual dislike between Andy Cole and him," he said. "I can shed no light on that allegation but they were the main culprits in the squandering spree in front of goal. It is possible they were just not a good partnership, full stop… Maybe the chemistry between them was wrong… I don't believe either would have sacrificed the team's interests because of personal animosity."

On the morning after the elimination against Borussia Dortmund, Ferguson's 1997 Diary *A Will To Win* recalled "an air of desperation at The Cliff", with Cantona in particular "in a broody mood". It seems Ferguson picked up on the Frenchman's dissatisfaction, although a specific desire to leave wasn't voiced. Talking to the press ahead of their next game, the United boss did concede: "It looks as if the chances he missed have prompted him to question his future."

It was enough to prompt one reporter to ask Martin Edwards about Cantona's plans. Edwards replied: "These matters are always reviewed in the close season. Eric Cantona is under contract for another year and there is no issue, no justification for this kind of speculation."

United drew their next two games, but on a pivotal night, Liverpool and Newcastle both lost, meaning the title was heading back to Old Trafford. Their final game was at home against West Ham, where the trophy would be presented.

On the day before the game, the *Mirror*'s Steve Millar ran

a prescient column where he asked "Cantona: is the United dream over?" "Wild celebrations are all around him, but Eric Cantona doesn't seem in any mood to party," Millar wrote.

"When the champagne corks were popping on United's training ground the morning after the title confirmation, Cantona was determined to get out of spray's way…. Cantona, stony-faced, was more interested in making a getaway than talking about the historic fourth title success… I remember talking to Cantona back in October when his below-standard form was eating away at him… (He) hasn't been able to shake himself out of that cocoon of mediocrity."

The Newcastle game had seen a new banner revealed at Old Trafford that said "Cantona: Our Man Forever" and Gary Neville echoed the message. "I think he's got to stay forever," said the right back. "He's been unbelievable for us. His presence is brilliant. His all-round performance and team effort is amazing. I would love Eric here next season."

So to 11th May 1997, the final day of the league season. As the players lined up in the tunnel, an absent-minded Cantona was tapped on the arm. It was opposition player John Moncur.

"I asked him in the tunnel if I could have his shirt and he said no," Moncur recalled. After the final whistle of an uneventful game, where United won 2-0 with the second goal created by Cantona, Moncur asked again. Eric was again reluctant.

Moncur: "I said, 'Remember the stamp Eric, come on mate!' He just looked at me and said 'Aah', and took off his shirt to give me." (Moncur later sold the shirt to *The Sun*, who contacted him offering to buy it and auction it for charity.)

The season over, Ferguson braced himself for the call he knew was coming. "As the season came to a close, Eric continued to have the air of a man for whom football had lost its appeal," the United boss said. "Seeing the dullness in his eyes, and the changing outline of his physique, I had to acknowledge perhaps he was right to terminate his career before blatant decline became an insult to the fierce pride that burned in him. But I clung to the hope his problems had some underlying cause and that once it was tackled he might rediscover the standards that had made him a legend.

"I feared the worst, however, when my secretary, Lynn, phoned me after our last league match to say that Eric wanted to meet me at Mottram Hall. Once we were in a private office, there was a hesitancy on both sides about how to start the conversation. But I was struck instantly by the look of resignation on Eric's face. He was totally straightforward with me. He did want to finish, he had been considering it for some time and now the decision was irrevocable."

Cantona then contacted the chairman to tell him face-to-face.

"Eric came to see me and said he had decided to retire," Martin Edwards says. "There was obviously no point in trying to talk him out of it. He was certain and absolute. I was disappointed, very disappointed, because he was our talisman. He was only 30. He probably wasn't as dominant in the last year as he had been previously. He hadn't really imposed himself in the Dortmund games and maybe it was around that time that he realised himself that he wasn't 100 per cent.

"Some players will play on for as long as their bodies will allow but Eric was always different. Once he felt his standards had dropped, then he would go away from the game, and what's more, I don't think it was a particularly difficult decision for him. I don't know, that's trying to read into his mind. But it still came as a very big shock."

The news had yet to hit the United dressing room, who still

had one more game to play – a testimonial for former Coventry defender David Busst, who had retired after the horrific injury at Old Trafford the previous year. United were trailing until an Eric Cantona penalty in the 69th minute levelled things up; four minutes later, Cantona was set up by Thornley to score a second. In the last minute, a contrived penalty was awarded to allow Busst to come on and score an equaliser. At the final whistle Busst approached Cantona for his shirt. Eric obliged.

Cantona travelled back with his team to Manchester. It is said he had let on to a couple that he was going to go. The rumour went around the bus, but he made no announcement.

According to Gary Neville: "He'd got off the bus and said, 'Have a good summer, see you later.' But the way he left was typical Eric. There would be no diminishing of his legend, no slide into mediocrity. He'd finish at the top or as near as he could make it – captain of a club that had won the Premiership. He certainly left us wanting more...

"I wished he'd stayed because I believe he could have been part of the European Cup-winning team. Failure hadn't been down to him; it was because we were a young, inconsistent side. His departure means that he fell short of conquering Europe, but it doesn't lessen his status in my eyes."

There was a mixed reaction to the news Eric had retired.

"Were we surprised? Life with Eric was one long surprise," Ryan Giggs said. "You never knew what he would do next. There were no farewells, and I didn't really believe he meant it until he failed to turn up the following season. He was a fit lad, and he could definitely have gone on longer."

Roy Keane wasn't absolutely shocked either: "... something Eric said earlier this year about United wishing to use him as a commodity, and the increasingly commercial nature of the club, provided a clue, perhaps, to the reason he chose to retire. Eric was a proud man. I think he decided if he couldn't play for United, he wouldn't play at all. I admired that."

Gary Pallister had picked up a similar vibe. "His departure didn't come as any great surprise," he said. "Even as he was playing his part in winning another title in 1996/97, he didn't look that happy in the dressing room. We didn't realise there were problems with the club over his image rights. Apparently the negotiations dragged on... I believe he felt he wasn't getting paid a fair enough percentage, as his image was the biggest selling point at the club and United must have made an awful lot of money out of him. The whole business struck him as unfair and it upset him, so that by the spring of 1997 he didn't look the same Eric, either on the pitch or off it."

Peter Schmeichel, who had roomed with him for so long, said of the news: "As befitted the man, the ending of his footballing career smacked of his individualism: he simply decided that he would prefer a life outside the world of football."

On Sunday 18th May 1997, the news of Eric Cantona's shock retirement was conveyed to world via a press conference in the Europa Suite at Old Trafford. The conference had been called that morning; journalists were caught on the hop but expected it to be a new signing. Martin Edwards and Alex Ferguson sat down. Edwards read from a statement.

"Good afternoon, ladies and gentlemen," he said. "We have asked you to come along today so that we may announce that

Eric Cantona has indicated his wish to retire from football with immediate effect. Eric is away on holiday with his family and is not planning to return to England in the near future... Eric Cantona has been a marvellous servant to Manchester United. This is a sad day for us and we are here to pay tribute to him, not to talk about his successor or successors."

Cantona's statement read: "I have played professional football for 13 years. I now wish to do other things. I always planned to retire when I was at the top and at Manchester United I have reached the pinnacle of my career. In the last four-and-a-half years I have enjoyed my best football and had a wonderful time. I have had a marvellous relationship with the manager, coach, staff and players, and not least the fans. I wish Manchester United even more success in the future."

It was Ferguson's turn to field comments. "Eric has helped to give us six trophies in four-and-a-half years," the United boss said. "And it's all for one million pounds. It's a sad day... Eric has had a huge impact on the development of our younger players. Eric has been a model professional and he has been a joy to manage. He's certainly one of the most gifted and dedicated players I have had the pleasure of working with. Whenever fans discuss United's greatest side, you can be sure Eric's name will be high up on the list. He leaves with our best wishes. He has left us with so many wonderful memories."

Edwards said the club would keep Cantona's registration and added: "If Eric changes his mind we would be happy for him to stay with us."

To reporters after the conference Ferguson admitted: "There were mutterings on the team bus on Friday after the Coventry testimonial. The lads had an inkling so maybe the news won't come as such a big shock to them all. The magnitude of the decision is a surprise, though, because he loved his football. But we can't stand still. Great players emerge all the time and we will try to get the best players here in his place."

If some of his team-mates had an "inkling", well, the unprecedented reaction from supporters was one of universal shock and heartbreak. Hundreds converged on Old Trafford, many of them in replica Cantona shirts. Why? Well, they did not know, really. Great players had been and gone, Ferguson had said so himself. There had never been this reaction. Not when George Best, or Bobby Charlton, or Denis Law, or Bryan Robson departed.

As Philippe Auclair reasons in his book on Eric, the atmosphere and response was almost funereal; Auclair uses death as a recurring theme partly in reference to Cantona's quote from 2006 when he said: "You quit and it's like a death."

And while there was no comparison with the tangible human grief felt in similar scenes after the Munich disaster and the death of Sir Matt Busby, it was in the absence of that feeling that those supporters could not comprehend, nor articulate, their very feeling of loss. And, as it was a loss, 'grieving' was the popular term to describe their reaction in captions of newspaper images over the coming days.

The King was dead. Long live the King.

# Wandering Star

**P**rior to Eric Cantona's arrival, one of the most popular songs on the Manchester United terraces was *Always Look On The Bright Side Of Life*; most football supporters tend to have a self-deprecating way of looking at their team. And though Manchester United were in the shadow of their Merseyside rivals for the '70s and '80s, they did win the odd cup, a level of failure most other clubs would trade their entire history for. The song remained in rotation in the Stretford End jukebox for some time after Cantona's arrival. It became something of an anthem of the 1994 FA Cup final as fans danced in the rain that reminded them of home. Though it occasionally makes an appearance now, it is now one that belongs to a different era (although United fans might feel that since 2013, the time is right to bring an old classic back).

Manchester United as a football club and commercial entity had grown more than ten-fold between November 1992 and May 1997. On the morning after the retirement announcement, share prices went down 6p to 628p, though plunged to 615p on early trading. Trying to rationalise Cantona's value in such terms is a pointless exercise. At the most recent estimate, he was still the most popular player and brought in around a quarter of the entire merchandising revenue by himself.

Having taken a pay cut in the summer of 1995, it perhaps stands to reason that even after exploratory talks, if Eric felt the club were so far away from what he felt was a reasonable offer, and that he was being exploited, then he would walk away. He had once said he would walk away penniless if it came to it, and whilst that wasn't quite the case, in the context of United's growing coffers, it may as well have been.

Transfer fees and wages were still on an incremental rise with figures that were almost insignificant compared to the revenues of the club. If Cantona's basic wage was £10,000 a week, or £520,000 a year, then those crude estimates of merchandise revenue alone meant that United had earned enough from Eric's image in the previous year to more than pay his salary for his entire stay at the club. When Roy Keane tested those waters in 1999, his new contract was rumoured to be worth £50,000 per week.

Cantona had expressed displeasure that he felt his image was being used without agreement. After speaking to Ferguson and Edwards, he did not feel suitably appeased. (Indeed, he later sued the merchandising arm of the club and was awarded £50,000.)

Despite this, one can't help but think Cantona's decision was ultimately a sporting one. Perhaps it was self-realisation and a loss of confidence. If he was conceding to anything, it was most likely time, the undefeated opponent.

According to Jean-Jacques Bertrand, Cantona's decision to

retire had ultimately stemmed from the moment he knew he would no longer be selected for his country in the role he wished to play. Eric wanted to go out on top. He could have done that in May 1996. He believed that he could go one step further and win the ultimate prize with his club. When that was not to be, he walked away. He had revolutionised British football in an unprecedented way.

"Cantona had a huge impact on United, most of which emanated from his talent and drive, but some from his attitude towards training," said Sir Alex Ferguson. "The young players thought of him as the king and hung on his every word and he captained the team in 1996 and 1997. As Cantona started to blossom at United, other clubs all wanted their own version of Cantona. By the time Eric retired in 1997, foreign players had become the backbone of top-flight football in England."

Newcastle signed Faustino Asprilla. Arsenal signed Dennis Bergkamp and, later, Thierry Henry. Chelsea bought Gianfranco Zola. Though these players had an impact on the success and the culture of those clubs, it paled in comparison to the remarkable transformation caused by Eric Cantona.

It is not an exaggeration to say that in a similarly concentrated period of time, no other player in British football history had as big an influence on their club's success as Eric Cantona did for Manchester United between 1992 and 1997. No other player in British football history could be cited as being so influential for so many brilliant young players who would also go on to dominate the British game. No other player in British football history had ever been as singularly responsible as Eric Cantona for the commercial growth of the club they play for, on the scale that the Frenchman was.

In the short-term, it seemed this commercial growth would

make it fairly straightforward for Cantona to be replaced. After all, by all accounts, his talent and contribution had diminished, hadn't it? Well, maybe not quite. Eric had scored 15 times in 50 games in his final season; one of those goals arguably the most-replayed since of his entire career.

There was also a direct correlation between his and his team's best performances that season, even if his team-mates had finally found a way to win in his absence.

Was it, then, a case of Cantona being judged by his own exceptional standards? "It's possible that people's expectations were too high," Ben Thornley says. "Every player goes through a period where they're not at their maximum. Maybe he'd hit this peak in the 1996 FA Cup final that would be impossible to improve. For me he bowed out far too early. He was only 30. He had another three or four years in him, he never played at 100mph so that wouldn't have affected him."

Over the days and weeks that followed the announcement, there were tributes and doubts aired in equal measure. It almost seemed reminiscent of the scene in *One Flew Over The Cuckoo's Nest* where the inmates learn that McMurphy has been defeated by Nurse Ratched, refusing to believe it and creating their own version of events instead.

United legend Paddy Crerand admitted his entire family had been in shock when they heard. "Cantona is a legend in Manchester," he added. "He'll not be forgotten." Graham Kelly, the FA chief executive who had once criticised the "appalling" example set by Cantona, gave an about turn: "He has a unique talent and has played a significant part in the development of young players. He has been a great example of skill, talent and vision and he will leave that great legacy behind."

But Guy Roux, Cantona's mentor in France, suggested it

might not be the end. "I'm not so sure about him retiring," he said that May. "Great performers always take several curtain calls. This is one of his first exits and I expect there will be more. I have become used to surprises from Cantona."

This was the belief of France manager Aime Jacquet, who said: "He is deeply in love with football and I certain that his love will make him come back."

Even Bernard Ferrer, the Marseille midfielder who was Eric's brother-in-law, agreed, saying: "It won't be once and for all. Eric is a bit tired after six massive seasons in which he has put in a huge physical effort. He needs a holiday."

Meanwhile, Gordon Taylor of the PFA said: "In football you are a long time finished. Eric is only 30 – I hope he will reconsider. Football will be the loser for him leaving the game. He has certainly brought colour as well as some controversy. That should not overshadow his achievements."

Liberia and AC Milan striker George Weah stated: "He has become the victim of injustice once again. If people have lost confidence in him in England he should move abroad. With his talents he could play anywhere in the world. It's a tragedy for football and a black day for everyone who loves the game. I hope with all my heart that Eric will change his mind. Millions of people love him and it is too soon for him to retire. My message to him is, 'Come back soon Eric'."

After this initial furore, though, the truth began to sink in. Cantona was pictured in the Alpine village of La Beaume taking his eight-year-old son Raphael for a spin on his Harley-Davidson. His mum was quoted by reporters as saying: "He is having a rest, he is hibernating, even if it is nearly summer. I don't really know what he is going to do now."

Both Manchester United and Eric Cantona made immediate

steps to try and show they were moving on. It was announced on 22nd May that Cantona would star alongside his brother Joel and actor Mickey Rourke (one of Eric's idols) in a boxing movie. "Mickey and Eric are delighted to be working together and I'm thrilled," Joel said.

Alex Ferguson, meanwhile, was in Belfast, where he was quizzed about talk that Middlesbrough schemer Juninho and Fiorentina striker Gabriel Batistuta were on their way to Old Trafford. "We had plans before Eric made his announcement and we will continue with those plans," Ferguson said. "We have to go on with life. He was a great player and we are all sorry to see him go, but we will now have to plan ahead."

Another target was reported to be Zinedine Zidane; Italian newspapers claimed United had made an £8m offer for the player who had inherited Cantona's international spot.

United retained Cantona's registration and the player was asked to participate in a testimonial in Lille on 25th May. He scored in the second half; around 100 United fans made the trip to be in the 9,000 crowd. On 30th May, Manchester's Key 103 radio station auctioned Cantona's shirt from the testimonial at Coventry, and raised £15,350 for David Busst.

Ferguson proceeded with his summer plans. In June, Teddy Sheringham was brought in from Tottenham Hotspur for £3.5m. Having been on the hunt for a goalscorer for so long, the unexpected absence of Cantona had presented a new creative void. At 31, he did not fit the manager's normal profile – this was an attempt to replace Cantona as best he could. Talks with Juninho had failed, with the Brazilian choosing the sunnier climes of Spain.

Sheringham, who had carved out a successful career in his own right, was immediately faced with questions about

Cantona. "I'm sure people will start making comparisons but I can only play my own game and hope it will be good enough for Manchester United," the England international said.

"Some will see it as a daunting task, but it's something I can handle." He would avoid one way of the press putting pressure on him: "I have always worn the number 10 shirt and I will have it again when I play for United. I think David Beckham will be swapping to the number seven."

That much was true. Beckham, having grown up adoring Bryan Robson and then worshipping Cantona, wanted the vacant shirt. "Robbo was around when Eric came in but it was really Eric who kicked it (the 'legend' of the number seven) all off," kit-man Albert Morgan said. "I can remember David Beckham when Eric left – he was desperate for that number seven shirt and he did very well when he got it. Eric though was the one that clicked everything together."

It was Manchester United and not Eric Cantona who headed for Japan and the Far East in the summer of 1997; the Lancashire club jetting off on their next step towards global domination. When they returned to face Chelsea in the Charity Shield, Gary Neville gave an interview describing life at the club without Cantona. "Manchester United is a cynical club, one that makes you think 'how unimportant am I?" Neville said. "Eric Cantona doesn't even get a mention. Basically it's a case of 'let's get on without him'.

"He has gone and it's not as if we're coming in every day

saying 'where's Eric?' It makes you think what it would be like if you left yourself. Nobody would give two hoots. But this is a club that has lost a big player every season and it was the same when Bryan Robson left, Steve Bruce, Mark Hughes, Paul Ince and Andrei Kanchelskis – and now Eric. Life goes on. We have got to improve as a club. Nothing less than reaching the European Cup final will do."

United started their season well enough. The Charity Shield was won on penalties (with Beckham suffering the embarrassment of his brand new shirt being labelled 'BECKAM') before routine wins over Tottenham and Southampton.

It was reported that Cantona would be invited to the West Ham game on 13th September and to a dinner the following day to celebrate the title win in May. Martin Edwards explained: "Hopefully, he'll be able to say his goodbyes because it was all done in a bit of a rush at the end of last season."

Five days after victory over the Saints, United boss Alex Ferguson was compelled to write to Cantona. He shared the letter for the first time in his 2013 book *Leading*:

*Dear Eric*

*Some months have passed since we last spoke and I felt that I should write to you as a mark of respect and esteem in which I hold you.*

*When we re-started training, I kept waiting for you to turn up as normal but I think that was in hope not realism and I knew in your eyes when we met at Mottram your time at Manchester United was over. Although, I still felt you should have taken both your Father's and my advice and taken a holiday before making such a major decision.*

*One thing, I would like you to remember is to remain active and fit. I always remember when I finished at 32 and I started management, I was more concerned about organising training and the coaching of players that I forgot about my own fitness and then when I realised about six years later what was happening, I started to train again to recapture my fitness and it was murder, so you do need to keep your fitness.*

*I am sure you have been keeping an eye on our results and as you can see we are doing quite well. As you know we have signed Teddy Sheringham to replace you but at the moment he is finding it difficult to find the space he got at Tottenham and is playing deep so we have some adjusting to do. Players sometimes don't realise how difficult it is to play at our level as every game is a Cup Final for our opponents so I just hope he can do it for us. Our pre-season tour wasn't too bad. The Far East tour was better than expected and our games against Inter Milan were very good. The Charity Shield wasn't a great performance but we were better than Chelsea and deserved to win, even though it went to penalties.*

*I still feel as we discussed at the end of the season that a top class striker is what is needed and that is always going to be the problem at our club as the financial restraints will always stop us getting the best because of our wage structure and it is such a pity because when you are at at the top you should buy the best to stop the others getting to you.*

*If I was younger, I suppose I would look at it differently, but from a personal point of view, I have not won the European Cup and it does get to me at times. However I just have to carry on and not put up a mental barrier and I have always had that belief and trust in my players and wish to continue to do so. I keep hoping that I will discover a young Cantona! It is a dream!*

*As I close this letter, I would like to hope that we will have a chat, a drink, or a meal together soon. I know the club has written to you about the forthcoming dinner and I hope you will manage it, but that is not the most important thing, for it is to remind you how good a player we were for Manchester United and how grateful I am for the service you gave me. I will never forget that and I hope you won't either.*

*You are always welcome here and if you just pop in unexpectedly for a cup of tea, no fanfare, just for a chat as friends, that would mean more to me than anything. Eric, you where I am if you need me and now that you are no longer one of my players, I hope you know you have a friend.*

> *Good luck and God bless,*
> *Yours sincerely*
> *Alex Ferguson CBE, MANAGER*

It is hugely revealing that even Alex Ferguson retained a hope, even until pre-season training, that Cantona would reappear. But Eric Cantona the footballer was no more. In an official capacity, at least. Because Old Trafford did bear witness to their former hero on several occasions in future years. As the club prepared for their first season after Eric, it seemed they were keen to erase all trace of his presence, at least going by the contents of the Old Trafford 'megastore'.

*The Guardian* reported that Cantona's lawyers had demanded £750,000 in merchandise royalties, prompting the club to remove all related goods from the shelves and take the rather drastic act of burning it. United apparently offered £250,000 as a settlement, but supporters who wanted to buy a shirt with Eric's name on the back were told they were unable to.

In December 1997, Cantona was interviewed by *GQ*, where he explained: "I stopped playing football because I'd done as much as I could. I needed something which was going to excite me as much as football had excited me."

In August 1998, Cantona was back on the Old Trafford turf for a fundraising game to mark the anniversary of the Munich Air Disaster. It had been a disappointing year for United, who failed to win a trophy for the first time since 1995. Cantona played for his select side but also pulled on the red shirt of United in the second half. Some 55,210 turned up to see Eric score a fantastic solo goal where he dummied past three players. He could have had a second, but youngster Alex Notman got there first, to affectionate jeers from the fans.

"It was just an amazing experience and to play in front of a full house at Old Trafford, and to get two goals was fantastic," Alex told me. "It's got to be one of the best feelings ever, and to share a pitch with the King made it an even more special occasion. I remember taking some stick off the lads for not leaving the ball for Eric to score, but I wasn't going to pass up the chance to get a goal on an occasion like that."

Post-match, Eric addressed the crowd: "It is a special night for me. I lost my passion for the game and I'm sorry about that," he said. "I gave everything for ten years and had five wonderful seasons here, the best of my career. I love you all."

A year later, Cantona turned out for a Rest of the World XI to take on United in a testimonial match for Alex Ferguson – or Sir Alex Ferguson as he was now known, following the incredible triumph of the Treble five months earlier.

Cantona had seen his replacement, Sheringham, score an incredible equaliser in the Nou Camp and then set up the winner for Ole Gunnar Solskjaer, just days after he had scored the winner in the FA Cup final. That could have been Eric; though it is doubtful he would have been happy with such a bit part role in the rest of that campaign. Furthermore, the testimonial appearances, while fun, showed the prospect of a playing return was a pipe dream. Eric's time had been and gone. As well as acting, he had spent time playing and coaching beach soccer, leading to some hoping that this rekindled passion for the game may lead to a coaching role at Old Trafford in the future.

United, meanwhile, continued to succeed. They broke records in their 1999/2000 campaign and were running away with the league the following season. A 6-1 win in February over Arsenal all but sealed the title and the club were in celebratory mood when Cantona attended a 2-1 win over Charlton Athletic on Tuesday 12th April. He had just been announced as the greatest ever player in the club's history, as voted by supporters, and more than 67,000 welcomed back their hero.

"That reception was tremendous and fitting for a man who was simply a magnificent player here," Sir Alex Ferguson said. "One of the great things about this place is that the fans do recognise the players who have made huge contributions to the club's history and success."

It seemed as if this return planted a seed. On 30th May 2001, four years and twelve days after Eric Cantona announced his retirement from playing, another bombshell was dropped at Old Trafford. It was the news all supporters had been longing to hear. The King was back.

Well, almost. But not quite. United announced Cantona would return as a youth team coach on an informal basis. "Eric wants to get back into the game so we've given him the opportunity to help coach the young players at the start of next season," Ferguson said. "It's not an appointment, but a casual arrangement to allow Eric to gain some experience."

United had won three consecutive Premier League titles. The players who Cantona had tutored had blossomed into some of the world's best. There was no player more popular worldwide than David Beckham; no captain more respected than Roy Keane. No winger more thrilling than Ryan Giggs. No midfielder in England with the brain of Paul Scholes. Even Andy Cole had rounded his game to become a success at the club. But Ferguson was planning for the future; he had announced he would retire in 2002, and the approach to Cantona was made with the idea that he could provide a good example for the next generation of young stars too.

On 3rd June, Eric spoke about his new role. "Alex Ferguson asked me if I want to manage one day and I said I wasn't sure," he said. "So he asked if I want to come for a week to see if I like to coach. I manage in beach soccer and I really like it, but in real soccer, I don't know."

Eric was asked if it would be similar to how his community service was in 1995. "I enjoyed it but I had to do it," he said. "Now I have to decide if I like it."

He did speak out about Ferguson's impending retirement and said he felt more should be done to keep him; but if not, he had a suggestion. "It's a shame… I would ask someone like Johan Cruyff to come. After Alex Ferguson you need someone with a very strong personality… But I am not the chairman of Manchester United. I am not rich enough."

Cantona and his hero Cruyff as custodians of the next generation? As it transpired, Ferguson remained for another 12 years after a u-turn in 2002. He went on to win six more league titles and another European Cup. (Cruyff was 66 when Ferguson eventually retired in 2013).

Three weeks later, the beach soccer tournament had journeyed to London's Hyde Park. Eric appeared to have gone cold on the coaching. "I'm not sure I will like it," he told *The Guardian*. "I will try it for one or two weeks. It is like a woman being seduced. She thinks yes. She thinks no. She thinks, do I need someone to seduce me? But I don't know. I am not a woman."

The *Express* carried more candid comments on 23rd June. "I have no arrangement with Manchester United and no ambition to return there," Cantona said. "Why would I when I can play beach football in the sun and sand of Brazil? I have a wonderful life and I don't follow football now. I did speak with Sir Alex and he asked if I wanted to be a manager one day. I told him I wasn't sure. He said for me to come to Old Trafford to see if I might like it and I said maybe I would. That was it.

"If I wanted to come back into football I would. I've had lots of offers. But I'm not sure I would like it. ... I have a vision of football. I would like to do something new and not the same regimented formula. The game played by United at their free-flowing best and Barcelona under Johan Cruyff is the type of game I would want to see a team play. I know why people loved me. People love somebody because they represent something at a particular time. But you cannot believe you are God when you are not. We are too small. We are nobody."

That summer, Cantona added to this theme, telling Greek media that if he went into coaching: "... I want to see a team play football as it has never been played before. I want it to be like an artist with a new movement, like a revolution."

However, soon after, Eric rediscovered just how dangerous talking to the British press could be. "I prefer someone who takes cocaine on a Wednesday and plays football on the weekend to win," he was quoted as saying. "He can still look himself in the mirror and be proud of himself if he has played hard for the team to help them win. Some people don't choose drugs like cocaine, but they use drugs to help them win.

"They are idols of people so how can they look at themselves in the mirror? I respect people that don't choose anything, but I respect someone like Maradona more than somebody who uses drugs to win."

However, *The Guardian* reported Cantona "could be in trouble" for his comments. This reminder that the press were keen to pick up on everything he said may have been enough to give Eric cold feet. While no announcement was made, Cantona never reported for coaching; or, at least, none of the academy players from the time can remember that happening.

Instead, the Frenchman made his next appearance as a guest rather than an employee a few weeks later when he was brought on for Paul Scholes in the 73rd minute of Ryan Giggs' testimonial against Celtic at Old Trafford.

Over the coming years, Cantona was asked for his opinions on various matters at the club. In April 2003, with Ferguson still going strong in the dugout, Cantona predicted his former manager would "die on the bench of Manchester United", admitting at the same time that he had his own regrets.

"He (Ferguson) likes other things but football is his life," Eric said after being named overseas player of the decade at a ceremony to mark the first ten years of the Premier League.

"There wouldn't be enough in his life without football. I quit and for the first two years it was very difficult. Playing football is something you dream about from when you are very young. When you quit it's not easy. Sometimes I think I quit too young because I love the game, but I didn't have the passion to go to bed early, not go out with friends, not drink and not do a lot of things. But Alex Ferguson can cope with that."

After the club was subject to a takeover from the Glazer family in 2005, some supporters hoped he would speak out against the new owners. "I can understand why the supporters are concerned," he told *FourFourTwo* in 2008. "The philosophy will never change while Alex Ferguson is at the club. After he leaves... that's what makes me worry. Ferguson is so strong, so popular. He can control everything. For the moment nothing has changed there – apart from in an economic way, and Ferguson does not control the price of the tickets for the fans."

Since Sir Alex retired, Eric has often talked about managing United one day, despite this seeming as unrealistic as the hope he would return as a player back in 1997.

In 1996, when describing how he would approach being a manager, he said: "If I did, it would be on the strict condition that I could bring something new to the game. I would never contemplate becoming a manager simply to do what other managers have done before me. All my life I've wanted to do new things, to break new ground. If ever I had the sense that I could do this as a manager, I'd certainly consider it."

In 2016, after Jose Mourinho was appointed, Cantona expressed concern. "I love Mourinho, but in terms of the type of football he plays I don't think he is Manchester United," Eric said. "I love his personality, I love the passion, his humour. He is very intelligent and he wins things. But I don't think it's the type of football the fans of Manchester United will love. I do many things and I'm very happy. But if they asked me to become the manager of Manchester United, I would. Because Guardiola is in Manchester City and they want someone to win things with wonderful football? It's me… Yes, I'm serious. I say that just because it's like when you are in the pub or the club. When you say you don't care, all the girls want you. Maybe if I say I don't care about that job, they will ask me. If they asked me I'd work very hard, of course."

His prediction of difficulty was proved true. In October 2018, Jose Mourinho was on the brink of dismissal after a long spell where fans complained about his style of football. Cantona was holding a talk at the Lowry Theatre in Salford and was asked if he would still take the job. "Of course!" he declared, to cheers. "You would see wonderful football, for sure."

Mourinho was dismissed in December 2018. While rumours swirled about the arrival of Ole Gunnar Solskjaer as an interim boss, former United merchandising executive Edward Freeman told the BBC that Cantona's interest in the job was serious: "Solskjaer doesn't excite me. I have an answer I don't think they would listen to, and you could turn it around very quickly. There's one player that no one has mentioned.

"He is a legend at United, he is worshipped by the fans, he is an intelligent guy. I know him very well and is the person who would make everything, not just on the field but off the field, work. That is Eric Cantona. I have been with Eric on a stage show and he has got up there and said how he loves United. He wanted to do the job and, certainly as an interim, what have you got to lose? He wants the job. He is desperate."

In December 2017, he had told the *Financial Times* he would never manage another club: "No. Only to manage Manchester United…They won't ask me. Maybe that's why they didn't win the Premier League. Only I could have made them succeed."

At those events at the Lowry, Cantona had, however, also expressed his fundamental desire that if not him, a former player should get the role. "At United, they never give a chance to a player who knows the club from the inside, who knows the identity and philosophy," he said. "I don't want people to think I'm saying this because I want to be manager of Manchester United. It's just the truth. Giggs? Any player who wants to be the manager, they should give them the chance."

Solskjaer was named interim manager and things started well, leading to calls for him to appointed permanently. Cantona supported those opinions, describing his former strike partner as "the spiritual son of Alex Ferguson". Of course, Solskjaer was appointed permanent United manager in March 2019.

To date, there has been no official working relationship between Cantona and Manchester United since 1997 and the hope-raising announcement of May 2001. So much time has passed that most people dismiss the idea of Eric returning as manager as an unrealistic eventuality; a pipe dream would likely go horribly wrong due to his inexperience and the changing landscape of football in the last two decades.

There is enough fantasy to entertain the daydream. Just what would Eric Cantona's style of football, taught as a coach, be like? It seems it would be like Cruyff, like Michels, and yet more economical than the elaborate interpretation of Guardiola; the perfect goal in eleven passes as opposed to one hundred and eleven. Speed, intelligence and penetration. All the hallmarks of Manchester United. All the hallmarks of Eric Cantona.

# The Expressionist

The Merriam-Webster Dictionary defines expressionism as "a theory or practice in art of seeking to depict the subjective emotions and responses that objects and events arouse in the artist".

Eric Cantona is not the club's most successful player. He did not win the most trophies, he did not make the most appearances and he did not score the most goals. He did not win a European Cup, and he did not win a *Ballon d'Or*. Others may contend that George Best and Cristiano Ronaldo had more natural talent than him.

But there was nobody quite like Eric Cantona; less a sportsman, more an expressionist who, for a period of his life, chose football as his medium. Faced with the safe option or the entertaining option; either bringing the ball down and surveying his options, or spinning his body four feet in the air so he could back-heel a pass to the left wing, Cantona would choose the latter. The Frenchman did not merely believe football was an art form. He described it as "the most beautiful of the arts".

"The more I find it easy, the easier it becomes," he said. "I try to convince myself it's easy. And when you're confident you find freedom, from freedom of expression comes genius, euphoria and fire...

"One day those who make football will have to understand that there is no salvation without the artist. Of course you have to win. But you also have to admit defeat so that football can again be a source of emotion."

Following his retirement, Manchester United's young players became the most revered and most loathed stars in the country. They were booed when they turned out for England. They were impossibly successful. Impossibly popular. Rival supporters were intensely jealous. They won the biggest trophies, they won the most games, they scored the best goals. It was relentless. Manchester United's Class of '92 went on to become the most successful group of home-grown players England has ever produced and while that is of course thanks in a large part to the coaching they received, Eric Cantona's own contribution to that is unquantifiable.

"There is definitely some of Cantona's influence which can be felt in United's success which followed," Martin Edwards says. "He was the catalyst for the change at the club, he introduced that arrogance, swagger and self-confidence that came into the style of play.

"Cantona's achievements speak for themselves. United going so long without winning the league, and then winning it every season he was there, bar the year when he was out with the suspension. Okay, United didn't win the league in 1998, but they won the Treble in 1999, and you can't help but feel he had a big influence on that because of how much he had inspired the young players. He was a huge character in that era."

Edwards believes the Frenchman is, simply, one of the greatest: "Cantona will always be mentioned whenever people discuss the influential players in British football history... I am biased, of course, but I would say Eric is as worthy as anyone.

"He was not only one of the most influential players in British football, but most definitely Manchester United's history too. You have different eras where players stand out. Best, Law and Charlton can't be split. Robson stands out on his own. So too does Eric. He is a big figure in the history of the game."

In a sense, though, talking about Cantona in such terms – discussing where he ranks among the great footballers, looking at trophies and statistics, even talking about his incredible influence on others – is a reductive exercise. Is it not the point that Eric Cantona was so special because he was unlike anybody else? Because it is impossible to compare? How is it even possible to comprehend or contextualise the difference he made when it was a journey nobody else had taken before?

That he walked into Manchester United, the biggest club in Britain, and still managed to appear as if he was bigger than the club is a story that is told through facts and context, and not comparisons. Nobody else has done it.

That he walked into a squad of mixed age and mixed ability, elevating the senior players to a level they had not previously reached to enjoy unprecedented success, and influencing the younger players to surpass that success is again, a story that can be told through facts and context, and not comparisons. Nobody else has done it.

A year after he retired, the club he joined for one million pounds was almost sold to BSkyB for more than one billion dollars. In 2019, United were valued at £5bn. Or, to put it another way – in approximately five years of Eric Cantona's time at Old Trafford, the club's value multiplied by approximately 20 times. In the roughly 20 years since he retired, the club's value has multiplied roughly five times.

Manchester United became a commercial machine after Cantona's retirement. On the first home strip they released after his retirement (aside from the special Champions League only shirt), the words 'Football Club' were removed from the crest. In some respects that represented a real changing of the philosophical guard at Old Trafford. History became a reference instead of part of the fabric. Perhaps that made sense. Manchester United were making history.

There remains that unshakeable feeling, though, that Cantona was the last of the great entertainers, before the pursuit of winning and profit was placed above almost everything else. Before a time where revenue was considered more important than trophies and glory.

You could be tempted to suggest Cantona is Frankenstein and modern football is the monster he helped create; but in spite of the great modern players and how entertaining the current product is, nobody has ever come close to having the same aura as the Frenchman, be it as an artist or as a personality. Nobody quite had that sense of drama, occasion and timing.

Eric Cantona left as he arrived; shocking, brilliant and in a style of his own.

# Bibliography

*Year In the Life – The Manager's Diary*
– Alex Ferguson/Peter Ball – Virgin Books
*A Will To Win – The Manager's Diary*
– Alex Ferguson/David Meek – Andres Deutsch
*Managing My Life* – Alex Ferguson – Coronet
*My Autobiography* – Peter Schmeichel – Virgin Books
*Russian Winters* – Andrei Kanchelskis – De Coubertin
*Giggs – My Autobiography* – Penguin/Michael Joseph
*Pally!* – Gary Pallister – Know The Score Books
*Heading for Victory* – Steve Bruce – Bloomsbury
*Keane – The Autobiography* – Roy Keane – Penguin
*Cantona – My Story* – Eric Cantona – Headline
*Cantona on Cantona* – Eric Cantona/Alex Fynn – Andre Deutsch
*Red* – Gary Neville – Bantam Press
*Red White & Blackmore*
– Clayton Blackmore/Wayne Barton – Empire Publications
*Cantona: The Rebel Who Would Be King*
– Philippe Auclair – Macmillan
*Leading* – Sir Alex Ferguson/Michael Moritz – Hodder & Stoughton
*One In A Million: The Trevor Francis Story*
– Trevor Francis /Keith Dixon – Pitch Publishing
*More Than A Match: A Player's Story*
– Lee Chapman – Stanley Paul
*Robbo: My Autobiography* – Bryan Robson – Hodder & Stoughton
*Glory Glory! Man Utd Players in the '90s*
– Andy Mitten – Vision Sports
*Football – Bloody Hell!* Patrick Barclay – Yellow Jersey Press
*FA Confidential* – David Davies – Pocket Books
*Fowler: My Autobiography* – Robbie Fowler – Pan Macmillan
*Tooting Common to the Stretford End*
– Alex Stepney – Vertical Editions